Routledge Revivals

The World Shipping Industry

First published in 1987, this book surveys the state of the world
shipping industry worldwide and the problems confronting it. It
reviews the expanding role of developing countries in shipping and
evaluates the contribution of shipping to development. The changes in
the institutional and environmental framework of shipping are discussed and the social impacts are assessed. Finally, the challenges,
opportunities and problems of the shipping industry are appraised and
future developments are postulated.

The World Shipping Industry

Ernst Gabriel Frankel

Routledge
Taylor & Francis Group

First published in 1987
by Croom Helm

This edition first published in 2011 by Routledge
2 Park Square, Milton Park, Abingdon, Oxon, OX14 4RN

Simultaneously published in the USA and Canada
by Routledge
270 Madison Avenue, New York, NY 10016

Routledge is an imprint of the Taylor & Francis Group, an informa business

ISBN 13: 978-0-415-61337-8 (hbk)

THE WORLD
SHIPPING INDUSTRY

Ernst Gabriel Frankel

CROOM HELM
London • New York • Sydney

© 1987 Ernst G. Frankel
Croom Helm Publishers Ltd, Provident House,
Burrell Row, Beckenham, Kent, BR3 1AT

Croom Helm Australia, 44–50 Waterloo Road,
North Ryde, 2113, New South Wales

British Library Cataloguing in Publication Data

Frankel, Ernst G.
 The world shipping industry : policy
 analysis and development : an industry at
 the crossroads.
 1. Shipping
 I. Title
 387.5   HE571
 ISBN 0-7099-1087-8

Published in the USA by
Croom Helm
in association with Methuen, Inc.
29 West 35th Street
New York, NY 10001

Library of Congress Cataloging-in-Publication Data

Frankel, Ernst G.
 The world shipping industry.

 Bibliography: p.
 Includes index.
 1. Shipping. 2. Shipping—United States. I. Title.
HE571.F7 1987   387.5   87-3608
ISBN 0-7099-1087-8

Photosetting by Mayhew Typesetting, Bristol
Printed and bound in Great Britain
by Billing & Sons Limited, Worcester.

Contents

Figures

Tables

Preface

The world shipping industry is in the midst of a major structural and operational change. Its roles, functions, and objectives are under review and sometimes even under attack, while its ownership, management, and organisation remain in a flux. Shipping makes a tremendous contribution to development and is an essential factor of international trade. Trade, in turn, has in recent years become the most important contributor to economic development. Yet, while the role of shipping should be obvious, and its organisation efficient and responsive to its tasks, the world shipping industry continues in turmoil. This turmoil is the result not only of current overcapacity and fragmentation in shipping, but also of the increased politicisation of the industry.

Shipping and economic development are increasingly linked. The health of the shipping industry is therefore of great importance not only to the major shipping nations but to all nations. While other modes of transport, such as aviation, trucking, and rail transport, have emerged from the recent recession with strength and vitality in most industrialised countries, shipping remains stagnant. Shipping has been subjected to more regulation and protectionism than other modes of transport, while being burdened by overcapacity and lack of adaptability because of restrictive operating and other rules.

The industry is truly at a crossroads now and must find an effective balance of service, technology, capacity, and regulation. The need for international and national public regulation as well as self-regulation, including service restrictions, is now being questioned. The recently introduced US Shipping Act of 1984, with its 'rights to independent action' as well as 'service contract' clauses is dealing a major blow to the traditional role of liner conferences. In fact, these changes may well form a radical shift in the structure of liner conferences.

At the same time renewed proposals for various technological changes in ship design, ship operations, and interface port operations are being advanced. Much of the maritime technology in use today is 10 to 25 years old and considered by many to be functionally obsolete. As a result, technological change – when it comes – will be pervasive and will cause a radical adjustment in the management and operations of shipping. The freedom of the seas, and in particular, free competition in shipping, is largely theoretical now as more and more countries adopt restrictive shipping practices. At the same time, the expanding role of developing countries in shipping is questioned, and the contribution of shipping to development is reevaluated. The changes in the institutional and environmental framework of shipping and its social impacts must therefore be assessed, and the challenges, opportunities, and problems of the industry appraised in order to evaluate future developments. This book is structured to meet these needs.

After an 'overview of world shipping' in Chapter 1, in which the status, development, and role of shipping as an industry are reviewed, Chapter 2 discusses institutional, policy, and regulatory issues affecting shipping. This includes an analysis of the administrative and organisational framework of shipping as well as of economic trends. Both public and private shipping policy are considered, and the implications of shipping nationalism are evaluated. Next we review trade and economic development in Chapter 3, with particular reference to its impact and demand on shipping. The changing role of shipping under increasingly volatile shifts in trading patterns is similarly discussed. The 'financial framework of shipping' has become a highly interesting and complicated issue in recent times, with the evaporation of traditional ship financing, and the emergence of many new and often quite imaginative methods of financing. Chapter 4 also includes a discussion of marine insurance and its various aspects.

As stated before, shipping operation and management is in turmoil now and subject to continuous change. This change, while dominant in liner shipping, has also started to affect other branches of shipping. Ship management, including shipboard social issues, are more and more affected by technological change, as well as by the integration of traditional shipping companies with other modal transport or industrial enterprises including mergers and joint venture operations.

Chapter 5 considers future developments in shipping. In light of these changes affecting ship operations and management, we look into the future and attempt to project challenges and opportunities to the turn of this century. Many believe that shipping, as we know it now, will be largely replaced by new types of integrated intermodal vessels. Chapter 5 tries also to convey the theories of technological, political, social, and economic factors which may radically change future projections. The aim is to excite the reader to think imaginatively and accept changes which are, at least to the author, inevitable in this most traditional of industries.

In Chapter 6 we discuss some of the policy alternatives, developments, and initiatives now under way or contemplated, and postulate their impact.

These projections pave the way for our final review, in Chapter 7, of the future prospects of world shipping, in terms of policy, regulatory, institutional and operational changes.

Acknowledgements

Creative work is never due solely to the efforts of a single person. This book is the result of interactions and discussions with many of my peers, colleagues, students, advisors, political friends and foes, as well as people far removed from any interest in the shipping industry who enlightened me by their pertinent or probing questions and productive criticism.

My particular appreciation is due to Dr Richard Goss of the University of Wales, who supervised and guided me in my research on the impact of protectionism on shipping; Dr Sidney Gillman of the University of Liverpool who read and reviewed that work; to Dr Ezra Bennathan, Economic Advisor at the World Bank, who was my mentor while I served the World Bank as Port and Shipping Advisor and enlightened me in the art and science of transport economics; to Dr Francis Ogilvie, Head of the Department of Ocean Engineering, who encouraged me in this work; Dr Robert Ellsworth, Director of Program Planning and Economics, at the US Federal Maritime Commission, who assisted me in understanding the often conflicting US policy objectives; to my beloved wife, Tamar, who always asked penetrating questions which required reflection and well thought answers; and, finally to Ms Sheila McNary whose infallible and cheerful editorial and production work made this book possible.

Finally, last but not least, I would like to thank Mr Peter Sowden, my editor, who originated this book project, for his ideas and editorial assistance in this venture.

Abbreviations

AAPA	American Association of Port Authorities
ADB	Asian Development Bank
ASEAN	Association of South East Asian Nations
CENSA	Council of European and Japanese National Shipowners Associations
CPE	Centrally Planned Economy
DFC	Development Finance Company
ECA	Economic Commission for Africa
ECDC	Economic Cooperation between Developing Countries
ECE	Economic Commission for Europe
ECLA	Economic Commission for Latin America
ECME	Economic Commission for the Middle East
EEC	European Economic Community
ESCAP	Economic and Social Commission for Asia and the Pacific
FIATA	International Federation of Forwarding Agent Associations
FMC	Federal Maritime Commission (United States)
FOC	Flag of Convenience
GATT	General Agreement on Trades and Tariffs
GDP	Gross Domestic Product
GNP	Gross National Product
HMSO	Her Majesty's Stationery Office (United Kingdom)
IAPH	International Association of Ports and Harbours
IBRD	International Bank for Reconstruction and Development
ICHCA	International Cargo Handling Coordination Association
ILO	International Labour Organisation
IMCO	Inter-Governmental Maritime Consultative Organisation
IMF	International Monetary Fund
IMO	International Maritime Organisation
INSA	International Shipowners Association
ISO	International Standards Organisation
ITF	International Transport Workers' Federation
LDC	Less developed country

MARAD	Maritime Administration (United States)
OECD	Organisation for Economic Cooperation and Development
PIANC	Permanent International Association of Navigational Congresses
TEU	Twenty-foot Equivalent Container
UNCTAD	United Nations Conference on Trade and Development
UNDP	United Nations Development Program
UWIST	The University of Wales Institute of Science and Technology
WISCO	West Indies Shipping Corporation

Shipping Terms

Bareboat charter	Charter arranged for a specific period under which the charter in effect takes control of the vessel, paying all operating and voyage costs
Bulk carriers/vessels	Vessels designed to carry dry or liquid bulk cargoes, generally in full ship loads
cabotage	Domestic trade/transport in coastal waters
c.f.	Cost and freight
c.i.f.	Cost, insurance, freight
Combined carriers	OBO or O/O vessels as defined below
Contract of affreightment	Contract providing a certain tonnage capacity to transport bulk cargo, during a specific period, between two ports or areas at agreed rates
Cross-trading	Transport between two foreign countries, and therefore not involving trade of the country whose flag the vessel is carrying
DWT	Deadweight ton
f.o.b.	Free on board
FOC	Flag of convenience
Freight	Charges levied by shipping companies for transporting goods. For liner vessels (liner terms), the cost of loading and discharge is normally included in the freight costs. In the case of bulk commodities, f.i.o. terms (free-in-and-out) or related terms are commonly used, whereby the cost of loading and discharge is not borne by the ship owner
grt	Gross registered tons. The total enclosed capacity (in units of 100 cubic feet) in a ship, less certain exempted spaces

Integrated barging	Fleet of barges or single barges semi-rigidly connected to push towing tug
Intermodal	Transport of goods using different modes of transport from origin to destination
LASH	Lighter aboard ship
Liner conference	A group of two or more vessel-operating carriers which provides international liner services or the carriage of cargo on a particular route or routes, within specified geographical limits. Each group has an agreement within which they operate under uniform or common freight rates and any other agreed conditions regarding the provision of liner services
Liner service	Regular scheduled service at fixed rates on a given trade route
LNG	Liquefied natural gas
LPG	Liquefied pressurised gas
mmt	Million metric tons
MT-NM	Measurement ton-nautical miles
Neo-bulk	Commodities which traditionally have moved on liner vessels, but which are often carried more effectively in part ship loads by specialised vessels (cars, latex, timber, solvents, etc.)
OBO	Ore/bulk/oil carrier. Vessels which are constructed in such a manner as to carry both oil and dry bulk cargo
O/O	Ore/oil carrier
POL	Petroleum, oil, and lubricants
Ro/Ro	Roll-on, roll-off
Seabee	A barge-carrying vessel
Space charter	Charter arranged for a fixed amount of space on one ship, or on a fleet of ships, for a single voyage or for a period of time

TEU	Twenty-foot Equivalent Container
Time charter	Charter arranged for a fixed period. Payment usually per DWT per month, excludes voyage costs
Tramp ships	Tramp ships are those which do not have to run on regular routes as liner ships, but run as required and when necessary to suit specific cargo
Trip charter	Charter arranged for a voyage specifying delivery and re-delivery ports or areas. Payments are per DWT per month, excluding voyage costs
ULCC	Ultra large crude carrier (generally crude oil tankers of 300,000 DWT or above)
VLCC	Very large crude carriers (generally crude oil tankers of 175,000 DWT or above)
Voyage charter	Charter arranged to carry a cargo on a single voyage between two specified ports or areas. Payment, usually on either a cargo ton basis or on a cubic capacity basis, includes voyage costs
Voyage costs	Vessel costs comprising bunkers, port charges, and canal charges
Worldscale	A freight index designed to express tanker rates, irrespective of vessel size and route, in terms of the costing of a standard vessel, Worldscale 100. It replaced the earlier INTASCALE (International Tanker Nominal Rate Scale) and ATRA (American Tanker Rate Schedule) in 1969

1

Introduction

There has been a general depression in the shipping industry since 1974. The prospects for a turnaround are difficult to assess in the best of circumstances, but in this case the difficulty is compounded because of cyclical developments that have been exacerbated by long-term structural changes in the shipping industry and in world trade, making adjustments a more lengthy, difficult, and complex process than in the past.

The rapid post-war expansion of world trade and its seaborne portion came to an end with the oil crisis in 1974. After an immediate decline in 1975, seaborne trade recovered slowly, but after reaching a peak of 3,755 million metric tons (mmt) in 1979, a sustained decline set in so that in 1983 it was somewhat below 1974 levels – 3,165 mmt and 3,248 mmt respectively. In 1984 world trade stabilised and experienced a slight increase in 1985. Unfortunately, the turnabout principally affected trade between developed nations.

The proximate cause of the developments in trade was the generally sluggish state of the world economy. Nevertheless it is possible to discern long-term trends in the economy that will affect shipping. While world trade appears to be revived now, at least among developed nations, it is not likely that we will see the sustained high growth rates of the past. The composition of trade has shifted in favour of more manufactured goods and partially processed raw materials – that is, higher value-added goods. The oil trade in particular has seen dramatic changes in volume, product mix, and trade routes. High prices and the economic slump have cut demand generally, and conservation efforts as well as technology have altered it in a fundamental sense. On the other hand, renewed growth will probably start from a lower level and is not likely to proceed at the high rates of the past – this notwithstanding the drastic change in oil price and glut of supplies experienced during the first half of 1986.

New sources of supply for many raw materials and finished goods have shortened many sea routes. The overall result is a large surplus of shipping, particularly in large bulk carrier tonnage. Demand for smaller tankers and bulk carriers is being bolstered by producers supplying products rather than raw materials – an example of the general shift to more value-added commodities in trade, but also an example of structural market change. When producer governments took control of production, as happened in most developing countries, they encouraged the entry of numerous buyers in order to free themselves from dependence on the few major buyers. The large number of new buyers caused shipments to be made in lots in liner vessels or by voyage charters instead of long-term charters. Such charters had previously been demanded by the large importers, many of whom owned and/or operated large portions of their shipping capacity requirements. In response to these changes, many companies let go of the major part of the fleet under their control. As a result the shipping market has been fragmented and remains essentially so today, although there is a tendency toward some concentration in certain producing countries who control their trade.

The tendency towards more trade in finished goods trade favours liner and neo-bulk shipping; most bulk trades tend, however, to be hurt by this development. Also, the growing use of recycled materials such as scrap, particularly in steel, copper and aluminium, does affect bulk trades in ores and in metallurgical coal. Steam coal seems destined to grow in importance since oil prices, even with a low rate of growth in demand, are bound to rise again in the future, but this may not occur until at least 1990.

In addition to these changes in traded products, there is a major development in the process of trading. Barter, or counter-trading, is rapidly becoming an important trade feature. While it has always been the preferred arrangement in East-West trade, it has also gained popularity in recent years in other trades, specifically trades among developed countries, and between developing and developed countries in both the West and East.

The world fleet has expanded over the years to meet the needs of the trade. However, the basic equilibrium between demand for and supply of tonnage was disrupted after 1974. Orders placed before the new trends were perceived caused the fleet to continue its rapid growth through 1977. Thereafter, the growth rate slowed substantially, but not enough to prevent the development of a very large surplus of tonnage, estimated worldwide at some 150–200 million

DWT, of which two-thirds are tankers.

The current situation is therefore characterised by a large surplus of tonnage in all types and sizes of ships. This has resulted in generally low freight rates, many lay-ups, low prices for secondhand ships, and accelerated scrappings – all of which are reflected in serious financial difficulties for owners. As many of the ships scrapped in recent years were younger than the average age of the world fleet, the actual average age of the fleet has gone up – both as a result of the scrapping of below average age ships, and of a less than proportionate addition of newbuilding deliveries. In early 1985, suggestions for institutionalised scrapping schemes were proposed by several owner associations, in which ship owners and governments would contribute to an international fund to induce owners to scrap vessels more rapidly. The establishment of break-up yards, requiring relatively little capital and skilled labour, but large numbers of labourers, would be encouraged in LDCs. Some LDCs such as Liberia and Kenya, where partial facilities appear to be already available, have become interested in active participation in larger scale scrapping operations.

While the depression in shipping is general the impact varies from market to market, as prospects for shipping vary with the industry's response to long-term factors of structural change. Thus, two major container operators, the US Lines and the Taiwan-flagged Evergreen Line, have inaugurated round-the-world services with new, very large, and economic containerships which are expected to be financially viable even under current conditions. A Japanese operator, K-Line, has announced similar plans, and others will undoubtedly follow.

In the bulk markets, freight futures contracts have been introduced. These allow charterers and operators to hedge against fluctuations in freight rates. Wide and successful use of such contracts may impart some stability to bulk shipping markets and ease adjustment. Clearly, economic imperatives of the market are bringing about structural changes in shipping patterns and operations.

Ownership of world shipping remains concentrated in developed countries and open-registry fleets, whose combined tonnage represented 75.0 per cent of the mid-1984 fleet capacity (DWT), as compared to 76.1 per cent in mid-1983. The 1984 percentage for developing countries increased only slightly, from 15.3 per cent in 1983 to 15.9 per cent in 1984. Socialist country participation in fleet ownership also increased marginally in percentage terms.

Developing countries generated 48.5 per cent of the world's

exports and accounted for 25.4 per cent of the world's imports in 1984. In other words, their percentage volume of the world's trade was more than 2.4 times the capacity of their fleet as a percentage of world fleet capacity.

The largest percentage increase was in containerships, where LDC capacity nearly doubled from 7.6 million DWT in 1980 to 14.3 million DWT in 1983. Nearly all the increase in LDC shipping capacity was by Asian LDCs, who increased their tonnage from 39.1 million DWT in 1980 to 73.3 million DWT in 1983. LDC tonnage in Africa, America, and Oceania remained level only with European LDCs showing any expansion in shipping capacity. African and American LDCs achieved no increase in capacity and only maintained reasonable participation in general cargo shipping capacity. Their severe lack of adequate container shipping capacity constrains their participation in liner trades increasingly served by container shipping. Similarly, bulk shipping capacity of African and American LDCs is highly adequate and actually declining.

PROFILE OF WORLD SHIPPING

Shipping is usually divided into major ship types and seaborne trades which ships serve. In the most basic terms it can be divided into tankers, combined carriers, bulk carriers, specialised carriers (tankers, automobile carriers, specialised bulkers, etc.), unitised carriers (containerships, Roll-on/Roll-off (RoRo) vessels, barge carriers, etc.), and general cargo vessels.

World seaborne trade did not increase between 1974 and 1985 in tonnage terms (Table 1.1 and Figure 1.1) and declined by about 20 per cent in ton-mile terms (Table 1.2). It reached a high of 3.7 billion tons and 17.5 trillion ton-miles in 1979, after which it declined to just 3.1 billion tons in 1983. After a small increase to about 3.3 billion tons per year, it has levelled off at this volume. Similar seaborne trade in ton-miles which declined to 12.58 trillion ton-miles in 1983 has only made a small comeback to just over 13 billion ton-miles currently.

It should be noted that while world seaborne trade is very gradually increasing again, the demand for shipping output in ton-miles is now, in 1986, just about equal to the level of demand in 1968, when the world shipping capacity was only about 73 per cent of its current level. This is obviously the major cause for oversupply in shipping, which in turn is causing low freight rates and a large

Table 1.1: World seaborne trade 1974–1985 (tonnes). (Figures in millions)

	Crude oil	Oil products	Iron ore	Coal	Grain	Other cargo Estimate	Total trade Estimate
1974	1,361	264	329	119	130	1,045	3,248
1975	1,263	233	292	127	137	995	3,047
1976	1,410	260	294	127	146	1,075	3,312
1977	1,451	273	276	132	147	1,120	3,399
1978	1,432	270	278	127	169	1,190	3,466
1979	1,497	279	327	159	182	1,270	3,714
1980	1,320	276	314	188	198	1,310	3,606
1981	1,170	267	303	210	206	1,305	3,461
1982	993	285	273	208	200	1,240	3,199
1983	930	282	257	197	199	1,225	3,090
1984	950	297	306	232	207	1,320	3,312
1985 Est.	910	288	305	248	188	1,350	3,289

Notes: Estimates for 1985 are based on statistics for the first nine to eleven months of the year for the most important countries as regards the specified commodities, supplemented with data from international associations. The 'Total trade' and 'Other cargo' estimates for 1985 are based on world trade growth as indicated by official sources
Source: *Fearnley's Review 1985*. Fearnley, Oslo, January 1986

Figure 1.1: World seaborne trade

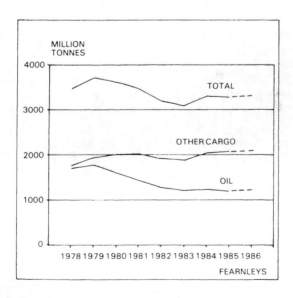

Source: *Fearnley's Review 1985*. Fearnley, Oslo, January 1986

5

Table 1.2: World seaborne trade 1974–1985 (ton-miles).
(Figures in billions)

	Crude oil	Oil products	Iron ore	Coal	Grain	Other cargo Estimate	Total trade Estimate
1974	9,661	960	1,578	558	695	2,935	16,387
1975	8,885	845	1,471	621	734	2,810	15,366
1976	10,199	950	1,469	591	779	3,035	17,023
1977	10,408	995	1,386	643	801	3,220	17,453
1978	9,561	985	1,384	604	945	3,455	16,934
1979	9,452	1,045	1,599	786	1,026	3,605	17,513
1980	8,219	1,020	1,613	952	1,087	3,720	16,611
1981	7,193	1,000	1,508	1,120	1,131	3,710	15,662
1982	5,212	1,070	1,443	1,094	1,120	3,560	13,499
1983	4,478	1,080	1,320	1,057	1,135	3,510	12,580
1984	4,450	1,140	1,631	1,270	1,157	3,720	13,368
1985 Est.	4,320	1,120	1,610	1,320	1,040	3,750	13,160

Notes: Estimates for 1985 are based on statistics for the first nine to eleven months of the year for the most important countries as regards the specified commodities, supplemented with data from international associations. The 'Total trade' and 'Other cargo' estimates for 1985 are based on world trade growth as indicated by official sources
Source: *Fearnley's Review 1985*. Fearnley, Oslo, January 1986

number of lay-ups. Some owners are trying to reduce their costs per ton-mile and stretch employment of their tonnage by slow steaming. But this approach is highly sensitive to fuel (bunker) costs. Recent drastic declines in fuel costs have made slow steaming much less attractive.

The world shipping fleet had a deadweight capacity of 606.2 million (DWT) tons, a reduction of 50 million (DWT) tons since it achieved a high of 657.4 million (DWT) tons in 1982. Assuming projected newbuilding deliveries and scrappings, capacity is expected to decline to 578.8 million (DWT) tons by 1989 (Figure 1.2 and Table 1.3). The largest decline is expected to occur in oil tankers, to only about 207.2 million (DWT) tons. Combined carriers are expected to decline in capacity as well. Dry bulk carrier capacity, on the other hand, is projected to increase slightly to about 206 million (DWT) tons with specialised, container, RoRo, and general cargo tonnage remaining at its current level of just under 133 million (DWT) tons.

Table 1.4 shows the laid-up tonnage. It is encouraging to note that the laid-up total continues to decline from the 80.2 million (DWT) ton high reached in 1982 when over 10 per cent of newbuildings delivered were immediately added to the laid-up tonnage pool. This

Figure 1.2: World shipping fleet

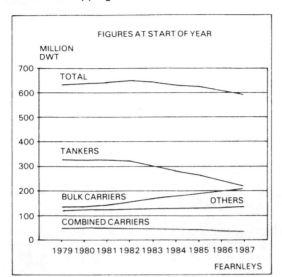

Source: *Fearnley's Review 1986.* Fearnley, Oslo, January 1986

Table 1.3: Estimated world fleet 1986–1989. (Figures in million DWT)

	Oil tankers	Combined carriers	Bulk carriers	Others	Total
1/1 1986	239.8	36.0	197.5	132.9	606.2
1/1 1987	222.8	34.4	204.2	132.9	594.3
1/1 1988	209.5	33.7	205.2	132.9	581.3
1/1 1989	207.2	32.8	205.9	132.9	578.8

Note: For each year the estimates are prepared by starting with the fleet at the beginning of the year, minus estimated demolition and losses, plus anticipated deliveries from the actual orderbook and possible new orders (not yet recorded) with anticipated delivery in the year of consideration
Source: *Fearnley's Review 1985.* Fearnley, Oslo, January 1986

decline is expected to continue as long as the rate of scrapping continues at a high level and newbuilding deliveries remain at a level of less than 25 million (DWT) tons.

The world shipbuilding orderbook (Table 1.5 and Figure 1.3) shows a drastic decline in tanker orders from a level of 19.7 million

7

Table 1.4: Tonnage laid-up 1974–1985. (Figures in million DWT)

End	Oil tankers	Dry cargo		Total	1985 End	Oil tankers	Comb. C.	Bulk C.	Others
1974	2.3	1.3		3.6	Jan	44.2	1.8	5.2	5.5
1975	41.3	7.4		48.7	Feb	44.5	1.9	5.1	5.5
1976	31.0	5.3		36.3	Mar	44.0	1.4	5.1	5.3
		Comb. C.	Others		Apr	43.8	1.0	4.6	5.3
1977	29.3	6.3	5.4	41.0	May	43.7	1.0	4.1	5.2
1978	21.4	3.2	4.3	28.9	Jun	43.2	0.5	3.8	5.3
1979	7.2	0.5	2.1	9.8	Jul	44.2	0.5	4.2	5.6
1980	6.1	0.4	1.8	8.3	Aug	43.6	0.8	4.3	5.7
1981	17.7	0.8	2.5	21.0	Sep	43.4	1.0	5.0	5.8
1982	55.8	6.0	18.4	80.2	Oct	44.7	0.8	4.6	5.8
1983	52.4	5.9	15.6	73.9	Nov	38.1	0.9	4.1	5.7
1984	46.0	2.1	10.2	58.3	Dec	37.3	0.9	4.0	5.5
1985	37.3	0.9	9.5	47.7					

Note: 'Others', in addition to dry cargo vessels, also include chemical tankers, gas tankers, etc.
Source: *Fearnley's Review 1985*. Fearnley, Oslo, January 1986

(DWT) tons per year in 1974 to only 9.7 million (DWT) tons in 1979. After a brief resurgence of demand in 1980/1, it has continued to decline to a level of 7.7 to 10.4 million (DWT) tons per year in recent (1983–6) years. The number of other ship orders declined as well, with the total number of vessels on order now hovering just above 1,000 per year, a loss of 60 per cent of the number of ships ordered per year only 10 years ago.

As ship deliveries usually lag behind ship orders by 2 to 4 years (now only 1 to 2 years), actual ship deliveries are much more even as shown in Figure 1.4. The distribution of new ship deliveries by type of country (or economy) is summarised in Table 1.6. The only increase in percentage participation of new deliveries is experienced by socialist and other (unallocated, mainly newly industrialised) countries as shown in Table 1.6.

A major development has been the drastic reduction in contracting prices for newbuildings (Figure 1.5). Both standard tanker and bulk carrier prices declined by nearly 50 per cent between 1980/1 and 1986. Specialised vessel, container, and RoRo ship prices declined by a smaller amount, yet their 1986 price is still only 65 to 75 per cent of the price of a similar ship ordered 5 to 6 years earlier.

Table 1.5: World orderbook 1974–1986/World contracting 1974–1985

1/1	Figures in number of ships and '000 DWT					Figures in million DWT				
	Oil tankers	Combined carriers	Bulk carriers	Others	Total	Oil tankers	Combined carriers	Bulk carriers	Others	Total
1974	1,131–196,915	73–10,217	528–23,838	871–11,354	2,603–242,324	27.1	2.4	7.1	9.1	45.7
1975	1,020–169,190	57– 7,480	468–20,762	1,036–14,728	2,581–212,160	2.7	1.8	13.7	7.8	26.0
1976	515– 77,327	55– 6,493	647–26,222	1,142–16,975	2,359–127,017	2.1	1.6	9.3	8.8	21.8
1977	241– 31,393	40– 4,488	603–23,425	1,317–19,890	2,201– 79,196	2.8	0.4	6.3	6.7	16.2
1978	147– 15,995	29– 3,075	398–13,496	1,185–17,556	1,759– 50,122	3.0	0.4	1.4	5.1	9.9
1979	110– 9,716	19– 1,942	176– 6,178	1,029–14,148	1,334– 31,984	14.2	1.4	10.4	4.1	30.1
1980	272– 18,438	27– 2,306	279–12,888	842–10,469	1,420– 44,101	9.0	1.3	18.7	4.9	33.9
1981	315– 17,876	34– 3,069	467–26,690	806– 9,436	1,622– 57,071	3.3	1.5	15.6	4.4	24.8
1982	234– 12,023	36– 3,148	608–31,679	811– 9,371	1,689– 56,221	1.4	0.6	5.8	4.6	12.4
1983	157– 7,717	30– 2,387	459–21,714	776– 9,463	1,422– 41,281	5.1	1.4	18.7	5.0	30.2
1984	158– 8,098	29– 2,423	663–28,406	717– 8,937	1,567– 47,864	3.9	1.7	11.2	4.2	21.0
1985	165– 9,274	27– 3,276	533–25,592	607– 7,110	1,332– 45,252	5.0	0.3	7.6	4.5	17.4
1986	157– 10,417	18– 2,778	302–17,967	575– 6,350	1,052– 37,512					

Note: Tankers, combined carriers and bulk carriers comprise vessels over 10,000 DWT. 'Others' comprises all other seagoing cargo carrying vessels over 1,000 grt. Figures as of 1/1 1986 and for the year 1985 are provisional, without deductions for cancellations and deleted orders
Source: *Fearnley's Review 1985*. Fearnley, Oslo, January 1986

Figure 1.3: World orderbook

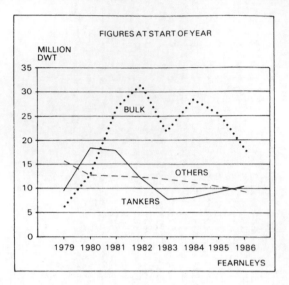

Source: *Fearnley's Review 1985*. Fearnley, Oslo, January 1986

Figure 1.4: Deliveries of newbuildings

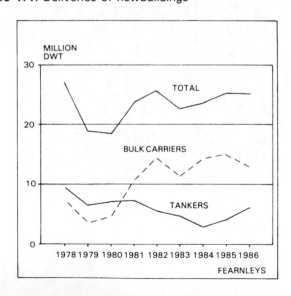

Source: *Fearnley's Review 1985*. Fearnley, Oslo, January 1986

Table 1.6: Distribution of deliveries of newbuildings by groups of countries of build, 1982–1984. (Thousands of grt)[1]

Country grouping	1982	1983	1984
Developed market-economy countries	9,898 (78.6)	10,443 (83.0)	10,012 (77.0)
Developing countries	1,519 (12.1)	975 (7.8)	1,263 (9.7)
Socialist countries	942 (7.5)	881 (7.0)	1,086 (8.4)
Other, unallocated	228 (1.8)	282 (2.2)	632 (4.9)
World total (100.0)	12,587	12,581	12,993

[1] The percentage shares of the world total are indicated in parentheses
Source: Compiled by the UNCTAD Secretariat on the basis of data contained in *Lloyd's Register of Shipping*. Merchant shipbuilding returns, quarterly issues of the respective years

Figure 1.5: Contracting prices for newbuildings

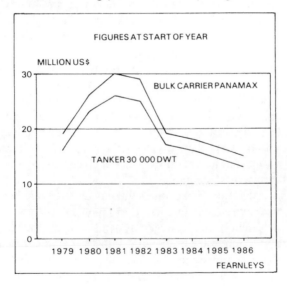

Source: *Fearnley's Review 1985*. Fearnley, Oslo, January 1986

Shipping productivity

The productivity of the world shipping fleet has declined steadily since 1970, from about 8.0 tons of cargo carried per year per DWT

11

in 1970 to about 4.92 tons in 1984. Similarly the ton-miles of production produced per available DWT declined from 32,670 in 1970 to only 1,936. During the same period the capacity of the world fleet more than doubled from 326.1 million DWT to over 674.5 million DWT. There are many reasons for this drastic decline in shipping productivity. Structural disequilibrium, oversupply, decline in world trade, dislocation or realignment of world trade and protectionism are only some developments which contributed. Over 64 per cent of the surplus tonnage consisted of tankers, with 31 per cent dry bulkers and less than 5 per cent general cargo and containerships.

THE STRUCTURE OF THE SHIPPING INDUSTRY

Shipping is structurally organised by function, performance, service, and technology. The structure of shipping is undergoing major changes now, as traditional functional organisation by liner, dry bulk, tanker, general cargo, and specialised shipping are increasingly merged into a multitude of diverse services and operation. Just as owner-operated vessels reacted to growing demands for regular larger-scale operations by forming liner or tramp shipping companies and major bulk material producers or users developed their own proprietary fleet 50 to 70 years ago, so now shipping companies are incorporated into large and often multimodal transport entities. While better integration of multimodal chains of transport links is usually the initial goal, many of these new entities often include major shippers or receivers, as well as large infrastructure owners/operators.

Shipping, as a result, is becoming not only an integral commodity distribution activity, but a major component of coordinated industrial production and delivery systems. While this trend is pronounced in the industrialised world, most developing countries, who have become active in shipping only recently, continue to operate their fleets under a more conventional structure.

Another major change in the shipping industry is increasing government involvement in ownership, operation, and regulation. Until the beginning of this century, shipping was largely owner-operated. The exception was shipping run by and for the use of large trading companies who transport goods to and from remote places often under the control of the trading company, according to some kind of sovereign writ granted by their national ruler. Trading and shipping companies were largely responsible for the colonisation of the rest of the world by European nations. Japan, on the other hand, did not use trade or shipping to extend its influence; the large Japanese trading and shipping firms of today grew out of large domestic businesses, manufacturing, and banking organisations.

The decline of colonialism and the inability of owner-operators to raise the capital to run a fleet of powered vessels – requiring major operating outlays for fuel, maintenance, and insurance, over and above the traditional crew wages and hull/cargo insurance – forced them to consolidate their operations in publicly-owned shipping companies.

The beginning of this century therefore saw the development of the dedicated, usually publicly-owned, shipping company. These usually concentrated their services in passenger (transocean, short ocean, or coastal), break bulk general cargo liner services, and general cargo tramp services. Chartering of ships began long ago when tramp vessels were hired for a voyage or for a specified time of service, but it became increasingly important in the hiring of ship capacity in the period between the two world wars with the emergence of dedicated dry and liquid bulk carriers. While some dry bulk trades, such as coal in North-West Europe, had been carried in dedicated colliers before World War I, the market really took off only with the large-scale use of specialised liquid bulk-carriers or tankers just before World War II.

The structure of the shipping industry has since been in constant flux, as traditional specialised service operators, such as passenger liner operators (Cunard, P&O, etc.) diversified their service by entering the liner and/or bulk services.

Still, until the mid-1950s, most world shipping was owned and operated by companies who usually only ran shipping. Government ownership or involvement, including protected shipping, was minimal. The US was among the first major maritime countries who found it necessary to provide both direct and indirect aid to its national shipping during and just after World War II. The US shipping or merchant marine acts involved were later changed or amended on various occasions, on the basis of their objectives of assuring defence readiness and reasonable control of transportation in foreign trade. Numerous countries have since enacted all kinds of legislation designed to support national shipping and to restrict participation of other, private shipping in its trade.

Also since World War II, an increasing number of shippers, particularly raw material producers, processors, or distributors such

13

as oil, steel, fertiliser, chemical, and other companies, became major ship owners. By 1960, these shippers controlled and operated over one-third of the tonnage needed for their shipping purposes. The governments of many newly independent, developing countries and centrally-planned economies – who were often major raw materials exporters – similarly tried to acquire tonnage to better 'control' the terms of their trade. It was then that large manufacturing, transport, and trading firms started to buy increasingly large interests in international and domestic shipping.

The structure of the shipping industry is now radically different. Less than 30 per cent of world shipping is today owned by pure shipping interests. A slightly larger percentage (about 32 per cent) is owned by trading, manufacturing, and transport companies, with only about 16 per cent owned by shippers and the rest by governments, government agencies, or non-shipping investors. This change in ownership has also affected operations, with nearly 22 per cent of world shipping operated by non-owning shipping companies, such as ship management companies or shippers.

The shift has had a profound impact on the structure of the world shipping industry, which has become increasingly institutionalised. The pure commercial independent ship operator who provided a basic transport service under fairly competitive terms, is largely a thing of the past. The reasons for these developments are political, financial, and operational. Increased capital intensity and modal integration demanded larger financial resources than most ship-owning companies could marshal. Political pressure often forced government, industry, and public participation in shipping, and shippers more often found it attractive to exert greater control. Technological and trade developments will probably continue to push this trend, and the traditional pure ship-owning operator will in the future be an interesting anomaly.

2

Institutional, Policy and Regulatory Issues

ORGANISATION OF SHIPPING

Shipping has moved from an owner-operated, free-wheeling, free trading, unregulated industry towards one that is largely institutionalised, regulated, and publicly-owned. Historically shipping regulated itself. Only insurers, who often consisted of pools of ship investors or owners, imposed certain conditions or regulations on the design, construction, and operation of vessels. Governments or government agencies sought a role in shipping only in times of emergency or war, when they requisitioned vessels for their purposes. In some cases, governments also acquired commercial tonnage for their purposes. There was for a long time very little difference between commercial vessels, most of which were armed, and purpose-built man-of-war or naval vessels. The distinction really only surfaced in the second half of the nineteenth century when fast sailing clippers and the new steam-propelled merchant ships fought for supremacy.

It was during that period that shipping became a transport service industry. Until that time, ship operators (usually owners) were also traders, colonisers, and entrepreneurs. The transport service function brought with it a need for regularity and quality of service, including the publication of commonly available freight rates. Liner shipping was the logical development. Associations of operators were formed, agreeing to provide a regular service (and capacity) on a defined route at agreed and published rates. These associations of shipping companies were called liner conferences. By 1980 more than 500 liner conferences provided regular services on the major trade routes. While most conferences have a closed membership, and new members are only admitted by consent of the existing members, conferences serving the liner trade of the US must by law be open, and thereby admit any qualified operator. Many conferences impose rules on their members and on shippers served by the conference. Among the most important are:

(1) Loyalty discounts, which provide shippers with deferred discounts after exclusive use of conference services for a certain period of time.
(2) Conference Loyalty, under which members undertake no independent actions.
(3) Conference Share Participation, under which members share conference business in terms of agreed-upon formulas, such as revenue sharing, cost sharing, etc.

Conferences also impose various conditions and agreements on members, and will often designate a member or a member's ships as 'fighting ships'. These are so named to offer services at a low non-conference rate, to underbid a non-conference operator who is trying to capture conference business by offering lower rates. Such 'fighting ships' are usually withdrawn as soon as the interloper is chased away. The operator of the fighting ship is usually reimbursed for his losses unless an overall conference revenue sharing agreement exists. If the intruder cannot be discouraged (particularly if he is powerful or government-owned), the conference will usually try to induce him to join the conference.

The liner conference system has been under attack in recent years. Developing countries have claimed that it is a discriminatory monopoly which overcharges for its services and discriminates against developing country trade and shipping. The Code of Conduct for Liner Conferences, adopted by UNCTAD in October 1983, was largely the result of pressure by developing countries to reduce the power and influence of conferences. A second blow to the conference system was supplied by the US Shipping Act of 1984. In addition to maintaining the continued requirement of open conferences in the US foreign trade, this act introduced other provisions such as the mandatory right to independent action by conference members, the ability of members to enter individually into service contracts, freedom to organise intermodal systems, and more. It also permitted shippers to organise in shippers' associations for the first time without concern of antitrust implications.

Various other developments now affect the organisation and function of liner conferences. Trade and shipping protectionism, such as bilateral trade and shipping agreements between countries, often influence the role and operations of conferences in that trade. The future of liner conferences is clouded even more by the fact that an increasing proportion of conference members are owned by governments, by large industrial or integrated transport firms, or by non-vessel operators (banks, investment companies, etc.). This trend affects the relations between conferences and their members, many of whom engage in liner shipping not only for profitability but for political, business, tax, and management control purposes.

Bulk shipping, including tramp shipping, has remained much less regulated. Although this industry has also seen a gradual shift away from owner-operator to government and trading/producer industry ownership, it is still largely unregulated in commercial terms. Pricing of bulk shipping (which is usually hired or chartered as complete ships) is still relatively free, and subject to supply and demand. Such vessels can be chartered bareboat or manned and managed by the operator. They are chartered for a particular voyage, over a number of voyages, or over a specified period of time.

Bulk shipping is under pressure now, with developing countries demanding an increasing role. While some insist on cargo reservation or similar protectionism in this market segment, others have proposed more formal organisation. As bulk shipping follows no fixed routes nor serves particular trades, imposition of protectionist or similar economic regulation may be difficult to enforce.

Currently all international shipping is regulated by various organisations and agencies, whose concerns may include vessel safety, shipboard labour or working conditions, pollution prevention, navigational control and safety, promotion of fair competition in shipping, and facilitation of cooperation in technical and operational matters.

Ship design, construction, and maintenance standards regulation are usually imposed by classification societies, which constitute official bodies in the major maritime nations. Government agencies often delegate some of their responsibilities to classification societies. Ship operation and safety is usually regulated by government departments or agencies, such as the US Coast Guard. These agencies are often also empowered to regulate environmental aspects of shipping. Many governments now subscribe to standards and rules promulgated by international organisations.

While some of these are strictly advisory bodies, others assume policymaking, regulatory, or implementary functions. The need both for international regulation and cooperation in shipping has long been recognised, and is now highlighted by the increase in specialisation

17

and integration of international shipping.

International organisations in shipping can be divided into two groups: intergovernmental organisations and agencies of international organisations, such as the United Nations. While the former function chiefly to make policy which will affect shipping among the countries of represented governments, the latter view their function as primarily regulatory.

Examples of intergovernmental organisations are the OECD, EEC, ASEAN, and similar regional or economic groupings. Their concern is mainly with economic issues affecting the shipping of their member countries. International agencies like IMO, ILO, and various purely technical agencies (in communications, etc.) are principally concerned with safety, workplace, environmental, and other standards. The IMO also recommends standards for ship crew qualifications, retention and discharge of pollutants, and the like. While the charter of the IMO initially included the promotion of fair competition in shipping and the facilitation of cooperation in technical and operational matters, it has seldom attempted to affect economic issues.

The reason may well be that a UN sister organisation, the UN Conference for Trade and Development (UNCTAD) has assumed a leading role with its Shipping Committee in operational and economic matters affecting shipping. UNCTAD now deals with issues of conduct, condition of shipping registration, facilitation of cargo flow, training of shipping and port staff, development of fleets in developing countries, international shipping legislation, relationships among shippers and among ship operators, conditions of service of seafarers, and other problems of concern to international shipping.

The ILO (International Labour Organisation), through its Joint Maritime Commission, has developed many conventions and recommendations for a comprehensive 'Maritime Labour Code'. The Code, which has been ratified by most important maritime nations, includes standardisation of working conditions such as work hours, pensions, vacations, sick pay, and the rights of seafarers. There are also numerous international bodies with interests or functions in legal or political issues affecting shipping. The Permanent Council of Arbitration (Hague), the International Hydrographic Bureau, and the International Court of Justice (Hague) are just a few of these.

The United Nations, through its Economic and Social Council, deals with many shipping policy questions through regional commissions such as the following:

ECE   — Economic Commission for Europe
ESCAP — Economic and Social Commission for Asia and the
          Pacific
ECME   — Economic Commission for the Middle East
ECA   — Economic Commission for Africa
ECLA   — Economic Commission for Latin America

All of these Commissions have shipping divisions who deal with particular issues of area or region. Finally, there are many non-governmental bodies or associations dealing with shipping. These include:

— The Baltic and International Maritime Conference
— The International Tanker Association
— The International Shipping Association
— The International Chamber of Shipping
— The International Chamber of Commerce

More specific technical and operational issues are usually addressed by other organisations, such as:

— The International Cargo Handling Coordination Association
  (ICHCA)
— International Association of Ports and Harbours (IAPH)
— The American Association of Port Authorities (AAPA), and
  other regional port associations
— The Permanent International Association of Navigational
  Congresses (PIANC)
— The International Standards Organisation (ISO)
— International Federation of Forwarding Agents Association
  (FIATA)
— The International Shipowners Association (INSA)
— The International Shipping Federation

The many trade, technical, modal, and specialised organisations are concerned primarily with policy, public relations, and government or intergovernment relations; there are also numerous national and local organisations.

STRUCTURAL CHANGES IN WORLD SHIPPING

In the last twenty years, the world shipping industry and world trade have undergone major structural changes. Shipping has also been subjected to major institutional and technological changes. This has introduced many new factors which influence the requirements of developing countries with respect to shipping.

Changes in trade routes, the physical form of commodities, origin-destination patterns, and shipment sizes, are some of the factors that have encouraged major technological changes in shipping and the shipping-port-inland interface. Shipping has become much more dependent on effective integration with these interfaces which, in turn, has introduced new, more advanced management, and larger investment requirements.

To cope with these expanded needs, liner shipping in particular has been largely containerised. Liner companies now increasingly consolidate their operation by forming consortia, joint ventures, joint services, or other joint arrangements which permit more effective use of economies of scale in this increasingly capital-intensive industry.

We now have multinational liner shipping consortia and multinational ship and container leasing companies. This is the environment in which developing countries try to operate their national fleets. The response of many developing countries has been to introduce protectionist measures. While these are largely designed to protect national fleet operations, they often affect the cost and effectiveness of services essential to their international trade.

Institutional changes in world shipping

The shifting pattern of ship ownership and its consequences are the most significant and sensitive of the structural changes that have taken place in the last twenty years. In this area there are more political than market-induced developments; they constitute a focal point in the North/South dialogue related to the call for a New International Economic Order.

The general pattern of ownership shows a significant decline in the share of world tonnage registered in the OECD countries – over 65 per cent in 1970 compared to 45.4 per cent in 1983 (Table 2.1). Tonnage under open registries gained, as did the socialist countries and the LDCs. The latter group, which accounted for almost 8 per cent in 1975, had raised its share to nearly 16 per cent in 1984. There is little doubt that UNCTAD's declared target of a 20 per cent share by 1990 will be reached. The distribution of tonnage between LDCs is quite uneven; excluding vessels under flags of open registry, more than two-thirds of developing country shipping is owned by Asian countries such as India, South Korea, Brazil, China, Singapore, Saudi Arabia, Kuwait, and so on.

Container shipping, which constitutes the most important technological change in recent years, has tripled in capacity between 1970 and 1984. While developing countries own 14.5 per cent of the world container shipping capacity (Table 2.2), nearly all of that capacity lies with the major developing countries of Asia (14.3 per cent of world total). South America has only 11 container ships, or 0.2 per cent of world total capacity, and African LDCs have none at all.

The traditional structure of international shipping, usually divided into conference liner shipping and bulk shipping, has come under increasing attack. Various restrictions, limiting access to cargo in ocean shipping or regulating use of port facilities, have been proposed or actually introduced; the operation of conferences and the free tramp and bulk markets are quite frequently subjected to government supervision or outright regulation. The fleets of traditional shipping nations, which provided efficient ocean transportation between many parts of the world, now face an uncertain future as their role in providing the links for international trade is questioned by many of their previous users.

The growing tonnage under LDC flags has been accompanied by measures to secure cargoes, resulting in the UNCTAD Code of Conduct for Liner Conferences (1984). The Code is an important element in the changing liner market, and is a manifestation of the issue that brought it about, namely the emergence of national merchant marines in the LDCs. One basic reason these fleets have been created is the widespread feeling that non-shipping nations are treated unfairly and arbitrarily by the liner conferences. The problem is not new; it arose shortly after conferences were established about a century ago. At that time, countervailing organisations in the form of shippers' councils were considered the proper solution.

The present Code calls essentially for a system of international regulation of conference trade. It accepts the conference system as a proper mechanism to render efficient service, but establishes the principles that:

Table 2.1: Distribution of world tonnage[a] (grt and DWT) by groups of countries of registration, 1970, 1983 and 1984 (mid-year figures)

Flags of registration in groups of countries	Tonnage and percentage shares[b]						Increase in tonnage (millions of DWT)	
	In grt (millions)			In DWT (millions)			1970–1984 (Average)	1983–1984
	1970	1983	1984	1970	1983	1984		
World total	217.9 (100.0)	416.9 (100.0)	412.8 (100.0)	326.1 (100.0)	686.0 (100.0)	674.5 (100.0)	24.9	− 11.5
Developed market-economy countries	141.8 (65.1)	197.3 (47.3)	187.3 (45.4)	211.9 (65.0)	322.4 (47.0)	303.4 (45.0)	6.5	− 19.0
Open-registry countries	40.9 (18.8)	107.3 (25.8)	110.0 (26.6)	70.3 (21.6)	199.8 (29.1)	202.2 (30.0)	9.4	2.4
Total	182.0 (83.9)	304.6 (73.1)	297.3 (72.0)	282.2 (86.6)	522.2 (76.1)	505.6 (75.0)	16.0	− 16.6
Socialist countries of Eastern Europe and Asia	19.5 (8.9)	43.1 (10.3)	43.5 (10.5)	21.7 (6.6)	54.4 (7.9)	55.4 (8.2)	2.4	1.0

Of which:								
in Eastern Europe	18.6 (8.5)	33.7 (8.1)	33.5 (8.1)	20.5 (6.2)	40.2 (5.9)	40.3 (6.0)	1.4	0.1
in Asia	0.9 (0.4)	9.4 (2.2)	10.0 (2.4)	1.2 (0.4)	14.2 (2.0)	15.1 (2.2)	1.0	0.9
Developing countries	14.5 (6.7)	66.3 (15.9)	68.0 (16.5)	20.5 (6.3)	104.9 (15.3)	107.1 (15.9)	6.2	2.2
Of which:								
in Africa	0.8	5.3	5.4	1.1	7.7	7.8	0.5	0.1
in America	6.4	14.9	14.8	8.7	22.3	22.2	1.0	−0.1
in Asia	7.3	45.0	46.1	10.7	73.4	74.6	4.6	1.2
in Europe	–	0.9	1.4	–	1.3	2.1	–	0.9
in Oceania	–	0.2	0.3	–	0.2	0.4	–	0.2
Other, unallocated	1.2 (0.5)	2.9 (0.7)	4.0 (1.0)	1.7 (0.5)	4.4 (0.7)	6.4 (0.9)	0.3	2.0

[a] Excluding the US Reserve Fleet and the US and Canadian Great Lakes fleets, which in 1984 amounted respectively to 2.2, 1.7, and 2.0 million grt

[b] Percentage shares are shown in parentheses

Source: 'Review of Maritime Transport 1984', UNCTAD, Geneva, August 1985. Compiled on the basis of data supplied by the Shipping Information Services of Lloyd's Register of Shipping and Lloyd's of London Press, Ltd

Table 2.2: Distribution of world fleet and TEU capacity of fully-cellular containerships by groups of countries, at mid-year 1982, 1983, and 1984

Flags of registration by groups of countries	Number of ships			TEU capacity and percentage shares[a]		
	1982	1983	1984	1982	1983	1984
World total	718	786	900	598,120 (100.0)	697,459 (100.0)	832,112 (100.0)
Developed market-economy countries	431	454	496	412,490 (69.0)	461,608 (66.2)	532,229 (64.0)
Open-registry countries	153	127	161	94,765 (15.8)	74,603 (10.7)	100,217 (12.0)
Sub-total	584	581	657	507,255 (84.8)	536,211 (76.9)	632,446 (76.0)
Socialist countries of Eastern Europe and Asia	35	49	61	15,934 (2.7)	26,525 (3.8)	33,340 (4.0)
Of which:						
in Eastern Europe	33	39	49	15,280 (2.6)	19,861 (2.8)	23,902 (2.9)
in Asia	2	10	12	654 (0.1)	6,664 (1.0)	9,438 (1.1)
Developing countries	76	128	147	53,814 (9.0)	104,264 (14.9)	120,968 (14.5)
Of which:						
in Africa	–	–	–	–	–	–
in America	16	11	11	1,529 (0.3)	985 (0.1)	2,048 (0.2)
in Asia	60	117	136	52,285 (8.7)	103,279 (14.8)	118,920 (14.3)
in Europe	–	–	–	–	–	–
in Oceania	–	–	–	–	–	–
Other, unallocated	23	28	35	21,117 (3.5)	30,459 (4.4)	45,358 (5.5)

[a] Percentage shares are shown in parentheses
Source: 'Review of Maritime Transport 1984', UNCTAD, Geneva, August 1985. Shipping Information Services of *Lloyd's Register of Shipping* and Lloyd's of London Press, Ltd

(1) Governments will have a role in relations between shippers and carriers.
(2) Conference membership shall be granted on the basis of some non-commercial criteria, one of which is the development of national shipping lines.
(3) Cargo allocations to aid national lines are acceptable – i.e., the 40-40-20 guideline.

Among other provisions, the Code justifies the reservation of cargo by trading nations, and suggests as a formula 40-40-20 per cent shares, with the two trading partners provided with a minimum of a 40 per cent share of their mutual trade, and no more than 20 per cent reserved for third-flag carriers.[1]

Several countries have not signed the Code, notably the US; others, like the EEC, will do so only with reservations expressed in the so-called Brussels Package. Under these reservations, the LDC partner's appropriation of its 40 per cent share is accepted, but the EEC partner's share is left free for competition among other EEC members. This free access is extended to any OECD member who offers reciprocity.

Many studies have attempted to assess the impact of the Code, or bilateral shipping arrangements in general. Under some special circumstances, it means that bilaterals may decrease the degree of non-competition. In general, however, there is likely to be upward pressure on the relevant freight rates because a given volume of trade is restricted to the trading partners' conference tonnage, which in all cases must be smaller than the world supply of shipping. To prevent this, rates are likely to become part of the trade agreements and to come increasingly under government control, as is seen in various countertrade arrangements, bilaterals, and the establishment of agencies to negotiate rates.

It should be noted that there have always been numerous methods for allocating cargoes within the existing conference system. Therefore, the Code is not achieving anything new. What it does, however, is to codify into international and national laws these methods of restricting competition. The government, instead of monitoring and controlling anti-competitive behaviour, now becomes a partner in it. The situation argues for extension of this approach into other areas of shipping, such as bulk shipping, and such attempts have been made.

With the Code in place, UNCTAD concerns and efforts have turned to achieve a similar convention for bulk cargoes. This so-called bulk sharing scheme has surfaced frequently at UNCTAD meetings, so far without notable success. However, in UNCTAD's view, such a scheme coupled with the closing of the open registries would provide LDCs with both ships and a cargo base, while the current focus is on the phasing out of the open registries. Several preparatory meetings have been held and some moves have been made towards an international convention for the registration of ships.

The fact that the Code applies only to conference cargoes (and now under the Brussels amendment and the US refusal of the Code excludes intra-OECD trade and trade with the US), as well as the increasing participation of independents, would indicate that the LDCs may not obtain the expected benefits from the Code. The Code suggests that 20 per cent of trade covered by the Code be made available to third-party carriers. Since at present third parties carry more than their suggested share on most trade routes, such tonnage would be surplus if the rule is strictly implemented.

Another initiative yet to affect the shipping environment is UNCTAD's Convention on Multimodal Transport, adopted in 1980, which appears to be a long way from ratification and coming into force. Its purpose is to regulate transport using several modes. The salient feature is that integration of several modes into one company may be held back. The convention calls for multimodal transport to be arranged exclusively by licensees and regulated Multimodal Transport Operators who would act as agents for shippers but not for carriers. On the face of it, the convention is counter to the observed structural changes in the industry. Multimodal transport is moving towards the creation of large multimodal transport companies and integration of multimodal transport operations as well as management.

In general, the LDCs have built up their fleets by relying on low, second-hand prices and easy financing on attractive terms for newbuildings from both domestic and foreign yards – that is, both domestic and foreign government subsidies to the yard have been available. In the operational context, they have had a comparative cost advantage in the crew component, although the advantage is often lost by overmanning. Other cost components are roughly comparable as they are incurred in similar markets. Also, wage rates and related costs have a tendency to rise, and even low rates are often at least partially offset by cumbersome excessive administration. As LDCs enter competitive markets and costs tend to equalise, they are likely to follow the path of the advanced shipping nations in using higher technology ships. Indeed, they would have to do so merely to be part of the international transport system – that is, smaller nations are affected by the technological developments in their major trading partners' systems. In addition, relatively large ships with small crews are of current interest in the EEC maritime nations. As concerns increase for their diminishing fleets, manning policies may also affect the current comparative advantage of the LDCs.

The LDC fleets as a group have grown rapidly in recent years, but, as mentioned earlier, the distribution of the tonnage is uneven. Some LDCs function as open registries, some have achieved status of major shipping nations (Brazil, India, South Korea, Kuwait, the People's Republic of China, the Philippines, Saudi Arabia, Singapore, and Taiwan), and yet others remaining essentially unchanged in these matters. The very fact that fleet expansion has been rapid and substantial in some LDCs does not prove that financing has not been a major constraint. The fleet expansion which has taken place rapidly in the last two years primarily in Asian LDCs only indicates the current acquisition opportunities that have benefited these countries. The majority of LDCs have not been able to take advantage of the lower new and second-hand prices available.

It is not clear to what extent the growth is achieved through purchases of second-hand tonnage, or from newbuildings. On the one hand, the supply of second-hand ships has been boosted by banks' repossessions. The consequent depressing effect on ship prices is offset by the banks' unwillingness to refinance these ships. In general, banks have become more cautious in ship lending, because the surplus of tonnage affects the value of financed ships. That is, the asset securing the loan becomes less important than shipping management, ship owners' skill and reputation, and his trading prospects, including non-shipping aspects that affect immediate cash flows. This tends to favour large, established, and intermodal companies. The small, unknown LDC shipping companies therefore have no ready access to ship financing. The same applies to LDC government-owned companies. Thus, the uneven distribution of tonnage among the LDCs carries its own momentum.

Developing country shipping policy

The current shipping depression, which is expected to continue for a number of years, will affect each LDC differently. Much depends on policy objectives and perspectives which give rise to the institutional support and control mechanisms for the fleet. Korea, for example, has a large surplus of tonnage, and recently tried to consolidate its fleet under a few companies after several smaller firms became insolvent.

In general, the greater the involvement of government through ownership or administrative controls, the more likely non-commercial support becomes to secure the fleet's survival. As a result, there is little LDC tonnage outside East Asia in lay-up. Also, LDC fleet expansion had not slowed down until quite recently, with some LDCs taking advantage of the depressed second-hand prices. Most of these were East Asian owners, many of whom are now suffering under surplus capacity.

What this may mean for the future – and whether it ought to be supported – is difficult to say. International shipping embodies a continuum of technology, from the old conventional carrier to the high-technology speciality ship. Where along the range will a particular LDC place itself? Each type and size of ship has its own cost structure and earning advantage. However, as mentioned earlier, this advantage of low wage rates is somewhat offset by large crews. Also, crew costs as a proportion of operating costs are smaller on new, high-technology ships because of the importance of capital or financial costs which dominate now. Does this mean that the LDCs are locked into the use of older ships? What are the implications for port infrastructure development?

Furthermore, new construction of ships has strong linkage effects in the country where they are built, and therefore contributes to economic growth. It also provides modern, efficient and competitive ships. In contrast, the purchase of second-hand ships is a redistribution of the existing world fleet. In a period of overtonnaging, this would transfer part of the surplus to the LDCs, resulting in costs which may or may not be recovered in a boom when newer vessels also operate. It seems, then, that the purchase of a second-hand vessel should be for an *existing* transport need, not merely to fulfil a *targeted* expansion of a fleet pending its future use. It is hard to make a case for a generally existing need in the present situation. However, some prospects for future use can be identified (whether suitable used ships are available is another question) in liner feeder services, bulk, and cross-trade shipping.

The LDCs have, for some time, argued that they have both a competitive edge and a right to expand their participation in bulk carriage. The competitive advantage is similar to that in liner shipping, i.e., mainly in the crew component. However, that edge is not pronounced when compared to open registry shipping (FOC). Hence, UNCTAD's efforts to phase out these registries must be seen at least partly as a way to improve their own competitiveness; as mentioned earlier, FOC ships are not likely to augment LDC fleets. Some LDCs have tonnage under FOCs. Reasons are often given as political – FOC allows trading that may be closed to the flag of ownership. An equally plausible explanation is the improved competitiveness FOC may offer even to an already competitive operator.

In turn, improved competitiveness may bring bulk cargoes to LDC ships. For the time being, however, UNCTAD is attempting to secure such cargoes through cargo allocation schemes. The reasons are based upon normative equity and 'fairness' criteria. In essence, the argument is that LDCs produce the major part of the bulk cargoes, and it is therefore both right and fair that they should carry an appropriate share of it. Clearly, there is little to say except that production *per se* conveys no particular right; it is ownership that confers right of disposal of the goods. Hence, once the commodity is sold, its transportation is in the hands of the buyer-owner.

This situation is reflected in real life: bulk carriage is usually in the hands of the importer, unless it is integrated transport. The arrangements for shipping must be set at the time of sale. Given that there are normally many sources of supply, the bargaining power lies with the importer.

Unless the LDC is a large bulk importer such as South Korea, there appear to be few prospects for LDCs in general tramp/bulk import carriage. On the other hand, integrated shipping or long-term arrangements in export agreements do provide opportunities. It is likely, however, that such arrangements will be more inspired by political than by market factors. Nevertheless, such arrangements become extensions of the bulk export sector of the country, and shipping facilities must be seen and treated as integral parts of the producing mine or plant.

Liner/cross-trading

Shipping policy debates are often confusing, not only because objectives are unclearly stated but because decision makers seem uncertain as to whether shipping is an export- or import-substituting industry. Most traditional arguments treat it as export, particularly when arguing for its effect on the balance of payment (BOP). With respect to cross-trading, however, the conclusion is unequivocal; it is a pure export activity directly reflected in the BOP. Nevertheless, many LDCs do not encourage cross-trading.

In terms of foreign exchange earnings, cross-trading ought to be encouraged. It has concrete and tangible effects on the BOP. While its linkages to the home economy are small, it also places few demands on domestic resources, particularly administrative, financial, and social.

29

There are a number of low volume liner cargo routes where the incentive to containerise is low. Container services, offered in conferences or independently, are generally overtonnaged and fiercely competitive – a situation which is not likely to improve within a reasonable time horizon. An exception to this situation may evolve within the emerging system of 'load centre ports' and the consequent demand for extensive feeder systems.

Liner/feeder service

This area of possible LDC involvement was mentioned in connection with the emerging 'load centre port' systems. That concept was discussed extensively in the early years of containerisation. Only now, however, is the concept materialising.

It is too early to assess the load centre/feeder concept, but its economic implications are compelling. The circular flow service obviates return voyages and allows for more intensive use of the ship's capacity. The improved service and lower unit cost should give a competitive edge if port transfer is done efficiently. With existing and projected container surplus, analysts expect very strong competition in liner trades and consequent weakening of conferences in general. In particular, it is expected that conference control of 'circular services' will be difficult at best, because each of these services will span the territories of several different conferences. Such developments will weaken the impact of the UNCTAD Code by removing more cargo from national shores by the co-mingling of cargo at the load centres.

Still, there are advantages in the feeder system of the circular service. These prospects exist whether or not the 'trunk-line' operators try to control the feeder system. Also, as more operators enter 'trunk line' services, new load centre ports and feeder systems will develop, all with potential for liner-feeder services.

Development of the feeder fleet is a more likely opportunity for LDCs than participation in mainline services, as it requires less investment and a lower level of technology and operational sophistication. Similarly, developed country operators with better access to developed country cargo will not oppose such participation to the same degree.

Feeder services may be somewhat less competitive than other international shipping because participants from non-feeder ports would be engaging in cross-trades. Acquisition and operation of the fleet may be facilitated by cooperative arrangements with the trunk link operators, or on a regional basis.

30

The system is not without problems, as is all change. The elusive but real prospect of a feeder port being perceived as a low status condition should not be overlooked. There is the potential waste of already completed port facilities based upon other expectations. The extent of that waste is, however, dependent on how the feeder system evolves. Ships, ports, and infrastructure must be consistent. With the feeder system, a new interface is introduced in the centre port; that is, the many different interfaces encountered in the various foreign ports under the old system are replaced by one interface in the centre port. It seems that this would facilitate consistency in the domestic system. Conceptually, the feeder service became an extension of a particular feeder port, thus expanding the domestic infrastructure to the centre port; the interface with international trade is at the centre port, not the feeder (domestic) port.

Application of the Code's 40-40-20 rule in feeder trades may raise complex issues, since the unequivocal identification of trading partners and cross-trades may be difficult.

Developing country shipping conditions

World ocean freight costs, as a percentage of c.i.f. value of imports, remained fairly constant at 6.6 per cent over the period 1980-3. While they declined slightly over that period for developed market economy countries, from 5.6 per cent to 5.4 per cent, the percentage figure for developing countries continued to increase reaching 10.8 per cent in 1983. Declining freight rates, resulting from excess shipping capacity, seem to have benefited developed country freight costs. Similar benefits were not derived by developing countries.

There are many complex reasons for this lack of price elasticity in developing countries (particularly in liner trades, which serve most of LDC import needs with the exception of oil imports). The following are a few examples, none of them mutually exclusive:

(1) Effect of protectionist policies.
(2) Age and condition of national fleet.
(3) Composition of national fleet.
(4) Management of national fleet.
(5) Effect of cost for service of national fleet on freight charges.

As pointed out before, the majority of LDCs have ratified the Code and have introduced various protectionist policies towards the implementation of clauses in this international agreement. Although the Code only applies to liner shipping and advocates the

31

use of conference systems in liner shipping, some countries have introduced legislation or announced policies affecting bulk shipping as well.

The major effect of protectionist policies so far has been the allocation or reservation of cargo shares to national shipping. Although the Code advocates a 40-40-20 split, some LDCs have announced cargo sharing objectives with a 50-50 split, particularly when bilateral shipping agreements do not form part of the general terms of the Code. Although the term 'national shipping' is not explicitly defined, it is generally assumed to apply to all shipping under effective control of a country.

In most LDCs, shipping is a public enterprise which may pose problems of management, control, and regulation. Measures to control competition between public and private national shipping enterprises become particularly costly when associated with competition between national and foreign shipping.

Conferences, as mentioned before, will usually set their freight rates (based largely on value and not cost of service) at a level required by the marginal member of the conference. When this member is the LDC national shipping company, rates will rise to a level which is very profitable for efficient or lower cost members of the same conference. This has been the case in many liner trades serving developing countries. While the cargo share reserved for national shipping at the conference rates provides some balance of payment and other advantages to the respective LDC, the loss in foreign exchange accruing from higher freight rates paid to more efficient foreign operators often offsets these advantages.

The average age of developing country fleets was only 10 per cent higher than that of developed country fleets (Table 2.3). This, however, is misleading, as most of the newer vessels (age 10 years or less) are owned by Asian LDCs. The average age of ships under African and American LDC flags is over 16.8 years, and well over one-third of the fleet has an age exceeding 20 years (20 years is normally considered the economic life of a ship). Furthermore, all of these ships are traditional general cargo vessels, only a few of which have modern cargo gear.

The condition of many of these vessels is below accepted standards. Although their wage level is low by comparison with those of developed countries' crews, they generally have higher crew components and higher maintenance costs because less on-board maintenance is performed by ship crew. As a result, average operating costs of African and American LDCs' liner vessels are usually higher than those of comparable vessels operated by developed country and FOC operators.

The composition of LDC fleets (with the exception of some Asian LDC fleets) is technologically backward. The African LDCs do not have any container ships in their fleets, while the American LDC fleets are composed of only 11 ships with a total capacity of 2,048 TEUs, or less than 0.2 per cent of world fleet capacity. Even major LDC maritime nations such as India and Brazil have only a few converted or multipurpose container vessels under their flags. With increasing containerisation of their liner trades, most of their competitors now employ container or RoRo vessels (often with their own cargo gear). Old general cargo vessels operated by LDCs have to carry containerised cargo as deck cargo, which is less efficient, costs more to load and unload, and requires more port time for an equal load of container cargo handled. As a result, operating costs of these LDC vessels are usually significantly higher per unit of capacity than those of vessels of competing conference members.

Tankers and bulk carriers constitute 44.3 per cent and 33.4 per cent of world fleet capacity (1984). LDC fleets own 12.1 per cent of the world tanker capacity and 17.1 per cent of the bulk carrier capacity, of which 8.1 per cent and 13.4 per cent respectively are owned by Asian LDCs. On the other hand, LDCs accounted for 83.1 per cent of the petroleum and 26.6 per cent of the dry bulk cargo loaded, and 29.4 per cent and 12.1 per cent unloaded. The Asian LDCs, as a group, have a net surplus of tanker and bulk tonnage, while the other LDCs have insignificant participation in bulk shipping. (The African LDCs, for example, only control 1.2 per cent tankers and 0.2 per cent of bulk carrier tonnage, or less than 7 per cent of their requirements.)

A reason for this slow adoption of technological change by LDCs is the lack of management skills. Container vessels require more effective cargo control, vessel and container routing and scheduling, and so on, than do general cargo ships. Most LDC operators require significant technical assistance to effectively manage modern containerised liner and bulk shipping operations.

The combination of used vessels, obsolete technology, high ship operations costs, and less than effective fleet management and maintenance results in the need for higher freight rates; these are usually negotiated and accepted by the conference. Even in bulk shipping, LDC operators usually have higher costs than the developing and FOC flag operators. Many LDC operators charter-in container vessels for their service. Because their charter costs are

Table 2.3: Age distribution of the world merchant fleet by type of vessel as of 1 July 1984. (Percentage of total in terms of grt)

Country grouping	Type of vessel	Total	0–4 years	5–9 years	10–14 years	15 years and over	Average[a] age (years) July 1984	Average age (years) July 1983
World total	All ships	100	17.5	30.6	27.5	24.4	11.16	10.98
	Tankers	100	11.3	41.1	31.7	15.9	10.40	9.98
	Bulk carriers[b]	100	23.4	24.8	29.7	22.1	10.63	10.61
	General cargo	100	13.9	24.3	19.7	42.1	13.60	13.58
Developed market-economy countries	All ships	100	18.5	31.4	28.6	21.5	10.73	10.61
	Tankers	100	11.6	40.4	32.0	16.0	10.42	10.05
	Bulk carriers[b]	100	23.3	25.9	30.6	20.2	10.39	10.42
	General cargo	100	17.5	27.7	17.8	37.0	12.56	12.65
Open-registry countries	All ships	100	14.9	33.0	31.8	20.3	10.89	10.69
	Tankers	100	8.7	44.0	37.1	10.2	9.95	9.40
	Bulk carriers[b]	100	22.2	22.8	31.4	23.6	11.00	11.11
	General cargo	100	11.1	23.5	23.2	42.2	13.93	14.18
Sub-total	All ships	100	17.2	32.0	29.8	21.0	10.78	10.63
	Tankers	100	10.4	41.8	34.1	13.7	10.24	9.80
	Bulk carriers[b]	100	22.9	24.7	30.9	21.5	10.62	10.67
	General cargo	100	15.3	26.2	19.7	38.8	13.04	13.16

Socialist countries of Eastern Europe and Asia	All ships	100	15.4	23.8	18.8	42.0	13.47	13.29
	Tankers	100	11.6	28.0	12.2	48.2	14.26	13.98
	Bulk carriers[b]	100	21.1	34.7	19.2	25.0	10.65	10.60
	General cargo	100	12.1	17.6	21.0	49.3	14.84	14.42
Developing countries (excluding open-registry countries)	All ships	100	19.8	29.8	22.8	27.6	11.29	11.05
	Tankers	100	15.8	41.9	23.9	18.4	10.16	9.68
	Bulk carriers[b]	100	27.4	22.6	27.3	22.7	10.40	10.05
	General cargo	100	12.2	25.7	19.0	43.1	13.80	13.79

[a] To calculate average age it has been assumed that the ages of vessels are distributed evenly between the lower and upper limit of each age group. For the 15 years and over age group, the mid-point has been assumed to be 22 years
[b] Including combined carriers
Source: 'Review of Maritime Transport 1984', UNCTAD, Geneva, August 1985. Compiled on the basis of data supplied by the Shipping Information Services of *Lloyd's Register of Shipping* and Lloyd's of London Press, Ltd

then loaded with a premium, the required freight rates are then even higher than those of their competitors.

Most LDCs protect their national shipping (owned or otherwise under national control) by various measures, including cargo reservation, cargo sharing, cargo assignment, differential port charges and port capacity assignment, and more. All of these measures cause an appreciable economic cost to the country concerned, particularly as they affect conference freight rates.

LDCs generally feel that they need this protection to allow their non-competitive shipping to stay in business. This maintains the vicious circle; LDC shipping is unable to improve its technology or management which in turn raises their costs which require more protection to assure survival. For some LDCs, shipping has become an important or potentially important export industry. The effort to foster or expand shipping as an export often contradicts protectionist measures advocated or imposed by the same nations. LDCs will have to deal with this dilemma and need help in resolving such policy conflicts.

One of the problems facing LDC liner shipping now is the introduction of large fourth-generation economic containerships into round-the-world service. Between 1984–7, container fleet capacity is projected to increase by nearly 40 per cent. These large vessels are expected to affect the structure of direct mainline container service to lesser trading areas, which would then be most effectively served by indirect, transshipment service via load centre ports.

This development offers LDCs an opportunity to participate in more efficient shipping services, by providing the feeder ship capacity. However, most LDCs do not have the capacity and integrate their current operations with efficient long-distance shipping to provide such a service, nor are they able to raise the capital necessary to acquire this new capacity.

RESTRICTIVE SHIPPING POLICIES

Numerous countries have introduced unilateral or bilateral policies on cargo reservation or other restrictive shipping practices. Yet only a few have enforced strict cargo reservation. To assess the impact of restrictive shipping regulations, a structural analysis of the relationship of different operational, financial, and economic factors is required. Shipping operations depend on many overlapping factors. The following are examples:

— shipping controls
— government shipping regulations, aids, incentives, and disincentives
— cargo demand and access control
— freight rate controls
— limitations on entry and merger by operators
— economic regulation
— cost and rate discrimination

The diagram in Figure 2.1 provides a rough representation of the relationships among different restrictive practices in shipping, and particularly factors limiting access to cargo. There are different levels of influence, and their interdependence can be expressed in hierarchical form. This implies that the factors and their impacts can be grouped into distinct sets, with factors of one set influencing those of one or more other sets.

Hierarchical representation of such practices in shipping offers a number of advantages to a study of the impact of such policies. First, it permits description of changes in priorities at various policy levels. It also enables a detailed analysis of structure and function in the system of policy hierarchies. Third, assembly of systems structure can be performed in modular form. Fourth and finally, it provides a mechanism for ready evaluation of the sensitivity of outcome to changes in policy issues or structure. A policy hierarchy, in our sense, is a model of our perception of the most important factors influencing shipping restrictions and their relationships.

Many restrictive shipping policies are closely related, and are often introduced as complementary elements of a country's shipping and trade policy. Some of these restrictive shipping policies have a direct effect on cargo access, such as operational controls on shipping, resulting in discrimination in the clearance of cargo or cargo controls, like transshipment and loading/discharging restrictions. Still others, such as shipping subsidies and restrictive trade financing and regulation, affect cargo access only indirectly. Some of the characteristics of the major restrictive shipping practices can be summarised as follows.

Cargo reservation

Cargo reservation can be introduced in different forms. Cargo may be reserved for a specific subset of ships, such as national flag foreign-going or national flag domestic shipping, regional shipping,

Figure 2.1: Relationship of factors in restrictive shipping practices and regulation

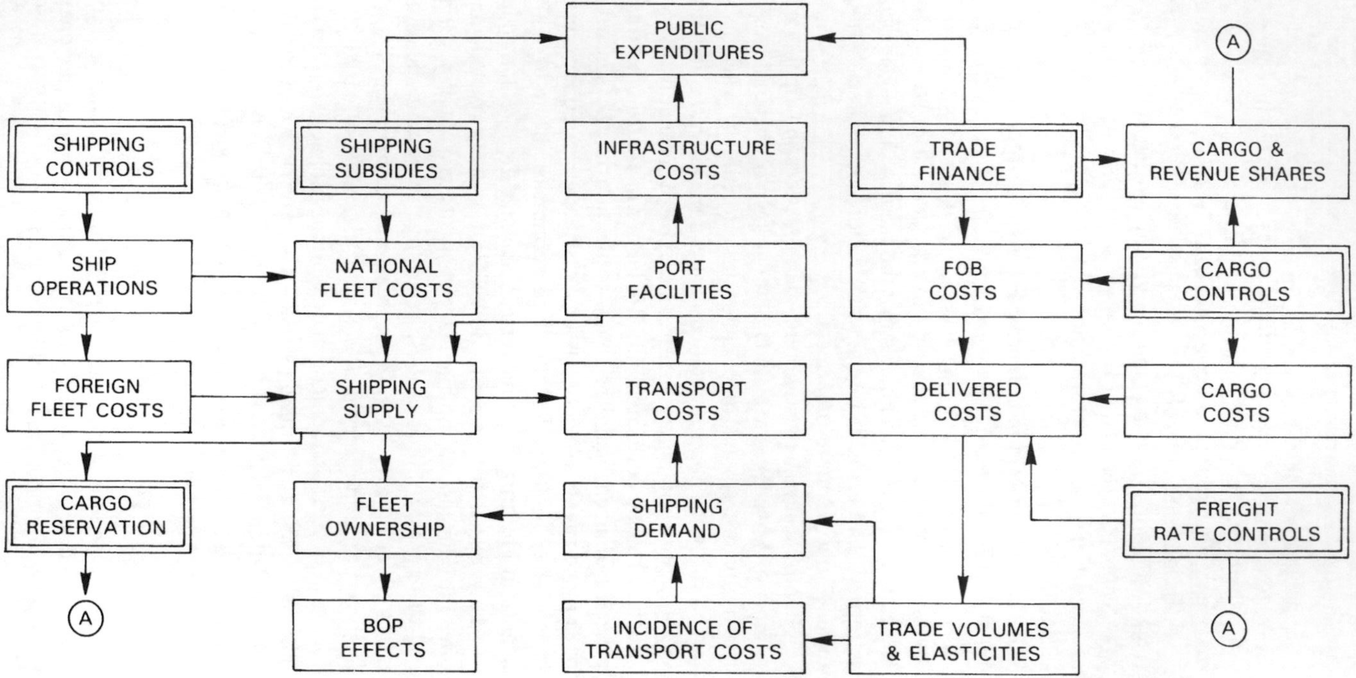

38

shipping of particular trading partners, developing country shipping, and more. The actual cargo reservation may be subject to various kinds of regulations:

(1) Bilateral agreements.
(2) Unilateral agreements.
(3) Multilateral agreements.
(4) International agreements.
(5) Pooling agreements on a national, conference, or operator level.
(6) Commodity or cargo form specific reservation policies or agreements.
(7) Cargo ownership or control specific reservation (government owned or impelled cargo).

Many countries employ several types of agreements.

Operational controls on shipping

These include the following:

(1) Port access restrictions.
(2) Port berth assignment restrictions.
(3) Restrictions in assignment of port labour, cargo handling equipment, or storage space.
(4) Discrimination in the clearance of export and import cargo.

These operational restrictions, sometimes imposed on 'foreign' ships, change the supply curve through shifting of the cost structure of the foreign-flag vessels (or conferences) in the trade. The impact of operational berthing controls can be evaluated using queueing network models which incorporate different priority rules.

Restrictions of port access are more difficult to analyse. Some network models are useful in such evaluations. Some port access restrictions may be absolute, while others are imposed during particular time periods, based on some priority policy, or simply random. All of these impact ship routing, scheduling, and operating cost in general.

Shipping subsidies

Shipping is subsidised in many countries. The application of such subsidies may take different forms:

(1) Operating cost or operation cost-differential subsidies.
(2) Construction cost or construction cost-differential subsidies.
(3) Fuel cost subsidy.
(4) Port dues and charges subsidy.
(5) Reduced taxation or other form of tax subsidy.
(6) Foreign exchange or currency subsidy.
(7) Preferential depreciation.
(8) Investment cost subsidy or preferred financing.
(9) Subsidised ship mortgage or mortgage insurance.

Shipping subsidies are usually introduced to reduce costs of national shipping.

Restrictive trade financing and regulation

Regulatory and fiscal incentives to shippers, exporters, and importers are common in national shipping. These may come in terms of low cost export/import credits, preferential access to foreign exchange, government insurance of transactions, and reduced regulatory trade controls. Also, typical of such incentives are tax and duty rebates, subsidised trade financing, and expeditious trading licensing.

Cargo controls

Cargo reservation may also be exercised through a number of direct cargo controls, such as:

(1) Cargo allocation policies or restrictive carrying licensing.
(2) Loading/discharge permit restrictions.
(3) Transshipment restrictions.
(4) c.i.f./f.o.b. policies.
(5) State trading which introduces state control over cargoes in international trade.
(6) Bills of lading control.

Such controls have an economic impact in terms of cargo delays and increased shipping costs.

Freight rate controls

Sometimes freight rate levels are controlled in order to promote stability in a trade and protect national shipping or shippers. These policies affect the delivered cost of goods, which in turn affects the volume traded and the demand for shipping.

Another kind of restriction is control of fleet ownership. Here the distribution of ownership of the ships active in the trade is regulated by one or both trading partners.

Balance of payments

The control of fleet ownership may have an impact on the balance of payments, foreign exchange requirements, and trade in invisibles. The impact will depend on the extent to which national shipping will meet its costs in domestic as opposed to foreign currencies.

Infrastructure costs

The type of quality of port facilities available to shipping are often affected by government controls and investment decisions. These facilities can have a direct or indirect impact on transport costs.

Public expenditures

Shipping protection usually requires the direct expenditure of public funds in three areas outside of costs entailed in the administration of regulations and policies. The three areas are:

— shipping subsidies
— infrastructure costs
— trade financing

Of these, the most difficult to estimate is the effect of trade financing, or of subsidy policies which are tied to shipping restrictions. Often such policies will have a dual role of stimulating trade as well as supporting national maritime objectives. The attribution of all of such expenditures to shipping protection costs may be a distortion; new means to account for these in an equitable manner are essential.

Transport costs

The true cost of sea transport will often diverge from the cost seen by the shipper, as a result of policy constraints imposed on freight rates.

Fleet revenues

The financial viability of shipping firms will depend on their costs and on the revenues actually generated by their operations. This viability is the ultimate test of the effectiveness of shipping protection measures, and thus is critical in the process of policy formulation.

41

Incidence of transport costs

Changes in shipping policy may result in increases or decreases in the transport cost of a country's trade. Depending on the elasticity of export supply and import demand, these costs may be passed on to the consumer or absorbed by the producer of the traded good.

Trade volumes and shipping costs

For some commodities, transport costs can be the single most important determinant of the level of trade. This is especially true of the bulk raw material (iron ore) and energy (coal) trades, where shipping costs are often equal to 30 to 40 per cent of the landed value of the commodity. But even liner cargoes (Table 2.4) often have appreciable freight costs. In fact, there appears to be an inverse correlation between the value of many commodities and the cost of ocean transportation. This is true despite the fact that the transport cost of many low-value commodities in liner trades is cross-subsidised by higher value commodities in the liner trades, as liner freight rates are largely based on the value of cargoes and not the cost of transport.

Predatory ratemaking

Similarly, international shipping regulation has skirted the various issues posed by the dumping of shipping or the gross underpricing of shipping services by state-controlled fleets.

Price competition which derives an advantage from being state-owned or controlled, or from flying the flag of a state which does not recognise the main IMO or ILO conventions, is often considered unfair; it frequently leads to predatory rates by non-conference operators who work under a state budget. Such protected and/or 'exempted' operators often charge non-compensatory rates. Some OECD members have recently proposed the use of anti-dumping and countervailing duty provisions in the GATT code to deal with such situations. It was found, however, that such an approach would be difficult: liners necessarily use complex rate structures, and it would therefore be problematic to prove the case without a comparison of all rates on all legs of the route.

Review of restrictive shipping policies

The direct and indirect interaction of the major restrictive shipping policies with cargo reservation can be represented in a hierarchical

Table 2.4: Ratios of liner freight rates to world prices of selected commodities

Commodity	Route		Freight rate/World price			
		1970	1979	1980	1981	1982
Rubber	Sing/Malaysia — Europe	10.5	9.7	8.9	7.3	8.7
Tin	Sing/Malaysia — Europe	1.2	0.9	1.0	1.2	1.2
Jute	Bangladesh — Europe	12.1	16.1	19.8	21.4	21.7
Sisal Hemp	East Africa — Europe	19.5	15.7	15.7	15.4	15.3
Cocoa Beans	Ghana — Europe	2.4	2.0	2.7	3.0	3.6
Coconut Oil	Sri Lanka — Europe	8.9	8.0	12.6	14.4	17.3
Tea	Sri Lanka — Europe	9.5	8.8	9.9	10.2	10.7
Coffee	Brazil — Europe	5.2	5.1	6.0	9.0	7.8
Palm Kernels	Nigeria — Europe	8.8	11.9	18.3	27.7	31.7
Coffee	Columbia (Atlantic) — Europe	4.2	3.0	3.3	3.8	4.2
Cocoa Beans	Brazil — Europe	7.4	6.1	8.6	9.3	11.9
Coffee	Columbia (Pacific) — Europe	4.5	4.6	4.4	5.5	5.0

Source: UNCTAD Secretariat, 'Shipping in the Context of Services and the Development Process', Geneva, November 1984 (GE 84–54143)

Figure 2.2: Interactions of restrictive shipping policies and effects on cargo access

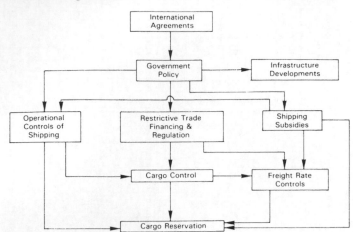

network as shown in Figure 2.2. While some of the interactions and resulting effects can be quantified, most are indirect and can only be represented qualitatively. Our principal interests here are the effect on cargo access and resulting costs.

Many developing countries introduced restrictive policies and regulations even before the Code came into force. They are now increasing the enforcement of their policies, which often go well beyond the recommendations or intent of the Code. Similarly, the interpretation of terms in the Code varies quite significantly among signatories. This is apparent in reviewing the policies introduced by such nations in response to or in supposed conformity with the Code. Many have already written amendments as conditions of their ratification of the Code, or have announced their 'interpretation' of the Code. Still, it must be admitted that the Code is intentionally vague in many respects, and provides recommendations in only a few major areas, such as cargo reservation.

Many developing countries now have a share in their liner trades which, according to a recent OECD report, approaches or even exceeds the 40 per cent recommended in the Code.[2] Notwithstanding these developments, various discriminatory measures continue to be advanced by some countries, even among those who already achieve the recommended participation by national shipping in the country's liner trade. In terms of bulk shipping cargo, reservation exists in many countries but is only sparsely applied. Nevertheless, there are instances, such as the case of full shiploads of neo-bulk import and certain export bulk cargoes, where some developing countries have imposed cargo reservation.

Protectionist or discriminatory measures in shipping

Although most developing countries have adopted cargo reservation in liner shipping, and some have passed laws restricting parts of bulk trades to their shipping, the actual implementation of these measures is usually quite lax. This is particularly true in bulk shipping. Nearly 30 nations, including practically all South American countries, reserve 50 per cent of all general cargoes to national shipping.

Many countries offer bunker and export subsidies to their shipping, and sometimes also extend tax rebates to nationally-owned shipping companies. Practically all the world's countries provide for cargoes owned, purchased, or sold by the government to be transported exclusively by national shipping (62 nations), or else offer national shipping the right of first refusal or a right to at least 50 per cent of all such cargoes. In countries with centrally-planned economies, government-controlled cargo is usually excluded from any cargo sharing agreements, and fully reserved to national shipping. This obviously implies that in many cases nearly all cargoes are excluded from carriage by foreign vessels.

Freight taxes on foreign flag vessels loading and discharging in a port is a measure used by Panama to increase national shipping participation in its trade. Some countries differentiate in their allocations. For example, Uruguay reserves 100 per cent of all imports and 50 per cent of all waterborne trade to Uruguayan ships. In some countries ships of particular nationality are excluded, usually for political reasons.

Another discriminatory measure used by countries such as the People's Republic of China is to restrict purchases to f.o.b., exports to c.i.f., and to fix freight rates. This provides China with complete control of shipping in its foreign trade.

Indonesia, in addition to imposing the 50 per cent reservation rule for national shipping on international trade, also reserves most feeder traffic to Indonesian ships. Similarly, the granting of loading/discharging permits is restrictive, making it difficult for non-Indonesian vessels to operate there. Other countries, like South Korea, reserve 100 per cent of all cargoes to their ships, and require special exemptions for foreign vessels to participate in Korea's foreign trade.

Most other developing countries enforce a 40 to 50 per cent cargo reservation as well as various other discriminatory measures. Developed countries (OECD, etc.) have generally been reactive and have accepted outright cargo reservation only as part of bilateral or multilateral agreements.

Bulk shipping restrictions are much fewer and usually less controlled than those applied to liner shipping. Although over 20 countries have explicitly defined bulk cargo shares to be carried exclusively by national shipping, only a few actually enforce these restrictions. The exceptions to this are countries like Brazil, Argentina, Indonesia, and others who reserve 100 per cent of specific commodities (Indonesian fertiliser, etc.) to foreign flag vessels.

Review of literature on restrictive shipping policies

Many authors have addressed issues of restrictive shipping practices in recent years. Economic and operational effects were among the most important aspects evaluated.

Wijkman,[3] using 1975 UN statistics, studied the effects of cargo reservation on the international distribution of tonnage and shipping income. He found that if a simple division of cargo volume among trading partners is assumed, developing countries (LDCs) would have an excess of over 10 million grt in general cargo tonnage, and nearly 9 million grt when general cargo and container tonnage are combined. When dry bulk tonnage is added, the surplus of LDCs grows to over 19 million grt. He included tonnage under open LDC register. If only closed-register LDCs are considered, these would have gained 3 million grt of general cargo tonnage and 18.6 million grt (or 25 per cent) if general cargo, container, and dry bulk tonnage are combined. Shipping income was assumed to consist essentially of tax and licence revenues, monopoly profits and natural resource rents. Wijkman concluded that cargo reservation would be accompanied by an increase in tax revenues of about US $700 m, of which the LDCs would gain US $576 m. The case for monopoly-profits income, from natural resource rents or other forms of shipping income redistribution (such as incurred through vessel sales, etc.), are more difficult to determine.

The study also enumerated possible reductions in efficiency that non-market induced transfers of registration or ownership may cause. Among them are the changes in ownership, changes in market form, traffic patterns, rent-seeking activities and operating costs. Another important effect is the changed balance of payments, which has been estimated by UNCTAD's Secretariat as 10 to 20 per cent of the gross freight receipts of the newly acquired fleet.

In an economic analysis of flag discrimination, Vanags[4] argues that changes in freight rates must be absorbed by changes in domestic prices, and that liner services should be treated as a homogeneous product of uniform quality to permit rational analysis. Also, average and marginal costs of providing liner services should be considered constant. He proposes that conferences serving a trade operate in such a way as to maximise joint profits of their members and set freight rates in terms of marginal revenues and costs.

Sturmey[5] argues that the Code deprives conferences of the right – which they had assumed – to make decisions that might fundamentally affect the welfare of the countries served, even in face of the opposition of those countries. According to Sturmey, the EEC's council regulation No. 944/79 of May 1979 undoes much of what the Code has tried to do.

Heaver[6] infers that the objective of conferences and the actions of member shipping companies are compatible with Banmol's theory, and claims that shipping firms maximise revenue rather than profit. This is a rather general statement and affects only a small number of firms. It also depends on the volume carried, as Laing points out.[7] He finds that conference members' profits vary, and are usually normal when carrying maximum volumes. Without conferences, however, liner companies would each show normal profits with smaller volumes of service.

In their fundamental work on the subject, Bennathan and Walters[8] assert that cargo reservation interferes with the efficient use of resources in shipping, and that marginal cost pricing becomes impracticable under such constraints. Bohme[9] also argues against artificial constraints. Devanney et al.,[10] in a case study of Conference Ratemaking on the west coast of South America, found that if the developing country's shipping is the high cost partner in a conference, cargo sharing may impose large additional costs. The result seems inevitable when conferences adjust their rates to be barely profitable to their marginal members. Ellsworth[11] concludes that the conflict between cargo reservation and rationalisation in liner shipping is real and pervasive. Frankel[12,13] studied the impact of cargo sharing and bilateral cargo reservation agreements on US liner trades, with particular reference to the US/Brazil-Argentina

47

trade, and found that it increased costs and rates significantly.

In other articles, Goss[14,15,16] analysed competition in liner shipping and its economics, as well as the effects of regulation and constraints on the efficiency of resource use in liner shipping. In his discussion of open conferences, Davis[17] concludes that such conferences often attract excess capacity which interferes with effective coordination and rationalisation. This is particularly common under regulatory supervision such as that imposed on US trades by the FMC, which forces conferences into a mould of artificially induced 'perfect' competition. Such arrangements would generally increase rates even more when combined with cargo sharing.

Earlier researchers like Walgreen[18] claimed that national flag shipping has a moderating influence on conference ratemaking policies, but this idea has since been rebutted. In an exhaustive study of the practices of conferences that serve the west coast of South America trade, Devanney et al.[19] concluded that when LDC national shipping is the high cost operator in the conference, conference rates will usually be adjusted to provide a marginal return to such operators. The result is a general increase of conference rates. Such an increase is often largely absorbed by the LDC economy in higher import and export costs.

This is particularly serious, as Zerby[20] points out, because LDCs export larger quantities of goods than they import. At the same time, most of their exports are bulk cargoes, while most of their imports are liner cargoes. As a result, they suffer under a chronic shortage of backhaul cargoes in all their trades, which makes cargo reservation even less viable from the point of view of shipping costs.

In recent years, many other authors have studied various aspects of restrictive shipping practices and their impact on shipping operations and economics. In general, they agree that government or intergovernment interference in shipping, through regulation or economic controls, adversely affects the costs and rates of shipping and the effectiveness of resource utilisation.

CARGO SHARING

Restrictions on competition have always been a fact of life in shipping – perhaps with good reasons, in light of the risks involved in this industry and the national interests that depend on it. In recent years cargo reservation, limited bilateral cargo access, and other methods limiting access to cargo in ocean shipping ('cargo sharing') have been introduced or proposed in many parts of the world. Developing and non-market economy nations have been among the principal proponents of these measures. The most important among these proposals are the cargo sharing provisions recommended under the 'Code of Conduct for Liner Conferences' developed by UNCTAD, which came into force in October 1983. This Code proposed cargo sharing among trading partners and third-flag carriers. Cargo sharing in bulk shipping is the next issue under consideration.

The concept of cargo sharing to advance national interest is not new, nor is the Code the first proposal for international acceptance of the concept. States used cargo sharing to reserve trade and water transportation for national shipping since colonial days. For example, in its trade with the American and Asian colonies, England limited other nations' shipping access to the trade with the colonies. England required this trade to be transshipped through her ports, without regard to origin or final destination of the cargo – thereby achieving *de facto* nearly exclusive cargo reservation for English shipping.

More recently, centrally-planned non-market nations made widescale use of bilateral cargo access agreements. The foreign trade of these nations consists chiefly of government-controlled (or owned) cargoes. Participants in bilateral cargo access agreements include countries whose policies leave little alternative to such agreements. These countries, such as Argentina and Brazil, adopted the policy of bilateral cargo reservation requirements nearly 15 years ago. A typical example is the policy of the People's Republic of China, under which imports are largely procured on an f.o.b. basis, while exports are shipped mostly c.i.f. The regulation of cargo access to international shipping is on the rise.

The reasons for this development include the increasing worldwide nationalism in shipping, the preoccupation of many developing and developed nations with participation in international shipping, and the integration of shipping with other national transport modes and national commerce. These factors (particularly in liner shipping) are manifested by restrictive practices and government policy designed to strengthen the development of national merchant fleets.

Cargo sharing, as a commercial concept, is based on the belief that a nation benefits when its shipping participates in its national trade. Developing nations have assumed the accuracy of this view,

49

and it has enormous political appeal. Cargo sharing fosters national control over price and service levels, protects nascent domestic shipping, retains profits for trading partners, and improves balance of payment while increasing employment in shipping by trading partners.

Market forces in shipping are also influenced by sharing, which regulates the competition among shippers and the quantity of affreightment in international trade. There are indications that cargo sharing also affects the shipping productivity, effectiveness and capacity assigned to carry the allocated shares. These in turn influence the cost of transportation. Finally, the limitations on competition and regulation (often associated with the introduction of cargo sharing and cargo reservation) tend to affect the shipping prices of goods covered by such systems, and consequently have an economic impact on the trading nations. In sum, cargo sharing affects the operation of free market forces in shipping by regulating the quantity and terms of shipment. It affects rates, shipper choices, quality and level of service, technological change, investments, and fleet expansion and contraction.

The subversion of cargo sharing is particularly acute in the case of developing countries. Few of their trades have the commensurate partners needed, or the balanced trade flow. These are necessary conditions if the strict forms of cargo sharing are to be efficient. Most forms of cargo reservation interfere with the rational use of resources; as a result, they increase costs, reduce service quality, and obviously limit competition.

There are a number of important basic facts, often overlooked, that influence the effectiveness of cargo sharing. First, once a ship is scheduled to undertake a voyage, 70 to 85 per cent of the voyage costs are normally fixed. Therefore the marginal costs of a voyage, incident with the carriage of cargo, are usually only 15 to 30 per cent of voyage costs.

Second, increases in freight rates or shipping costs must actually be absorbed by increased domestic prices. Therefore, the increased freight costs are more often than not borne by the importer. Similarly, in liner shipping, conference behaviour is usually interpreted as maximising the joint profits of members through an attempt to assure minimal profit for marginal members of the conference. As a result, in the absence of an uncontrolled operator in the trade, rates will usually increase to assure the marginal conference members financial viability, while adding to the profit of the remaining members.

The purpose of this study is to investigate the effect of cargo sharing on the cost and price of shipping and thereby evaluate the economic impact of such systems. We must then seek to answer two questions:

(1) How can the negative effects of restricting cargo access be avoided or minimised?
(2) What attractive alternatives can be developed to achieve the goals of cargo access restrictions more effectively?

Probably the most important international agreement affecting shipping is the UNCTAD Code of Conduct for Liner Conferences, but a major ambiguity in the Code is the definition of 'national shipping'. The Code implies that the head office, that is, effective control and a substantial share of ownership, must be within national jurisdiction, but that joint ventures (space charters, etc.) may be given the status of national shipping. As a result, a flag of registry may not be important, and various approaches have been devised to satisfy the basic provisions of the Code qualifying a shipping company as 'national shipping'.

Allocation of international shipping

Let us first consider the various methods by which international shipping is allocated. By shipping we mean the liner and bulk or tramp sectors of the industry.

Liner shipping in particular routes can be allocated in the following ways:

(1) Open market competition among liner operators.
(2) Independent action conference. (Members are free to set their own participation.)
(3) Open single rate conference. (Qualified operators may join, subject to their acceptance of a single rate and conference rules.)
(4) Open dual/multiple rate conference. (Qualified operator may join, subject to the acceptance of multiple rates and conference rules.)
(5) Closed conference. (Closed to new members unless voted by quorum of members.)
(6) Rate agreement between conference and independents.

51

(7) Interconference agreements.
(8) Cargo sharing agreements.

Shipping terms under cargo sharing agreements often use *ad valorem* or value of cargo sharing, revenue of volume of cargo sharing, and percentage fee redistribution. Countries may also use port dues differentials, preferential assignment of berths, cargo restrictions, and special fees or penalties, as well as taxes or dues to assure compliance with cargo sharing legislation.

Cargo sharing and related agreements also affect the allocation of trade, the relations with shippers, freight rates, terms and quality of service, and terms of trade. The forms this takes may be broken down into categories:

(1) Institutional arrangements for conducting the trade:
(a) membership of conferences/pools
(b) share of trade
(c) pooling mechanisms
(d) decision-making procedures
(e) sanctions
(f) self-policing
(g) conference agreements
(2) Relations with shippers:
(a) loyalty agreements
(b) dispensation
(c) availability of tariffs and related regulations
(d) annual reports
(e) consultation machinery
(3) Freight rates:
(a) criteria for freight rate discrimination
(b) conference tariffs
(c) general freight rate increase
(d) promotional freight rates
(e) surcharges
(f) currency changes
(4) Terms and quality of service:
(a) fighting ships
(b) adequacy of service (frequency and volume offered)
(c) quality of service
(5) Provisions and machinery for settlement of disputes
(6) Terms of trade (trade in which shipping terms form an integral part of the terms under which goods are traded)

There is an infinite variety of methods by which trade between regions can be artificially allocated among various parties. Cargo sharing will here be considered in its broadest sense, including all such allocation agreements. By their nature, these agreements restrict competition, but the degree of cooperation involved varies.

A distinction should be drawn between 'cargo reservation' and cargo allocation schemes. Cargo reservation is usually applied to particular commodities or to government-controlled shipments. In these cases, carriage of the specified goods is reserved for particular carriers (usually the national flag fleet). These preference schemes are typically administered by governments through legal statutes and regulations. Cargo allocation, on the other hand, is the assignment of cargo to specific operators. Sometimes cargo allocation is used in conjunction with cargo preference; however, the two remain distinct in concept.

An example of cargo reservation is 'equal access' agreements, whereby national carriers are granted transferable national flag status under national cargo preference laws. (Each such carrier may transfer his allocation to someone else.) One such 'equal access' agreement is the 'Agreement Between the United States of America and the Union of Soviet Socialist Republics'. This document states the intent of the US and the USSR to carry equal shares (or at least one-third) of all trade between the two nations. Shares are computed separately for liner and non-liner carryings, and are based on weight tonnage.

Meanwhile, allocation schemes represent agreements between carriers to limit competition amongst themselves. The parties to the agreement will still generally compete for the unallocated portion of the market. Thus trade carried by the parties to the agreement is allocated amongst them. No prohibition of carriage by non-parties is implied by the term 'allocation'. Cargo preference reserves an entire market (or market segment) for a particular carrier or set of carriers, thus offering the greatest degree of security to the preferred carriers on a trade route.

In an effort to classify the types of possible cargo sharing arrangements, we will describe the alternative administrative frameworks and operational bases on which allocations can be made. Broadly, arrangements will be considered in order of the increasing degree of cooperation implied. Operational implications and considerations of market structure will be considered in greater detail later in this chapter.

Table 2.5 presents a simple outline describing alternative cargo

Table 2.5: Dimensions of cargo sharing: Possibilities, criteria, issues

Item	Comments/Examples
A. Traffic subject to the sharing agreement	
1. All cargoes (liner and non-liner)	
2. Liner-type cargoes	Require government cargo reservation. Example: Korea's Maritime Promotion Law. By specifying *commodities*, can avoid losses in covered cargo due to changed mode of carriage (e.g. liner to tramp service for neo-bulk commodities)
3. All liner services	Would require closed trade for sharing agreement (i.e. no outsiders allowed)
4. Conference-carried cargoes	In general, would entail multi-lateral sharing
5. Conference subset	Typical for pooling agreements
B. Definition of trade route coverage	
1. Direction of trade	Imports only versus imports and exports
2. Transshipped cargoes	Origin/destination basis versus port of lading/unlading
3. Between two super-national regions	Northern Europe to Far East
4. Between single nation and trade region	US to ASEAN
5. Strictly bilateral	Indonesia to US
6. Between a port range and a single nation	US Pacific to Japan
7. Between specific ports	New York, Philadelphia, Baltimore to Tokyo, Kobe, Osaka
C. Criteria for qualification for national-line share	
1. Nation of incorporation of liner company	
2. Nationality of owners (controlling interest) of liner company	
3. Nationality of management ('Effective Control')	
4. Location of company headquarters	
5. Payment of local taxes	
6. Membership in joint venture with a national line	
7. Vessel registry	
8. Crew nationality	

54

D. Share allocation basis
   1. Sailings
   2. Capacity (measurement tons per year provided)
   3. Cargo weight
   4. Cargo value
   5. Revenue tonnage
   6. Freight revenues
   7. Revenues and volume
   8. Revenues less certain costs
   9. Earnings
E. Administration of shares
   1. Renegotiation period
   2. Criteria for changes in shares
   3. Criteria for entry into scope of sharing agreement
   4. Terms and conditions of adjustments for over/underperformance

55

Table 2.6: National cargo preference policies of 55 countries*

Unilateral		Bilateral	
100% reservation, all or part of trade	6	50/50	14
50% reservation, all or part of trade	11	40–40–20	4
Preference for national fleet carriage of government cargo	19		

*OECD and major developing countries
Source: Totland, 'Protectionism in International Shipping and Some Economic Effects'. *Maritime Policy and Management, 7*, 2:103–14, 1980

sharing characteristics according to the dimensions of cargo type, trade route coverage, nationality of carriers, share allocation basis, and administrative issues.

Table 2.6 shows the 1980 features of five major types of reservation policies. Two-thirds of the policies identified in 1980 included a degree of unilateral reservation, i.e. reservation of cargo to the promulgator's national flag vessels, irrespective of the cargo's origin or destination. More than a third of the policies completely excluded cross-traders. Only four instances of discrimination policies conformed to the popular 'Codist' interpretation, i.e. 40-40-20.

More recent cargo reservation policies, particularly unilateral cargo reservation law, reflect the growing influence of the Code as a model, but it is clear that many such policies will be difficult to implement. Frequently key definitions are vague, and administration/enforcement provisions are inadequate or are delegated to inexperienced agencies.

As of this writing, the patterns of reservation policies have polarised. Allowing for the fact that many of the policies studied exist only on paper and are ambiguous in some respects, the trends by LDCs are apparently toward more extreme positions (50 to 100 per cent reservation), and while developed countries tend towards the Code, only with reservation provisions. Table 2.7 shows developments in the adoption of national cargo preferences of 71 countries by 1983. It indicates a distinct move towards more bilateral rather than multinational or Code cargo preference.

Cargo sharing agreements

Cargo sharing agreements can be entered into by operators serving or interested in serving a trade, by treaties between two or more

Table 2.7: National cargo preference policies of 71 countries (1983)

Unilateral		Bilateral	
100% reservation for all or part of trade	10	50/50	25
50% reservation for all or part of trade	8	40–40–20	9
Preference for use of national vessels for government cargo	19		

Source: Author's review of (31 December 1983) maritime laws
OECD and major developing countries

trading countries, by unilateral laws imposed by a sovereign country, or by rules or codes negotiated by international organisations empowered with the responsibility. Cargo sharing agreements can be divided into those covering liner trade and those covering non-liner (tramp or bulk) trade.

Liner shipping serving liner, scheduled break bulk, or unitised trade is often organised in conferences of shipping companies serving particular trades. Such conferences frequently include cargo sharing or allocation as part of their agreements. Similarly, governments may impose unilateral cargo allocations or enter into bilateral or multilateral agreements with regard to cargo sharing. Finally, international agreements may impose cargo sharing or reservation requirements, such as those introduced by the UNCTAD negotiated 'Code of Conduct for Liner Conferences'.

Few, if any, operator negotiated cargo sharing agreements exist in tramp/bulk shipping. Exceptions are volume contracts, long-term charters, and similar service contracts. Although some governments have recently imposed unilateral policies regarding bulk cargo reservation and a few bilateral bulk cargo sharing agreements have been negotiated, the bulk trade remains largely free of protectionist measures. This situation may not continue much longer, since a Code similar to the Liner Code enacted in October 1983 is now under discussion.

General framework of liner operator agreements in liner shipping – conference agreements

A conference agreement is the basic document defining the contractual relationship among the members of a liner conference. It is essentially a compromise among competing member lines, designed to restrict or eliminate competition between the member lines and to

57

meet the existing and potential competition from outside lines. Most conference agreements are confidential documents.

The scope of conference agreements differs widely. It depends largely on the competition between the member lines, and the existing and potential competition between conference members and outsiders. At a minimum, conference agreements require members to (i) charge uniform rates and (ii) follow the same rules and regulations for calculating and collecting freight charges. This applies to all cargo shipped in vessels owned, controlled, chartered, or managed by the members in the area of operation covered by the conference agreement. Further, in some conferences, the members agree separately to pool either their total freight earnings, or those deriving from some specific area or from specified commodities within the conference operation, and to divide the earnings among the members according to agreed percentages.

A conference agreement[21] may cover some or all of the following matters:

(a) the sphere of the conference, i.e. the range of ports and activities which come within the purview of the agreement

(b) the types of memberships, such as full and associate members, their rights and obligations, terms and conditions of membership (viz. admission fee, security deposit, faithful performance bond)

(c) admission, withdrawal, suspension, and expulsion of a member

(d) procedures regarding conference meetings and voting

(e) conference secretariat, their officers and duties, and appointment of committees

(f) obligations of members regarding rates and operation of conference services

(g) practices of members which are prohibited under the conference agreement

(h) self-policing provisions such as investigation of and penalties against malpractices of the member lines

(i) arbitration of disputes between members

(j) members' participation in other agreements

Pool agreements by liner conferences

Pools are a natural outgrowth of conferences, inasmuch as they serve primarily to limit service competition while the conference limits price competition. Pooling represents one type of cooperative arrangement among carriers. The details of the pooling agreement determine the degree to which competition among pool members is eliminated.

Many bilateral pooling and equal access agreements have been adopted in response to cargo preference laws, import quotas and fees, and other barriers to market entry imposed by the governments of some trading partners. A number of pools are designed primarily for rationalisation purposes, including the Israeli, Italian, Calcutta and Bangladesh, and Japanese pools.

Pooling agreements include provisions regarding the following categories:

(1) Coverage:
  — carriers
  — ports or coastal range
  — commodities
  — separate pools by commodity group
(2) Operational requirements:
  — minimum number of sailings
(3) Pool shares:
  — basis
  — renegotiation period
(4) Contribution rates (revenue pools) may or may not include:
  — bunker, currency adjustments
  — taxes
  — *ad valorem* charges
  — heavy lift charges
  — container rental
  — port differentials
  — deductions/additions for non-pier-to-pier container rates or free-in, free-out, free-in-and-out rates
(5) Penalties:
  — forfeiture for undercarriage
(6) Pool transfers:
  — frequency of settling accounts

Pools covering a particular trade route can be either 'blanket' regional pools (covering all points within a coastal range) or port-specific pools. Pools generally apply to the trade between specified ports only. Some conference ports may cover non-pool ports, and different pools may exist for different sections of the trade covered

59

by the conference. Some conference members operating in a particular section may work outside the pool covering that section. This situation usually arises when a carrier has access to cargoes that others do not (through cargo preference, in particular).

An example of pooling is Article 2 of the Liner Code of Conduct for Liner Conferences. That article implies that the traffic subject to share allocation is the trade between two countries which meets these criteria:

   (a)   it is covered by the conference (Article 2, paragraph 4(a))
   (b)   it is covered by the pool or berthing, sailing or other cargo allocation agreement operated by the conference (Article 2, paragraph 2)
   (c)   it is generated by the mutual foreign trade of the two countries (Article 2, paragraph 4(a))

Item (c) thus means that national shipping lines have rights to carry cargoes originating in or destined for their country – cargoes which are transshipped at ports of other nations. However, Article 2, paragraph 17 is somewhat confusing on this issue, stating that 'the provisions of Article 2, paragraphs 1 to 16 inclusive, concern all goods regardless of their origin, their destination, or the use for which they are intended, with the exception of military equipment for national defence purposes'. Note that this article of the Code would affect reservation indirectly since it leaves almost all cargo liable to cargo sharing provisions.

'Cargo pools' usually cover a particular commodity or commodity group, and are based on a freight-ton allocation of carriage. Under the agreement, each member has the right to carry a specified percentage share of the freight-tons of the commodity.

In a revenue pool, each member is entitled to receive a specified percentage of the total freight revenue earned by all the pool members.[22] Generally, the revenue paid into the pool is either a fixed percentage of total revenue or the total revenue minus certain expenses.

Revenue pool agreements usually exempt certain special stowage/handling cargoes and other cargoes for which there is little competition between lines. Some pools require that members meet extraordinary cargo movement requests. Sometimes associate membership in a pool is granted whereby the associate member receives more than some small fraction (say, 2.5 per cent) of total gross pool revenues, but the excess (less carrying allowances) is due to the pool account. Pool shares can be fixed for a specified period and subject to regular negotiation, or can be changed only by the petition of members.

Sailings may be allocated in the form of berthing rights. Some pools also stipulate an even spread of sailings over the period. If a member carries less than the minimal amount, he will not be compensated unless he can prove that *force majeure* prevented him from filling his quota.

Thus, allocation can take place based on the share of sailings made, capacity provided, tonnage carried, revenues earned, or some combination of these. The most typical arrangement is a combined cargo/revenue pool, which allocates revenues but provides adjustments to encourage a similar split of tonnage carried.

Ultimately, the members of a pool are interested in their net revenues from providing liner services. It is in arranging this division that the terms of pooling agreements become complex. The costs of carriage of various commodities differ. Revenues from various commodities vary according to tariff schedule. Also, serving different ports changes carrier costs. At the same time the pool must take care to avoid arrangements which might incite members to use outside lines.

Pool applicants invariably emphasise that the pool is intended to reduce malpractices and otherwise stabilise the real rates assessed – a symptom of overtonnaging. In general a pool has three objectives:

(1) To increase the pool's share of the market.
(2) To provide an equitable distribution of benefits among members.
(3) To satisfy these two goals in the most efficient manner possible.

This third objective can be restated as an attempt to remove incentives for inefficient competition within the pool. That is, the pool seeks to rationalise its operations.

Pools cover only a small fraction of the US liner trades. In general, the FMC has approved pools which result from foreign government unilateral actions. In foreign-to-foreign trades, pool participation by US operators is more common. These pools emerged naturally from closed-conference environments in foreign countries. Since pools represent a significant reduction in competition, they are in conflict with the basic philosophy in the United

States. The US Code of Federal Regulations permits only a limited type of pool. It defines a pooling agreement as one which 'provides for the division of the cargo carryings or earnings and/or losses among the parties in accordance with a fixed formula'. This agreement may take several forms.

Administration of pools

The administration of the pool itself is usually conducted through a pool committee of members or their agents. This body typically keeps track of cargo movement and vessel scheduling, and monitors members' performance. The conference secretary is sometimes the pool secretary. When many ports are covered by a pooling agreement, there will often be several pool committees.

The fixing of pool shares is a critical part of port administration. Where two or more lines of the same flag are members of a pool, the shares are first fixed on the basis of flag group and then between members within each flag group. Shares may be allocated among others on the basis of various factors:

— negotiations between pool members
— commercial and other requirements of the trade
— past performance of each member
— future potential of each member
— capacity of a line to compete as an outsider if agreement cannot be reached, and
— national aspirations of different members.

The UNCTAD Code suggests that pool shares would be revised at two-year intervals and that new shares should be based on performance but subject to national flag share guidelines. Further, any member line dissatisfied with its share should have the right to international arbitration.

All the pooling agreements filed with the Federal Maritime Commission, pursuant to Section 15 of the Shipping Act, are revenue pooling rather than cargo pooling agreements. The revenue shares of the pool members are sometimes matched by a corresponding obligation to carry about the same percentage of cargo as their share of the revenue pool. This arrangement is similar to the Chilean and Peruvian agreements, but not to the agreements with Argentina, Brazil, and Japan.

Cooperative agreements

Cooperative agreements between carriers vary in the degree of cooperation involved, from simple rate agreements through allocation of sailings, revenue pools, joint service agreements, and, at the other extreme, outright merger between liner shipping firms.

The basic types of commercial operating agreements are outlined below.

Joint service agreements

A joint service agreement is defined as one which 'establishes a new and separate line or service to be operated by the parties as a joint venture'. The new and separate service fixes its own rates, publishes its own tariffs, issues its own bills of lading, and acts generally as a single carrier.[24] The agreements must be filed with and approved by the Federal Maritime Commission before they become effective. There are presently 12 joint service agreements covering the US-Far East trade on file with the Federal Maritime Commission.

The parties to a joint service agreement agree to establish and maintain a joint cargo and/or passenger service, and cooperate to supply tonnage for the joint service. However, profits and losses are borne solely by the owner or charterer of the vessel.

Usually, each party delegates all management and organisational responsibility of the joint service to a separate corporation. This corporation would handle the solicitation and booking of cargo and passengers as well as the collection of freight and passenger revenues.

A joint service may become a party to other agreements (including agreement to establish a conference, a pool, a joint service, or any other lawful arrangement). In such cases, the joint service acts as a single party or member. The authorised signatory for the joint service is designated by the joint service agreement.

Although the parties participate in a joint service, their bills of lading, dock receipts, and passenger tickets must show the name of the party for whose account the vessel is operated. These papers may be terminated either by mutual consent of the parties, or by required notice given by one of the parties to the other and to the government agency involved.[25]

Consortium

In a consortium providing liner shipping services, only the ships generally remain under separate ownership.

Joint venture

In this closest form of cooperation between independent liner companies, the participants jointly own or lease vessels, equipment, and terminals. The venture has its own management. Tax considerations dictate that most joint ventures arise between companies from a single country.

Merger

When two firms merge, they no longer have separate corporate identity in any respect and become a new single entity.

As we have seen, the closer forms of operating agreements – joint service, consortium, joint venture – implicitly satisfy the objectives of a pool. Pools merely represent one form of carrier cooperation, short of a joint service. Some form of operating agreement is required to implement a bilateral agreement (see below).

General framework of non-liner operator agreements: Tramp/bulk carrier agreements

Tramp and bulk shipping operators are not organised in conferences or other groupings for particular trades or services. As a result, there exist few, if any, operator agreements on cargo sharing. Some national operator organisations have attempted to influence governments to reserve shares of cargo in various countries, frequently resulting in unilateral or bilateral allocations of cargo. At the same time, there exist no known inter- or intra-operator agreements on cargo allocations within the tramp/bulk shipping industry.

The trades served by tramp/bulk shipping (reefer, dry bulk, oil, gas, chemicals, etc.) depend on a competitive free market system. In turn, the prevailing market mechanisms hinge on the demand for primary commodities in quantity and on the supply of shipping capacity for these commodities at a particular place and time. Since bulk commodities are usually traded in worldwide markets that are subject to multiple sources of supply, the variations of demand and the economies of the world commodity trades make these trades more vulnerable to free market forces. Dedicated ship movements are usually not possible except for a particular service (such as supplying a fixed amount of coal annually to a power plant), which would usually be arranged for under a shipping contract or charter.

General framework of government and inter-government agreements for liner shipping

As described earlier, the most important international agreement affecting liner shipping in recent years is the UNCTAD 'Code of Conduct' enacted in October 1983. Developing country members of UNCTAD were the strongest proponents of the Code, expecting it to provide a means for change in existing practice, including ownership, ocean rights, and in particular, liner shipping. Among its various terms, the Code (Appendix A) recommends a cargo sharing formula by which each trading partner would set aside 40 per cent for its national shipping, with up to 20 per cent of the trade left for carriage by cross-traders.

The Code implies the existence of viable conference arrangements while recognising participants in non-conference shipping within the environment agreed upon by the liner conference in the trade. The Code's 54 articles cover economic, regulatory, and operational issues, including:

— The role of national shipping lines in determining conference policy, including the degree of participation in the trade (40-40-20 or otherwise) and allocation by freight or volume of cargo. National shipping lines have a dominant role in determining service levels in a trade, and can veto conference decisions.

— Third party rights (20 per cent, unless different levels are accepted by national shipping lines).

— Shippers' councils, consultations among conferences, and shippers' organisations, in matters of mutual interest. The Code recommends the establishment and strengthening of shippers' councils in areas where they are lacking.

— Freight rates, to be decided by commercial considerations and set as low as possible. (Three months' notice is required of a conference's intent to change the level of freight rates, with an additional ten months required between the date of the notice and the date the increase takes effect.)

— Arbitration and settlement of claims or disputes between conference members, conferences, shipping lines, shippers' councils, and individual shippers. The role of government in code enforcement is to be minimised, with national or international arbitration preferred.

Cargo sharing under the UNCTAD Code[26]

The Convention, in accordance with its Article 48, was open for signature from 1 July 1974, through 30 June 1975. Since that date the convention has been open for accession. By 3 August 1983, 59 countries had made definitive signatures, approved, accepted, ratified, or acceded to the convention (see Table 2.8).

The Convention came into force on 6 October 1983, according to the conditions fulfilled the previous April from Article 49(1), when countries representing 25 per cent of the world tonnage had become 'contracting parties'. This tonnage requirement of the convention is that the contracting parties shall own not less than 25 per cent – i.e. 18,173,548 grt – of the relevant world tonnage (72,694,191 grt). The 59 countries listed in paragraph 3 above own 20,848,476 grt, or 26.8 per cent of the relevant total.

At the same time, by early 1983 some members of UNCTAD still had not become contracting parties to the United Nations Conference on a Code of Conduct for Liner Conference. Thus, at its sixth session in Belgrade, Yugoslavia in the summer of that year, the United Nations Conference on Trade and Development drafted a resolution (144:VI) urging these members to join. It also called on members already parties to the Convention to take prompt measures to implement the Code on a national level, bearing in mind the annexes to the Final Act.

The Brussels package. The EEC countries have adopted regulation 965/79, which established the guidelines for members' ratification of the Code. The so-called 'Brussels package' accepts the Code as governing the OECD countries' trade with developing/Codist countries; nevertheless, it '. . . opts for continuation of the "status quo" for trade between the community and developed countries which accept the code with "reciprocity" agreements among developed countries to allow cross-trading in each other's developing country trades'.[27] The main provisions can be summarised as follows.[28]

(1) In trades where one country is not a party to the Liner Conference Code, the Code will not apply at all.

(2) 'National line' status, under the Brussels package, is not confined to companies owned in the country concerned, but is extended under the same conditions to all shipping established in that EEC member state.

(3) Under the Brussels package (unlike the Code), 'national line' status does not automatically guarantee a right of conference membership to all national shipping lines: this is a matter for

commercial negotiation between lines.

(4) In conference trading between countries adopting the Brussels package, the cargo sharing provisions of the Code will not operate at all.

(5) In a conference trading between countries adopting the Brussels package and a Codist developing country, member lines from EEC countries and other OECD reciprocating countries will redistribute the shares which are allocated to them under the Code. This redistribution, like all cargo sharing agreements within liner conferences, must be unanimously agreed. Unless all conference members agree to dispense with it, it must follow principles which already apply in normal commercial conference negotiations.

(6) Lines from other OECD countries (whether Codist or not) will in any case remain free to operate as cross-traders outside the Conference. They will remain free to compete as cross-traders within the Conference on the same basis as European lines in the trades covered by (4); they will also be able to share on the same basis as European lines in the commercial redistribution process in the trades covered by (5). However, these rights depend on the reciprocal treatment of European cross-trading lines by the OECD country concerned.

Although the 'Brussels' amendment was generally accepted by EEC countries, not all have acceded to the Code, as Table 2.8 demonstrates.

Institutional and organisational settings

There are many institutional frameworks within which cargo sharing arrangements can take place under the Code, varying broadly in terms of their scope and also government involvement.

The amount of change required in the institutional framework to accommodate cargo sharing arrangements will depend largely on the existing liner industry environment.

Competition in the liner trades can be limited through government cargo preference schemes that run from limited preference laws to extensive reservation of cargoes. Where the government has a strong involvement, the trade is more likely to be closed. Similarly, cargo sharing pools are a more natural development in closed-conference trades than in open-conference trades.

Where all trading nations desire a strict sharing formula like the Code's, its efficiency declines when more countries are involved

Table 2.8: Countries' signatories and ratification of liner code (August 1983)

Ghana	24 June 1975	r
Chile	25 June 1975	s
Pakistan	27 June 1975	s
Gambia	30 June 1975	s
Sri Lanka	30 June 1975	s
Venezuela	30 June 1975	s
Bangladesh	24 July 1975	a
Nigeria	10 September 1975	a
Benin	27 October 1975	a
United Republic of Tanzania	3 November 1975	a
Niger	13 January 1976	r
Philippines	2 March 1976	r
Guatemala	3 March 1976	r
Mexico	6 May 1976	a
Cameroon	15 June 1976	a
Cuba	23 July 1976	a
Indonesia	11 January 1977	r
Ivory Coast	17 February 1977	r
Central African Republic	13 May 1977	a
Senegal	20 May 1977	r
Zaire	25 July 1977	a
Madagascar	23 December 1977	a
Togo	12 January 1978	r
Cape Verde	13 January 1978	a
India	14 February 1978	r
Kenya	27 February 1978	a
Mali	15 March 1978	a
Sudan	16 March 1978	a
Gabon	5 June 1978	r
Ethiopia	1 September 1978	r
Iraq	25 October 1978	a
Costa Rica	27 October 1978	r
Peru	21 November 1978	a
Egypt	25 January 1979	a
Tunisia	15 March 1979	a
Republic of Korea	11 May 1979	a
Czechoslovakia	4 June 1979	app
Honduras	12 June 1979	a
Union of Soviet Socialist Republics	28 June 1979	acc
German Democratic Republic	9 July 1979	r
Sierra Leone	9 July 1979	a
Uruguay	9 July 1979	a
Bulgaria	12 July 1979	a
Guyana	7 January 1980	a
Morocco	11 February 1980	a
Jordan	17 March 1980	a
Yugoslavia	7 July 1980	r
Guinea	19 August 1980	a
Mauritius	16 September 1980	a
China	23 September 1980	a
Barbados	29 October 1980	a
Romania	7 January 1982	a

Table 2.8: *contd.*

Lebanon	30 April 1982	a
Jamaica	20 July 1982	a
Congo	26 July 1982	a
Malaysia	27 August 1982	a
Federal Republic of Germany	6 April 1983	r
Netherlands	6 April 1983	a
Trinidad and Tobago	3 August 1983	a

(s = signature; app = approved; acc = accepted; r = ratified; a = acceded to)
On or prior to 30 June 1975, the Convention had been signed by a number of countries which by 31 August 1984 still had not deposited an instrument of ratification, acceptance, or approval with the Secretary-General of the United Nations. The countries, arranged in chronological order of signature, are:

Iran (Islamic Republic of)	7 August 1974
Ecuador	22 October 1974
Malta	15 May 1975
Brazil	23 June 1975
Algeria	27 June 1975
France	30 June 1975
Belgium	30 June 1975
Turkey	30 June 1975

within a natural (geographic) trade region. However, if regions organise into trade 'associations' to negotiate as a bloc, this problem could be mitigated. The feasibility of this approach depends on the economic integration achieved in the region (ranging from customs, unions, free trade areas, common markets, and economic unions, through full economic integration).

Resolution of disputes

Disputes among shipping companies or between shipping companies and shippers can be resolved by direct conciliation, arbitration, or legal process. Similarly, cargo reservation agreements must provide for the resolution of disputes between various groups – a shipping line and a conference, a shipping line and a shipper or shippers' organisation, between members of a conference, and between conferences themselves. Several mechanisms exist. (See Figure 2.3).

The UNCTAD Code provides for direct negotiation and, failing that, non-binding mandatory conciliation. The EEC has established the International Chamber of Shipping as a conciliation resource; otherwise, binding arbitration can be sought with the consent of both parties.

69

Figure 2.3: Dispute resolution

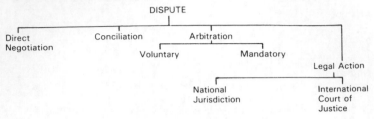

Enforcement. Several countries who have signed the Code, including the People's Republic of China, Indonesia, and the West African countries, have required importers to purchase f.o.b. and exporters to sell c.i.f. Nevertheless, we have no detailed information available on the extent to which this is enforced or what sanctions are applied to offenders. It is clear that West African countries are using manifest data to enforce penalties for the infringement of cargo reservation agreements. Fines proportional to the value of the merchandise – up to 25 per cent of the value – and higher port dues are among the means employed.

Many other countries assess a flag *ad valorem* percentage 'fee' on any foreign trade cargo carried by a foreign ship, with smaller fees for ships carrying cargo within their national quota or share. For example, the People's Republic of China levies a fee, while carriage outside the agreed-upon share (unilaterally or bilaterally enforced) is assessed at a higher rate. Other enforcement measures include preferential assignment of berths and other facilities to vessels carrying reserved cargo, with top priority often given to national shipping.

Ambiguities. Cargo reservation agreements must begin by defining 'national' shipping capacity. The Code embodies the most influential definition to date:

> [a national shipping line is] . . . a vessel-operating carrier which has its head office of management and its effective control in that country and is recognised as such by an appropriate authority of that country or under the law of that country.

> Lines belonging to and operated by a joint venture involving two or more countries and in whose equity the national interests, public and/or private, of those countries have a substantial share

and whose head office of management and whose effective control is in one of those countries can be recognised as a national line by the appropriate authorities of those countries.

Problems may arise in the definition of 'head office', 'effective control', and 'substantial share', although in most cases, the nationality of a carrier is fairly clear (in particular for state-controlled lines).

The definition of a 'national shipping line' involves the following considerations:

(1) Joint ventures may be granted 'national line' status as long as a national line participates.

(2) Space chartered by a national line on a foreign-owned vessel may be considered part of the national share.

(3) Vessels' flag of registry may or may not be important in their assignment to national share. For example, under the Korean government's Revised Maritime Transportation Promotion Law, exemptions to the Korean-carrier requirement are available for carriers whose governments have negotiated agreements with the Korean government, and are based on the flag of the main line vessel used. While this allows flag-of-convenience (FOC) feeder operations, carriers with FOC deep-sea tonnage would be excluded.

(4) The extent of ownership interest may be specifically accounted for in assigning national shares (e.g. 51 per cent of 'ABC Lines' would be considered part of the fleet of nation 'X' and 49 per cent of that of nation 'Y', if such was the ownership split).

(5) In Item (4) above, ownership might depend on the nation of incorporation of the company, or the citizenship of the individual corporate shareholders.

(6) Location of management headquarters may or may not be considered in assignment.

(7) The national line definition may be modified over a 'phase-in' period; space chartering would be considered part of the national fleet only as an interim measure until the owned fleet expanded sufficiently.

(8) Since it is the recognition by an appropriate government authority in each nation which establishes national line status, it is important to note that conditions of such recognition may not be uniform for all nations.

We must note, too, that the Brussels package departs from the Code in the matter of national lines. It maintains that:

> The status of 'national line' in itself does not entitle a shipping company to be admitted to the conference. Whether it is a subsidiary of a European line or of a US line established in an EEC country, access to a conference will be dependent on commercial negotiations between the national lines applying for membership or between these national lines and the national line (or group of lines) already belonging to that conference. If these negotiations fail, there may be governmental settlement of the dispute in a non-discriminatory way. . . . As in the past, the principal factor governing a conference attitude to a new applicant will be its assessment of the applicant's capabilities as a competitor and hence of the desirability of including it within the conference instead of competing with the conference from without.

Other government or inter-government agreements – Liner shipping

The most important type of government agreement is the unilateral introduction of protectionist measures based on government legislation. Unilateralism, while attractive and often an only choice for a government, introduces many difficult problems, particularly for countries which have highly imbalanced trades or depend on trading partners for various economic concessions.

The dangers of unilateralism are many, but the most important effects are usually countermeasures by the trading partners.

Unilateral action often includes a 100 per cent cargo reservation to national shipping, which is not only unrealistic but obviously results in adverse reactions. Other measures may introduce all kinds of preference for national shipping.

Bilateral agreements

A bilateral agreement, as applied to liner shipping, is any plan mutually acceptable (to the two governments involved) for the allocation of liner cargo carriage between two countries. While allocation is normally on a 50-50 or 40-40-20 basis, any combination of shares is possible. This includes unequal allocations, as well as a range defining maximum and minimum participation by the fleets of the two countries. Similarly, cargo shares could be defined by volume, weight, or revenue, any combinations of these, or by the amount and type of capacity and service offered. Finally, cargo shares can be reserved for 'government-controlled cargo', 'government-owned cargo', 'government-subsidised cargo', certain types of reserved cargoes, or all cargoes. Reservation of shares may also be affected by ports of origin or destination, or even by places of origin and destination. Other reservation clauses have also been used, such as type and form of cargo, method and form of affreightment, method of purchase and payment, and so on.

In summary, there are many formulas which can be used to structure bilateral cargo sharing agreements. There are also conditional bilateral cargo sharing agreements in which parties agree to shares providing that other economic, trade, or shipping benefits will be offered. Examples of bilateral agreements in the US-South American trade are listed in Table 2.9.

Multilateral agreements

There are similarly many formulas for structuring multilateral agreements. The Code, for example, is essentially a multilateral cargo reservation/equal access agreement.

Multilateral agreements basically involve three or more countries who agree to share their cargo in some form. They can take place between two or more blocks of trading countries, comprising two or

Table 2.9: US–South American agreements

Country	Agreement number	US coastal region	Share allocation Northbound agreements	Share allocation Southbound agreements
Brazil	10027	Atlantic	40–40–20	–
	10320	Gulf	40–40–20	–
	10330	Pacific	50–50	–
	9847	Atlantic	–	50–50
	9848	Gulf	–	50–50
	9873	Pacific	–	50–50
Argentina	10386	Atlantic	40–40–20	–
	10382	Gulf	40–40–20	–
	10388	Atlantic	–	50–50
	10389	Gulf	–	50–50
Peru	10041	Atlantic	–	50–50
	10044	Gulf	–	50–50
Chile (agreements expired 31 December 1980)	9941	Atlantic	–	50–50
	9942	Gulf	–	50–50

more trading areas. The purpose is to assure 'fair' participation in the mutual trades, while providing more effective use of shipping capacity than is usually feasible under bilateral cargo sharing agreements, cargo reservation schemes, and particularly the Code-type formula. It recognises that most trades are highly imbalanced, both in volume and form of trade, and also that ships which serve trade efficiently in one direction may be unsuitable to serve in the other. Therefore, under most existing bilateral agreements, the choice of ships and ship capacity is usually a compromise which severely affects the cost and quality of service.

Under multilateral agreements, such inefficiencies can often be reduced or eliminated by structuring the agreements (including the selection of partners) in such a way that the trades complement each other, and assure a 'best' use of shipping capacity employed. The potential savings in costs are variously estimated from 10 per cent to well over 50 per cent. Such multilateral agreements furthermore offer opportunities for the use of semi-open conferences (the term implies openness to ships registered or controlled by all parties to the multilateral agreement).

Government or inter-government agreements –
bulk shipping

Although there are no international agreements with respect to bulk shipping reservation, numerous countries have introduced unilateral legislation in this area. Many developing countries, particularly commodity exporting countries, have passed legislation reserving 40 to 100 per cent of bulk cargo (usually exports) to national shipping. Still, in most cases the countries lack the capacity to actually have their national shipping carry the reserved share. As a result, many of these countries issue temporary exemptions, permits, or licences to foreign shipping, or encourage national shipping companies to charter or lease the necessary tonnage.

Impacts of cargo sharing

The impacts of cargo sharing can range from the cost of shipping and the quality of services provided to balance of payment in the countries involved. Cargo sharing may affect the employment of nationals of these countries, as well as countries providing seafarers to other nations' shipping; security of shipping services as well as cargo shipped; participation in fleet operation and control, and many other areas. These impacts may be temporary or permanent, indefinite or fixed. They also have secondary and tertiary effects which can be even more difficult to identify and quantify. In this section we will briefly review the most obvious – not necessarily most important – impacts of cargo sharing, with an emphasis on liner shipping, the only shipping sector which has accumulated real experience with cargo sharing.

Impacts of cargo sharing in liner shipping

There are a significant number of potential impacts imposed by cargo reservation measures. These fall into the following general groups:

(1) Impacts on liner operations.
(2) Impacts on relations with shippers.
(3) Impacts on freight rates and general costs of shipping.
(4) Impacts on the terms and quality of service.
(5) Impacts on the methods for the settlement of disputes.
(6) Impacts on the terms of trade.

Limiting access to cargo will affect the number and frequency of port calls and the port pairs served, consequently influencing the technology used and the rate of technological change. For example, recent studies of the impact of bilateral cargo sharing agreements found that the protection provided under these agreements resulted in the use of older ships than would be employed if the trade were open to third-party competition. The studies concluded that containerisation was not effectively employed, and members of the conferences generally used their older (often fully depreciated) tonnage to serve the particular trade. The same study also found a significantly higher freight rate level than should be expected in the service if it were opened to competition.

The reasons behind these statistics included the lack of effective competition, the essential protection provided, the high costs of the protected marginal operators, the lack of rationalisation of tonnage and schedule of services, as well as the less than efficient use of port infrastructure and support services. Differences in freight charges of 20 to 40 per cent appear to be common, but equally important from the shipper's point of view are the reduced frequency of service, as well as slower or less direct service. Cargo sharing operators usually

75

limit their port calls and often use greater selectivity in accepting cargo.

Considering the organisation of conferences with cargo sharing or cargo reservation agreements, the effectiveness of self-policing seems compromised; the conference feels threatened by the shippers' councils which are usually essential to cargo reservation schemes. Sanctions and other intra-conference policing measures are infrequently employed, particularly against major national shipping companies covered by the agreement.

Developing countries and their trades are usually affected more by these operational impacts for various reasons:

(1) LDC operators are often the marginal members of the conference with the highest operating costs.

(2) LDC liner trades which are nearly exclusively with developed countries are highly imbalanced, with an average import/export balance of 7:1 by volume and nearly 9:1 by value. This occurs despite great effort at industrialisation and use of container and other liner shipping for pseudo-bulk cargo and semi-finished materials. The lack of rationalised use of tonnage also increases freight rates.

(3) LDC operators often employ obsolete and inefficient tonnage, encouraging other conference members to do likewise. Higher than necessary freight charges are usually combined with higher port throughput and feeder costs, making LDC trade even more costly and less competitive. This is often exacerbated by the lack of incentives for additional port calls, or calls at smaller ports, as well as by the level and quality of service.

All of the above factors result in significant increases in transport and trading costs which are practically always borne by the LDC economy.

Another important issue concerns relations with shippers. Conferences usually employ loyalty or service agreements – which also often include dispensations and discounts – to tie shippers to the conference. Obviously, under cargo reservation agreements, these type of arrangements are not necessary.

Most cargo reservation agreements, as well as the Code, require shipper/conference rate discussions (and often shipper or government approval). Various forms of consultation machinery are frequently included also. Similarly, there are often requirements for the advance notification of tariff or rate changes. Many of the agreements require notices like the Code's of as much as 150 days, which, given unpredictable factors like port congestion, fuel cost changes, etc., can result in unduly large preemptive rate increases. These were initially designed to assure the conference of an effective rate in preparation of changes in conference members' costs which may never materialise.

The quality and terms of service nearly always decline under non-competitive service conditions imposed by cargo reservation. Even on routes covered by closed-conferences, there is always the potential for non-conference operators to offer services in competition with the conference. This ever-present danger usually provides a measure of service and freight regulation offering reasonably competitive terms. On the other hand, closed-conferences have traditionally offered loyalty discounts, service agreements, and other forms of rebates to retain shipper's business. They also often delegate fighting ships or fleets to undercut any non-conference competitor in their trade, until the competitor either is driven out of the trade or comes to terms with the conference.

An increasingly important issue is the cost of shipping. Commercial credit is more and more difficult to obtain for second-hand ships, and terms of ship financing have stiffened significantly. Under these conditions, LDCs attempting to increase their ship ownership to carry 'their share' of cargo find it difficult to obtain ship financing, particularly as many large foreign debt problems of many LDCs frustrates their situation. As a result, they either accept high cost financing or use joint venture, charter, space charter, joint service, or similar agreements to get the tonnage capacity required to carry their share.

Cargo sharing and reservation agreements affect liner operations and economics. They also have secondary effects on port usage, progress toward universal intermodal operations, and mode of shipment of neo- and pseudo-bulk commodities. The greatest impacts can be expected in trades where competition was initially low, or wholly excluded following implementation of the agreement. Economic and operational impact of cargo sharing is affected by various factors, as shown in Table 2.10.

The imposition of cargo reservation agreements on various routes is expected to significantly reduce the number of ports served in a particular trade, by removing the incentive to serve any but the primary ports. The elimination of some ports in a given trade will not only reduce service and affect the economic viability of by-

Table 2.10: Circumstances governing the impact of cargo reservation schemes

Significant impact	Circumscribed impact
— open conferences are the rule — significant non-conference competition exists — operational agreements among carriers are limited in scope — no shippers' representation exists — government regulation is present to a high degree	— trades are characterised by closed, highly integrated conferences — shippers along the route are organised, whether in Shippers' Councils or in some other form — carriers and shippers negotiate directly, outside a legislated framework

passed routes, but may also drive up point-to-point costs to shippers because of further feeder costs.

Cargo reservation agreements have promoted a marked increase in the move of pseudo- or neo-bulk cargoes, traditionally carried on liner vessels, to parcel bulk carriers. This trend can be expected to continue, particularly if the imposition of cargo reservation results in deterioration of reliability, frequency, and quality of service, or a large increase in freight rates.

Intermodal transport is essential for effective containerised liner operations. The UNCTAD Code, and most cargo reservation agreements, make no provisions for intermodal operations. Thus, they would only encourage national flag operators to invest in intermodal facilities, if at all.

Impacts on costs and revenues. Cargo reservation agreements affect costs and revenues by limiting carriers' control over rate setting, thereby regulating the supply of vessels, particularly of lower-priced marginal tonnage. The relationship between the rates charged for shipping services and the actual costs of supplying transport is determined by the mechanism of rate setting. These rates have a number of forms: conference rates, bilateral shipping arrangements, short- and long-term charter rates, and non-conference liner rates.

While conference rates and bilateral arrangements for US trade must be reviewed by the FMC, charter rates are determined in an open market. Under free competition, prices are based on marginal costs. Non-conference liner services usually offer rates set below those of the conference lines. (Some non-conference lines are operated by subsidised national fleets and offer rates below marginal costs.)

The impact of the cargo reservation agreements on freight rates will depend on the interaction of many factors, but will probably increase rates. Cargo reservation may directly encourage the use of inefficient, high operating cost, national flag tonnage, which would drive up conference rates. Since third-party shares can be unilaterally adjusted by national flag carriers, participating third-party carriers would tend to allocate only inefficient tonnage to the trade. The extent to which rates will change obviously depends on the degree of reallocation of tonnage, *vis-à-vis* current allocation.

Generally, all restrictions on third-party carriage will tend to reduce competition and efficiency, raising freight rates. In addition, the 5-month delay on rate increases imposed by the Code will induce conferences to 'play it safe' by introducing increases far above those necessary for expected near-term cost increases. The resulting rate increases could often be contained or limited if the period of notification were reduced.

On the other hand, while closed-conferences will reduce competition and drive up rates, at the same time they could permit more rationalisation on a bilateral basis to reduce freight rates. However, effective rationalisation is not generally possible in bilateral liner trades, particularly if containerised. Therefore, the introduction of closed bilateral conferences may be expected to increase freight rates.

The US stance in opposing cargo reservation and enforcing open conferences in its trade can be expected to affect freight rates in two general ways.

First, they will shift the concentration of beneficial ownership of liner capacity, therefore changing the market power of carriers. Second, they will affect the absolute supply of vessels available to the US market, altering the marginal cost supply curve for the industry and the production curves for each carrier.

However, if cargo allocations by other nations increases the supply of shipping available to the US market, and if this shipping is technically efficient, then the general effect will be a drop in freight rates.

Of the alternatives shown in Figure 2.4, the only ones detrimental to the US would be the adoption of cargo allocation without an ensuing increase in available capacity, or with a subsequent increase in demand for container carriage. Either result would strengthen the market position of the steamship companies without

Figure 2.4: Possible outcomes of cargo allocation options

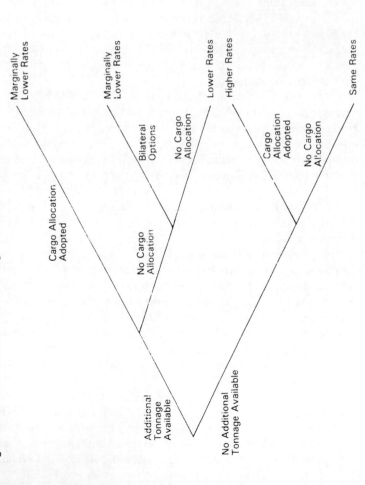

yielding any benefits through cost reductions.

The probability of these outcomes cannot be determined without a global survey of major foreign routes, particularly those in the European and the Far East foreign trades.

Impacts on level of service. Service levels can be expected to go down as operators provide only a minimum of capacity and frequency in line with their allocated share. A national flag shipping company under the protection of a cargo sharing agreement would be encouraged to assign its oldest or least efficient shipping to the service, with resulting degradation of service quality and reliability. This might then induce shippers to channel their cargo to more efficient and reliable services offered by cross-trading, third-party shipping. The resulting imbalance in assigned capacity utilisation might eventually by equalised by revenue sharing or similar clauses. There is little incentive, particularly to government-owned shipping companies, to improve level, frequency, or quality of service.

Another important effect of cargo reservation is the imbalance of trade routes served by container shipping. Most bilateral trades suffer a severe imbalance in containerised cargo shipping demand; cargo reservation would therefore either build up empty container inventories in one country or else require substantial haulage of empty containers. Most container operators agree that only multilateral (including round-the-world) shipping routes permit effective rationalisation of container shipping and utilisation of expensive container inventories.

A severe constraint may arise where the existing shipping capacity of agreement partners is inadequate to carry their share. Should general multilateral cargo sharing agreements come into force, the US and many of the LDCs lack sufficient fleet capacity to carry their share of their trade. Since the demand for marine transport is subject to fairly wide swings, especially in the bulk commodity shipments, the supply of vessels can shift from scarcity to excess capacity in a relatively short time. If partners to bilateral or multilateral cargo sharing agreements limit their capacity to national fleets, they will expose themselves to even greater fluctuations in demand and available capacity. Many countries (particularly LDCs who lack the capacity to carry their share in cargo reservation agreements), define 'national shipping' as in-charter or space charter of capacity, joint venturing, or other methods of increasing capacity without investing in additional tonnage.

The major operational areas where cargo sharing agreements may require specific stipulations are chartering, routing, scheduling, and vessel characteristics. Lines which presently charter, either to fulfil their conference/pooling agreements or to gain time while contemplating newbuildings or conversions, may find they need to own their tonnage under future cargo sharing agreements. This has obvious implications for the structure of the liner industry.

As members of conferences, liners usually follow a fixed route with minor variations in the order and number of port calls, including the number of times a port is visited during a round-trip voyage. On many trade routes, calls are made at a port either outbound or inbound.

If control of market share is attempted through operational regulation, participants' routes and schedules will have to be supervised. The transshipment role of participants would also require supervision, something not presently attempted.

Practically all US liner operators serve more than one country or trading partner. Bilateral cargo sharing agreements could seriously hamper optimum scheduling and capacity allocation on all legs of the route. This is especially likely when (i) cargo sharing agreements exist between the US and other countries served by a particular liner trade route, or (ii) bilateral cargo sharing agreements are in force between all countries on the liner trade route.

Routing and scheduling of liner services subject to several cargo sharing agreements may become quite difficult, unless the agreement includes revenue sharing. On the other hand, revenue sharing – as a part of a bilateral cargo sharing agreement – introduces many drawbacks.

Effects of cargo sharing on competition – conflicts with rationalisation policies

The arbitrary division of the freight market according to the 40-40-20 ratio is in direct conflict with a policy of rationalisation. The principle of rationalisation is based on minimising costs, and implies that each vessel in a given service is operated at the same marginal cost. This is necessary to maintain minimum costs.

Because of technical and relative scale differences among existing companies, operation at equal marginal costs does not result in a 40-40-20 division of cargo on most routes. On Far Eastern routes, for example, in order to operate at equal marginal costs, the US would have to provide 60 per cent of the capacity and Japan 40 per cent. Currently, if the two countries were to expand to carry their 40 per cent share, a 30 per cent increase in capacity would be required for both.

The hypothesised expansion of US capacity would be new tonnage, whose long-term marginal cost must equal competitors' marginal costs for an optimal solution. This means that reductions in US operating costs through the use of diesel propulsion and larger ships would have to make up the additional financing costs. Given present interest rates and construction costs, it seems unlikely that this can be done with US-built tonnage unless the subsidy rate is increased. Thus, it appears impossible for the US to consider ratification of the UNCTAD Code unless subsidised US operators are allowed to acquire foreign-built vessels, among other things.

Potential magnitude of impact of cargo reservation

The total amount of dry cargo (bulk and liner) transported in seaborne trade in 1982 was 1,760 million tons, of which about half 850 million tons) consisted of dry bulk commodities. Table 2.11 shows dry cargo trades by major regions.

LDCs (region 1-4) load or export 29.2 per cent of dry cargo, and 32.5 per cent of dry bulk cargo; they unload or import 28.8 per cent of dry cargo, and 20.6 per cent of dry bulk cargo. However, some regions such as Africa export mainly dry bulk cargo (95 per cent of dry cargo exports) and import mainly general cargo (70 per cent of dry cargo imports). This obviously leads to a gross imbalance: general cargo and container ships run largely empty on their return trips from Africa while dry bulk carriers are empty on return trips to that country. The same problem exists – though to a smaller extent – in other parts of the developing world.

Rationalisation of shipping under bilateral or other cargo reservation schemes is quite difficult. Generally the cost of both liner and bulk shipping in these trades exceeds similar trades where some return cargo balance exists, or where lack of cargo reservation allows operators to engage in cross-trading to obtain some return trip revenues. Strict enforcement of the Code and other cargo reservation schemes may introduce other constraints on effective management, affecting both the cost and price of shipping.

To study this problem, we have investigated the implications on tonnage redistribution under a strict interpretation of cargo sharing.[29] Average ton-mile capacity estimates were used to adjust the tonnage of the different LDCs to those required for the respective countries to carry 50 per cent of their seaborne international trade. Table 2.12 shows that their bulk tonnage would have to increase marginally from 14.7 per cent to 16 per cent of world total, while general cargo tonnage would have to decrease from 26.4 per cent to

Table 2.11: Dry cargo seaborne trade 1982 (millions of tons)

Region	Loaded				Unloaded			
	Total		Bulk		Total		Bulk	
	Tons	%	Tons	%	Tons	%	Tons	%
Africa	81	5.1	77	9.1	94	5.4	28	3.3
Central America and Caribbean	40	2.1	9	1.1	28	1.6	7	0.8
South America	181	10.1	115	14.2	60	3.4	8	0.9
Asia	218	12.0	65	8.1	318	18.1	132	15.6
Oceania	7.4	0.4	–	–	3	0.3	1	–
Europe	474	27.1	70	8.2	751	42.7	318	37.4
North America	455	26.1	284	33.4	162	9.2	188	22.1
Australia, NZ, Japan and South Africa	305	17.1	220	25.9	363	20.6	168	19.8
Total	1,760	100.0	850	100.0	1,780	100.0	850	100.0

Source: *Maritime Review 1983*

Table 2.12: Redistribution of tonnage 50/50 share (000 DWT)

Country group	Present DWT				1982 Dist. with 50/50			
	Bulk	%	G.C.	%	Bulk	%	G.C.	%
Africa	300	0.1	2,647	2.2	9,450	4.5	3,560	3.0
Central America and Caribbean	272	0.1	1,518	1.2	1,050	0.5	2,160	1.8
South America	9,945	4.8	11,411	9.5	14,850	7.2	4,578	3.8
Asia	20,662	10.0	17,847	14.9	8,400	4.1	17,040	14.1
Oceania	60	–	107	–	68	–	112	–
Europe	84,720	41.1	49,796	41.5	83,210	40.0	51,610	43.0
North America	1,200	0.5	4,242	3.5	1,200	0.6	4,380	3.6
Other Dev.	25,600	12.4	9,004	7.2	25,420	12.3	9,200	7.7
Open Registry	63,400	31.0	23,392	20.0	62,511	30.8	27,324	23.0
Total	206,159	100.0	119,964	100.0	206,159	100.0	119,964	100.0

21.5 per cent of world total. Obviously, it was necessary to make simplifying assumptions, such as equal productivity of tonnage registered under LDC or developed country flags.

There are some significant fleet deficiencies in regions such as Africa, which totally lacks participation in its bulk trades, and surpluses in regions such as Asia, which has a significant excess of bulk tonnage. However, it would be necessary to investigate the redistribution requirements on a nation-by-nation basis to fully analyse the implications of strict cargo sharing.

Effects of cargo sharing. The imposition of some sort of cargo sharing in dry and liquid bulk shipping, similar to the recommended cargo allocation under the Code, has been under discussion by UNCTAD for several years. Various proposals have been advanced and several countries, including Brazil, Ecuador, Korea, the Philippines, Indonesia, and Venezuela, have introduced regulations to that effect. In many developing countries the government, or government-owned entities, have a monopoly in the transportation of petroleum and other bulk commodity imports and exports; in others, national regulations only allow vessels under flags of the bilateral trading partners any access to bulk trades. Still others, such as Indonesia, give priority to national flag vessels and allocate the rest by quotas on a bilateral basis. On the other hand, Korea uses a system of waivers for bulk cargo carriage on foreign flag vessels, with all major bulk commodities basically reserved to Korean shipping.

Many nations are experimenting with different forms of cargo reservation in bulk shipping. The major dilemma is that a significant proportion of the world bulk fleet sails under open registry flags, as opposed to the almost exclusive registration of liner vessels under flags of trading nations.

UNCTAD has recently developed guidelines for registration of ships which would require a 'bound' between beneficial ownership and flag of registration. (The beneficial owner is the person, company, or organisation which gains the pecuniary benefits from the shipping operation.) There are obviously many different reasons for owners' use of open registry. Likewise, many countries which are not usually considered to provide for open registry do permit foreign minority or majority ownership of vessels registered under their flag. Many LDCs, who are staunch supporters of the Code and other UNCTAD proposals, also beneficially own significant fleets operating under flags of open registry countries (Table 2.13). In some cases the reasons for open registry are political, while in others economic advantages are uppermost.

Abolition or restriction of open registry, and the imposition of a direct link between ownership and registry, would affect about one-third of the world's bulk shipping fleet. It is difficult to estimate the resulting impact on costs since bulk shipping has traditionally been served by a mix of fleets: some operated by cargo owners, by contract carriers, or by independents offering vessels for short-, medium-, or long-term charters. Approximately one-half of the world's bulk carrier tonnage trades in the competitive charter markets. This tonnage would be most affected by a change in the rules of registry and bulk cargo reservation.

There is a general feeling that under bulk cargo reservation the charter market would be affected most, with an increasing percentage of bulk tonnage engaged in contract and long-term charter trading, as well as an increase in charter rates given a declining fleet of bulk carriers available for spot or short-term charter. Another factor affecting the future development of charter or negotiated (contract) rates may be the decreasing ability to rationalise bulk tonnage under bulk cargo reservation regulations.

The obvious conclusion is that cargo reservation, limited ship registration, and other restrictive practices will in general result in higher ocean transportation costs and lower quality of service. On the other hand, we cannot ignore the fact that more equitable control of shipping by trading partners, including terms and costs of shipping, is necessary to assure development of international trade.

There is currently a surplus of shipping capacity. Some reorganisation of international shipping structure may be possible to provide meaningful control over the terms and costs of international shipping for countries with insufficient participation in their foreign trade. Such measures might avoid the tremendous penalties that would be incurred if proposed cargo reservation and ship registry agreements are rigidly enforced.

Shipping regulation

Paradoxically, international shipping is one of the most and yet least regulated transportation industries. Its design, manning, cargo handling, stowage, and other technical and operational aspects are highly regulated. At the same time the industry is largely free of economic or management regulation. Various international bodies,

Table 2.13: Beneficial ownership* of open-registry fleets, 1983. (Number of vessels and thousands of DWT)

Country or territory of beneficial ownership	Liberia		Panama		Cyprus		Bermuda		Bahamas		Total	
	No. of vessels	DWT	No. of vessels	DWT	No. of vessels	DWT	No. of vessels	DWT	No. of vessels	DWT	No. of vessels	DWT
United States of America	429	44,558	293	7,166	2	5	16	85	8	324	748	52,138
Hong Kong	452	29,427	460	10,112	4	56	–	–	1	–	916	39,595
Greece	237	18,730	462	8,441	278	3,647	–	–	1	17	978	30,835
Japan	204	10,736	792	10,816	1	4	–	–	–	–	997	21,556
Norway	138	6,113	39	931	–	–	1	13	5	95	183	7,152
Unspecified	95	3,943	172	2,709	–	–	–	–	–	–	267	6,652
Germany, Federal Republic of	81	1,923	196	3,302	87	999	1	7	1	6	366	6,237
Switzerland	69	4,008	81	1,401	3	26	–	–	4	48	157	5,483
United Kingdom	35	2,106	120	1,164	16	100	14	442	7	186	192	3,998
China**	4	140	134	3,225	–	–	–	–	–	–	138	3,365
Republic of Korea	10	1,053	75	1,403	–	–	–	–	–	–	85	2,456
Italy	18	1,175	45	447	6	122	3	9	–	–	72	1,753
Netherlands	18	1,050	78	547	1	3	–	–	3	4	100	1,604
Canada	13	855	7	53	1	1	15	677	4	8	39	1,593
Israel	25	1,148	7	180	1	16	1	2	–	–	34	1,346
Denmark	24	892	16	60	4	16	–	–	17	251	61	1,219
Indonesia	23	401	62	798	–	–	–	–	–	–	85	1,199

Monaco	16	1,023	6	86	–	–	–	–	1	29	23	1,138
Pakistan	31	849	22	226	–	–	–	–	1	–	53	1,075
France	9	879	30	144	–	–	–	–	1	18	40	1,041
64 countries, entities, or territories, each beneficially owning less than 0.5 per cent	77	3,712	458	3,432	32	158	5	65	4	16	576	7,383
Unidentified	13	533	231	1,728	42	947	4	6	3	15	293	3,229
Total	2,021	135,254	3,786	58,371	477	6,099	60	1,306	59	1,017	6,403	202,047
Percentage share in total open-registry fleets	31.6	67.0	59.2	28.9	7.4	3.0	0.9	0.6	0.9	0.5	100.0	100.0

* The beneficial owner is the person, company, or organisation which gains the pecuniary benefits from the shipping operations

** The Government has advised that many of the vessels attributed to China are chartered ships, being operated by the China Ocean Shipping Company

Source: Based on data supplied to the UNCTAD Secretariat by A. and Appledore Limited

governments, and industry groupings are responsible for these regulations.

The functions of government-imposed shipping restrictions can be summarised as follows:

(1) *Policing*. Usually implies a 'public interest' image of shipping; that is, under government direction shipping would be enforced to pursue goals of public concern, which they might not otherwise. This can also be interpreted as the exercise of sovereign power of the state, whereby governments give power to or remove power from shipping, through their regulations.

(2) *Rationalisation*. Is often assumed to be a cause for regulation, whereby governments attempt to assure efficient use of resources in the provision of essential shipping services.

(3) *Standard setting*. Includes rules to maintain service, quality, environmental, and other standards.

(4) *Interest representation*. Regulations which monitor participation of representative suppliers of shipping capacity or users.

(5) *Economic*. Includes measures to maximise the perceived economic need of the country in terms of transportation costs, national participation in shipping, control of shipping terms (and therefore often terms of trade), employment in shipping, and balance of payment effects.

(6) *Defence*. Goals of regulation which affect availability and control of adequate shipping capacity to meet defence needs.

International shipping regulation is usually designed to satisfy the perceived interest of a majority of member countries of an authoritative body such as UNCTAD or IMO. Such regulations are often a compromise of the many national interests. International shipping regulations seldom address issues of economic efficiency or rationalisation. Rather, they usually reflect policing, standard setting, and interest representation functions interpreted as public goals represented by members of the body.

RATIONALISATION IN LINER SERVICE

Rationalisation is generally defined as an approach minimising the resources required to supply a service (or product). In liner service it could imply reduced fleet size, increased ship utilisation, and decreased operating costs for liner operators to assure adequate capacity and quality of service to both shippers and authorities.

Rationalisation in liner shipping can be accomplished in a number of ways. Some maintain frequency, speed, and diversity of service, while others maintain capacity. Rationalisation efficiency can similarly be measured using several approaches. Shrier[30] defines it as the 'total of measurement-ton nautical miles (MT-NM) sailed by the fleet'. Other measures could include the ratio of ton-miles utilised divided by ton-miles provided, which relates rationalisation efficiency to fleet utilisation; the product of the ratios of port calls/years made after and before rationalisation; the ratio of ton-miles utilised divided by ton-miles provided. However, neither of these really provides an effective measure of quality and level of service.

Such a measure should evaluate both the savings from better use of assets in the service and the costs resulting from degradation in service (such as reduction of number of port calls, increased time of delivery of cargo, and less offered capacity at particular ports). Obviously, ports which do not provide adequate cargo-volume inducement cannot justify service. Therefore a ratio of cargo offered to capacity and service available at a particular port must be included in the measure. Removing a marginal port from service may allow more valuable increases in service at other ports. Obviously, shippers and ports both prefer to have frequent service from all loading to all destination ports by all types of ships. Fast ships, as well as ships with enough excess capacity to accommodate all cargo offerings, are also preferred. Of course all these desired service features are costly, resulting in unrationalised shipping services and shipping costs far in excess of those necessary to provide comparative, yet rationalised, service.

Rationalisation of liner shipping requires participating operators to cooperate in establishing such service. Institutional guidelines or arrangements are necessary in terms of access to cargo, service requirements, and legal rights (or restrictions) on participants in the trade. These must also take into account any government regulations affecting the rationalised trade and service. In other words, it determines:

— liner operator participation
— cargo reserved for participants
— price setting and reporting

Table 2.14: Government involvement in rationalised liner shipping

Permissive
1. completely free trade
2. unregulated conference
3. commercial combining agreements
4. no imposition of shipper assent

Delegative
1. shipper council involvement
2. closed conference
3. restricted trade
4. required filling of tariffs

Regulatory
1. regulated tariff agreements
2. regulated carrier combinations
3. regulated trade
4. closed conference restricted to defined carriers

Controlling
1. unilateral agreements
2. bilateral agreements
3. multilateral agreements
4. other types of restrictive trade agreements
5. controlled trade
6. defined carriers
7. assigned shares

— loyalty, discount, and other commercial rules
— relations with any shippers' councils
— inter- and intra-coordination among operators and shippers
— relations with government
— government regulation and supervision.

Government roles can vary from permissive to delegative, regulatory or controlling involvement. In recent years, we have gradually moved towards more regulatory and controlling involvement, particularly in trades between developing and developed countries. The forms of possible government involvement are summarised in Table 2.14.

Framework for rationalised liner service

Rationalisation requires that interdependent operators work together to improve their joint utilisation of resources to provide required service and capacity. Yet this appears to be in direct conflict with pure economic competition. Existing constraints in international shipping usually prevent 'the invisible hand of competition' described by Adam Smith in *The Wealth of Nations*, producing a market for shipping services on specific trades without large excess capacity. This applies to most liners, in which the demand for reliably scheduled service requires allocating any excess capacity, unless rationalisation is introduced.

Most liner services, particularly between developed and developing countries, are highly unrationalised in terms of resources applied to the service. Cargo access restrictions and direct service requirements have been shown to make this problem even worse. The increasing capital intensity of liner shipping, with greater use of mixed or full containership, implies additional allocation of under-utilised resources.

It can be shown that even on nearly balanced North Atlantic[31] liner routes a 20 to 30 per cent cost reduction could be obtained by rationalisation of services. The savings possible for developing country trades may exceed 50 per cent. In the study of rationalisation benefits achievable in North Atlantic liner trade, the approach taken was to:

— identify large volume 'load centre' ports;
— limit ports of call to port pairs that are the largest, directionally-balanced traffic generators;
— limit service to achieve high utilisation of ships and cargo facilities; and
— implement feeder and intermodal services for distribution/collection of cargo.

In that analysis, the commercially-closed trade concept was applied to each of several sub-conferences covering a specific set of port pairs, with all operators working as a coordinated service. The characteristics of the service in terms of frequencies, rates, ship types, etc. would be determined by negotiation with shippers' councils.

Rationalised liner service requires many changes in the traditional structure of liner shipping. For example, intra-regional feeder and assigned inter-regional port pair services would essentially constitute sub-conference agreements. Such agreements would have to be mandatory, with participation imposed on 'assigned' conference members. On the other hand, rationalisation, particularly in liner shipping, will be essential if we are to contain the increasing cost of services, particularly in developing country trades.

To indicate the potential impact of rationalised liner shipping on developing country liner trades, we projected the cost for liner shipping in a hypothetical trade. In this simplified analysis, two 'load centre' ports were selected in each trading area while feeder services to the other four ports in each area were introduced to lower the costs of long distance main line service. Service frequency was maintained constant, as were delivery time and port, ship, and cargo handling rates. It is noted that the savings are quite substantial.

Method for rationalising liner shipping

Rationalisation can include reducing fleet size, changing service itinerary and schedule, increasing fleet utilisation, and lowering operating costs, while assuring sufficient service to transport the cargoes offered. Methods used by liner operators to rationalise their service include:

— reduction of frequency of sailing at ports
— reduction of number of ships in service
— slow or optimised ship speed and size
— adjusting shipping capacity to actual need at certain ports or on certain legs of the route
— reduction of number of port calls
— integration of feeder and land transport services
— replacement of parts of main line itinerary by feeder services.

These methods are not mutually exclusive, nor are all applicable to every situation. Optimum methods, of course, may change seasonally or over time.

The approach to structuring a rationalised service depends on the balance of cargo movement between port pairs and groups of ports; the ability to replace main line by feeder line service; fleet composition; flexibility in ability to service frequency; and the capacity to exchange frequency of port calls for reduced time of delivery. Finally, specific regulations or other imposed requirements often constrain possible changes.

Operations research techniques, such as maximum flow

algorithms based on the maximum flow/minimum cut theorem, prove useful in deriving preliminary minimum capacity allocations to various links of the network, consistent with service frequency and cargo demands. Ultimately, however, simulations of alternative rationalisation schemes must converge on a rationalised solution which is realistic and considers the particular characteristics of the services demanded and the ships available. A number of studies have been performed.

Binkley[32] studied six alternative rationalisation plans for the North Atlantic. These demonstrated that rationalisation would either produce substantial excess capacity, if the number of port calls were reduced, or lower the fleet size and ship speed requirements. The combination of about 15-knot service and rationalised itineraries could reduce fuel consumption as much as one half, although with some reduction in shipper service. Using normal sea speeds and reducing ports of call to less than three at each end of the route, would achieve similar results.

Hapan-Lloyd AG[33] analysed coordinated competition on the North Atlantic container trade for 1975, when liner traffic was largely balanced. Through use of extensive feeder services they were able to show that a 27 per cent saving, equal to US$200 million in estimated total system cost (including container handling, leasing and ownership, positioning and feeder charges) was possible. Service frequency at individual ports was maintained, but 40 per cent of the port calls were by feeder ships.

Gilman et al.[34] also performed an analytical study of container shipping on the North Atlantic. The rationalisation scheme developed reduced the fleet in service by about 60 per cent while providing weekly service at all ports of call which had been served weekly or more often, with less frequent service at other ports. However, the 'typical' ship used in that study was larger than the average ship actually in service at that time. The resulting savings therefore were probably in the order of only 30 per cent.

Bast et al.[35] evaluated a seven-country trade route of small traffic, under bilateral agreements with equal cargo reservations to trading countries made under UNCTAD 40-40-20 rules. Assuming exclusion of cross-trading, even by neighbouring country fleets, they found that more and smaller ships would be required to carry the trade efficiently. Costs were estimated to be at least 25 per cent higher and transit time would be expected to increase.

In this study we considered both the US North Atlantic to North-West Europe and the Brazil/Argentina to US Atlantic liner routes.

The rationalised fleet and route assignments were developed to meet the requirements of comparable capacity, port call frequency and transit time of the existing service. The available ship mix was used as far as possible for the main line service. Feeder vessels, or smaller or less efficient main line vessels assigned to feeder services, were added wherever feeder services provided significant cost savings without a degradation in service quality.

The service assignments in converging on the rationalised liner service consisted of the following steps:

(1) Develop service frequency, capacity, and transit time requirements for each port and port-pair.

(2) Rank the ports by cargo flow (import plus export).

(3) Determine the minimum required number of link transits and link flows in the network representing all port-pair flows, consistent with port service frequency, and cargo flow requirements.

(4) Assign capacity (ships) to the network links, with the largest and most efficient ships assigned to serve only one or at most two ports at each end of the route. The number of ships assigned should reflect port service requirements.

(5) Assign less productive ships where needed to carry unassigned traffic, according to port service frequency and level of service.

(6) Next, select the smallest (traffic) port not yet served by feeders and connect it by feeder to the nearest main line port. Determine number and size of feeder vessels required.

(7) Compute the new minimum requirement for main line vessels, starting with assignment of most productive vessels to largest ports and their port pairs.

(8) Select the next smallest port and also connect it to the nearest main line port with its own feeder service or one combined with the smallest port.

(9) Continue this process until only one or two main line (load centre) ports are left on each side with all other ports served by feeders.

(10) Determine minimum ship production required and compute port capacity requirement for each level of rationalised shipping. Starting with no-feeder and continue to an all-feeder regional service (where as few as one or as many as all ports are main line ports).

(11) Compute for all feasible rationalised solution (those which

are within existing fleet and port capacity) the resulting total cost. Select least cost alternative.

Using the above repeating simulation technique, the two liner routes were analysed assuming mid-1982 service conditions.

The US Atlantic–North-West Europe route analysis resulted in a 41 per cent reduction in the number of main line ships required and the addition of 8 per cent of feeder vessels, for a total saving in the number of vessels of about 33 per cent. Ship capacity utilisation went up from 63 per cent to over 84 per cent average, and total cost savings were of the order of 19 per cent. This was based on a constant level of port-to-port service. If service frequency to smaller ports is reduced to a level more consistent with their demand (say, port calls only for an average of more than 200 TEU) then additional savings of 7 to 8 per cent are possible.

Even greater benefits could be achieved on the Brazil/Argentina to US liner trade, as the current route structures permits major rationalisation.

Methods for rationalising liner services

Any method aimed at rationalising liner services must have an objective and a well-defined set of constraints. The objectives could be the owner's goal to minimise costs, for example, subject to the constraints that capacity offered, transit time, and frequency of service in the trades is not reduced. Under such conditions, it is usually fair to assume that the cargo offered and the revenues would remain constant. The model presented here is deterministic, and considers the effect of changes in routing and scheduling. It includes both direct services between all ports (with or without separation of services), as well as indirect services where cargo from lesser ports is transshipped through large ports via feeder vessels.

We used a simple integer linear programming or dynamic programming model to calculate the savings possible from rationalising the US-Brazil/Argentina trade, based on the assumptions that:

(1) Sufficient capacity is provided to carry cargo offerings (assumed to be within ±20 per cent of the average cargo offering between any two ports).
(2) There is no intra-regional and intra-national (cabotage) trade.

97

(3) Transit times are not increased and frequency of service is maintained.

Savings of about 18.6 per cent were obtained when using costs of typical vessels currently serving the trade. An almost equally good solution would simply separate US-Argentina and US-Brazil service, and assign load centre status to one Brazilian port (Santos).

The West Africa-North Europe liner system can be analysed using a multi-vehicle routing problem (including a special travelling salesman algorithm), since return cargoes from each port are generally less and the problem can therefore be solved as unidirectional.

CARGO SHARING IN BULK TRADES

Bulk shipping is much more fragmented than liner shipping. This makes computing the capacity requirements under any cargo sharing or reservation agreement more difficult. Many bulk trades are seasonal and the markets of suppliers change frequently. Only a small fraction of the world's bulk trades are performed under long-term contracts. As a result, bulk shipping usually plies wide-ranging routes.

The first step is to obtain an idea of the magnitude of change required in bulk capacity under different flags, to provide national shipping with the required capacity to carry, for example, a 50 per cent share of the nation's bulk trades. To this end the bulk trades of all the major nations were studied, and the average ton-mile shipping capacity needed for bulk imports and exports was determined. This was then translated into an equivalent bulk shipping capacity (DWT) requirement, and compared with existing national capacity. Table 2.15 summarises the resulting deficits and surpluses in tonnage.

The total shift in tonnage required is 231.5 million DWT, with a shift to developing countries of 105.7 million DWT of tankers and 12.9 million DWT of dry bulk carriers. The largest surplus is under open registry, with 100.2 million DWT of tankers and 65.7 million DWT of dry bulk carriers. The surplus of dry bulk carriers under flags of developed market economy countries nearly balances their deficit in tanker tonnage. The problem is obviously that significant segments of open registry shipping are beneficially owned by interests in developing countries (Table 2.16). As a result, it is extremely difficult – if not impossible – to estimate the economic impact of cargo sharing in bulk shipping. Reflagging may not necessarily involve change in ownership for more than about one-half of the ships currently under open registry.

Table 2.15: Summary results. Flag distribution of bulk shipping capacity by ship type

Country/Region	Present (% of world)		Potential with 50/50 (% of world)		Actual change in		Absolute shift in ownership of tankers and bulkers (000 DWT)
	Oil tankers (%)	Bulk ships (%)	Oil tankers (%)	Bulk ships (%)	Tankers (000 DWT)	Bulkers (000 DWT)	
World total	100	100	100	100			288,549*
Developed market economy countries	50.20	45.80	40.86	60.33	−28,521	−31,280	
Open registry countries	33.28	31.41	0.47	0.87	−100,192	−65,756	
Socialist countries of Eastern Europe	3.15	4.19	9.04	13.45	18,008	19,948	
Socialist countries of Asia	0.79	2.11	0.75	1.78	−117	−709	
Developing countries of Africa	1.19	0.17	7.21	4.31	18,373	8,923	
Developing countries of America	2.58	3.06	9.73	8.39	21,848	11,471	
Developing countries of Asia	8.50	11.85	29.94	8.42	65,472	−7,399	
Developing countries of Europe	0.00	0.26	0.00	0.00	−12	−551	
Developing countries of Oceania	0.00	0.04	0.00	0.12	−10	165	

* About 60 per cent of world fleet of tankers and bulk carriers will change ownership/flag (in the limit)
Note: Calculations do not consider:
1. trade in products
2. trade in timber
3. vegetable oils, tapioca (imported for some countries)
4. effect of domestic trades (cabotage)
5. length of haul

Source: Original data. Present per cent of world total. 'Review of Maritime Transport 1985'. UNCTAD, New York, 1986.
Computations by author

Table 2.16: Beneficial ownership[a] of open-registry fleets, 1984. (Number of vessels and thousands of DWT)

Country or territory of beneficial ownership	Liberia Number	Liberia DWT	Panama Number	Panama DWT	Cyprus Number	Cyprus DWT	Bahamas Number	Bahamas DWT	Bermuda Number	Bermuda DWT	Total Number	Total DWT
United States of America	366	38,151	304	7,447	3	7	25	4,078	16	83	714	49,766
Hong Kong	410	27,214	440	9,990	3	34	1	14	–	–	854	37,252
Greece	247	18,407	516	9,877	368	8,049	2	60	2	19	1,135	36,412
Japan	199	10,216	964	12,705	1	5	–	–	–	–	1,164	22,926
Norway	158	6,275	47	862	3	625	5	196	1	13	214	7,971
Germany, Federal Republic of	88	2,190	184	3,130	85	680	1	6	1	7	359	6,013
Unspecified	69	2,850	164	2,825	–	–	–	–	–	–	233	5,675
United Kingdom	39	2,348	128	1,935	16	60	16	377	22	843	221	5,563
Switzerland	57	3,322	82	1,268	5	58	1	2	–	–	145	4,650
China[b]	5	171	114	2,926	–	–	–	–	–	–	119	3,097
Republic of Korea	10	989	73	1,156	–	–	–	–	–	–	83	2,145
Pakistan	38	1,292	25	466	–	–	–	–	–	–	63	1,758
Israel	25	1,356	5	140	2	32	–	–	1	2	33	1,530
Italy	16	950	34	380	5	120	–	–	3	9	58	1,459
Indonesia	21	309	68	1,015	–	–	–	–	–	–	89	1,324
Netherlands	18	729	60	481	7	22	8	7	–	–	93	1,239
Monaco	17	1,053	7	59	–	–	1	29	–	–	25	1,141
Denmark	21	766	16	55	5	16	17	251	–	–	59	1,088

Sweden	13	939	23	70	4	1	36	1	3	–	41	1,048
75 countries, entities or territories, each managing less than 1 million DWT	75	3,068	492	3,610	43	17	396	16	113	422	643	7,609
Unidentified	10	335	210	1,683	46	1	854	3	–	4	270	2,876
Total	1,902	122,930	3,956	62,080	596	96	10,994	65	5,136	1,402	6,615	202,542
Share in total open registry fleets	28.8	60.7	59.8	30.7	9.0	1.4	5.4	1.0	2.5	0.7	100.0	100.0

[a] The beneficial owner is the person, company, or organisation which gains the pecuniary benefits from the shipping operations
[b] The Government has advised that many of the vessels attributed to China are chartered ships operated by the China Ocean Shipping Company
Source: 'Review of Maritime Transport 1984', UNCTAD, Geneva, August 1985

3

Trade and Economic Development

International trade has assumed increased significance in recent years. Trades of some countries have acquired values as large as their GNP, while even the US now has a foreign trade equal to over 16 per cent of its domestic product. On the other hand, the composition of international trade and the trading routes have changed greatly since 1970. Air cargo transport has captured well over 40 per cent of long distance, high value cargo (US $25,000/ton plus) and the percentage continues to increase. As of 1985, in ton-miles air cargo constituted nearly 4.4 per cent of total international goods transport. At the same time, pipelines for gas and oil (transmediterranean, transpanama, etc.) have captured over 4 per cent of ton-mile transport previously performed by shipping.

Another major development is the participation of raw material producers in the processing and manufacture of the material. This not only reduces shipping volumes, as in the conversion of bauxite to alumina (a 4 to 1 weight reduction), but also affects the distance over which the processed material is shipped. It frequently eliminates steps between the original transport of the raw material to processing plants and subsequent shipping of the semi-finished or finished product.

Other developments affecting shipping demand are the successful energy conservation and substitution measures introduced by many major oil and gas importing countries. While total world energy consumption has levelled off and now increases below the rate of population growth, imports of petroleum and gas have actually declined in recent years, largely due to the price escalations experienced in the late 1970s. Some countries, such as Brazil and South Africa, developed conversion methods for economic production of substitute fuels such as methanol or gasohol, while others invested heavily in new domestic petroleum or gas production.

Grain trades have also declined as a result of massive food self-sufficiency developments in countries such as India and China, which were previously large grain importers. As a result, international trade has moved from supplying countries with major commodity and transportation deficiencies to a role of responding to comparative advantages.

Nevertheless, various nations have imposed trade barriers which create increasing threats for the shipping industry. Some of these barriers are explicit, while others may be only indirect. They may apply to the goods traded, their transportation, or both.

DEVELOPMENT OF SEABORNE TRADES

International seaborne trade has increased by over 27 per cent between 1970 and 1984, or at a compound rate of barely 1.51 per cent per year during this 15-year period. Petroleum trade actually declined from 1.440 billion tons to 1.407 billion tons during that period, dry bulk cargo increased from 0.488 billion tons to 0.790 billion tons, or by 61.9 per cent. General, container, specialised, and minor bulk cargoes increased from 0.677 billion tons in 1970 to 1.103 billion tons in 1984, or by 62.9 per cent (Table 3.1). Therefore, excluding petroleum, world trade actually increased at a much more healthy compound rate of 3.46 per cent. In value terms, trade developments are even more impressive with overall trade growing at 3.6 per cent; excluding petroleum this translates into 4.48 per cent per annum in constant dollar terms. Of course, the recent devaluation of the US dollar against currencies of other major industrialised nations makes it difficult to judge trade values in constant dollar terms realistically. Within this trade expansion, world container cargoes grew from 48 mmt to just over 305 mmt between 1970 and 1984 or by 535.6 per cent, or at an annual growth rate of nearly 12 per cent.

While container shipping originated in the US, the percentage of world container traffic generated by US trade has slipped from 92 per cent in 1960 to 76 per cent in 1965, 35 per cent in 1970 and just 17 per cent in 1984. Both Western European and Far Eastern container traffic volumes now exceed those of the US (Figure 3.1). The transatlantic and transpacific container trades, which grew at over 15 per cent a year in the early 1970s, are now slowing significantly. (These mature liner trades are now over 76 per cent containerised.)

103

Table 3.1: Development of international seaborne trade: 1970 and 1980–1984[a]. Estimates of goods loaded

Year	Tanker cargo		Dry cargo				Total (all goods)	
			Total		Of which: main bulk commodities[b]			
	Millions of tons	% increase/ decrease over previous year	Millions of tons	% increase/ decrease over previous year	Millions of tons	% increase/ decrease over previous year	Millions of tons	% increase/ decrease over previous year
1970	1,440	13.1	1,165	13.0	488	16.0	2,605	13.0
1980	1,871	−6.6	1,833	3.3	796	4.5	3,704	−2.0
1981	1,693	−9.5	1,866	1.8	806	1.3	3,559	−3.9
1982	1,480	−12.6	1,793	−3.9	759	−5.8	3,273	−8.0
1983	1,400	−7.4	1,710	−2.8	714	−5.9	3,110	−5.2
1984 (Est)	1,427	1.9	1,893	10.7	790	10.6	3,320	6.7

Sources.
(i) For tanker cargo, total dry cargo and all goods, base data were communicated to the UNCTAD secretariat by the United Nations Statistical Office. Owing to possible subsequent revisions or other factors, these detailed data may differ marginally from the aggregated figures reported in the United Nations, *Monthly Bulletin of Statistics*, January issues
(ii) For main bulk commodities: *World Bulk Trades 1983* and *Fearnley's Review 1984.* Fearnley, Oslo
[a] Including international cargoes loaded at ports of the Great Lakes and St Lawrence system for unloading at ports of the same system, but excluding such traffic in main bulk commodities. Also including petroleum imports into the Netherlands Antilles and Trinidad and Tobago for refining and re-export
[b] Iron ore, grain, coal, bauxite/alumina and phosphate

Figure 3.1: World container traffic

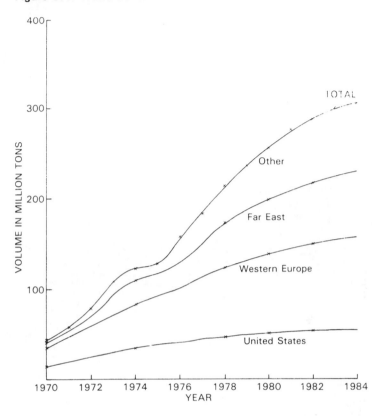

The largest increase in containerised trades in recent years has taken place on Pacific routes. Far Eastern and South-East Asian container trades, for example, increased by over 400 per cent in the last eight years. The future thrust, however, is expected in North-South trades, such as North America and North-West Europe to South America and Africa, or Far East to South Asia.

Some areas, such as the Near/Middle East, have seen spectacular increases in container traffic — from zero in 1970 to over 16 million tons in 1984. Yet in the last two years this trade has declined significantly, since many development projects in the region have been halted.

Another area of great future potential for container traffic is Eastern Europe and mainland China. Eastern European container trade only reached 2.4 million tons in 1984, while China's container

105

Figure 3.2: Bulk shipping demand

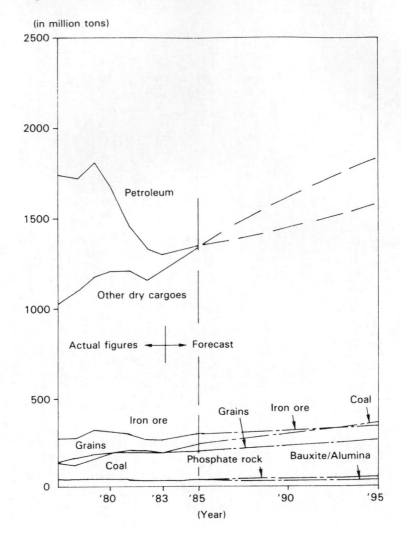

(in million tons)

2500

2000

Petroleum

1500

Other dry cargoes

1000

Actual figures ←——|——→ Forecast

500

Iron ore

Grains

Iron ore

Coal

Grains

Coal

Phosphate rock

Bauxite/Alumina

0

'80 '83 '85 '90 '95

(Year)

Figure 3.2: *contd*.

(in million tons)

List of articles	'79	'80	'81	'82	'83	'85	'90	'95	Annual compound growth rate (%)			
									'79–'83	'83–'90	'90–'95	'83–'95
Petroleum	1,817	1,638	1,482	1,328	1,292	1,360	1,450	1,500	Δ8.2	1.7	0.7	1.2
Iron ore	327	314	303	273	268	297	316	349	Δ4.9	2.3	2.0	2.2
Coal	159	188	210	208	208	223	247	301	6.8	3.0	3.3	4.7
Grain	182	198	206	200	195	217	239	271	1.7	2.9	2.5	2.8
Phosphate rock	48	48	42	40		48	53	59	Δ5.8	2.16	2.16	2.16
Bauxite/Alumina	46	48	45	38		42	42	42	Δ6.2	0	0	0
Other dry cargoes	1,176	1,214	1,218	1,162	1,220	1,352	1,698	2,131	Δ0.4	4.62	4.62	4.62

Source: Figures of actual results are according to Fearnley's. The 1983 figures are the estimate value

Note: Annual compound growth rate of Phosphate rock, Bauxite/Alumina and Other dry cargoes is calculated taking 1982 as a reference point

trade was less than a million tons. Both of these trades operate at less than 20 per cent of containerisable cargo and therefore offer large opportunities for future development. China is accelerating the development of both its container shipping fleet and container terminals to facilitate rapid expansion of containerised trade.

Bulk trades consist of major commodities such as petroleum, iron ore, coal, grain, phosphate rock, and bauxite/alumina, and minor bulks. As shown in Figure 3.2, petroleum is only expected to increase at a rate of 1.2 per cent between 1983–5, with coal demand slowing to a 3 to 3.3 per cent growth rate during that period. Similarly, grain and iron ore demand is likely to grow at rates of only 2 to 3 per cent per year during that period. Other bulk cargoes such as bauxite/alumina indicate zero growth in demand. The only real growth is expected in other dry cargoes which include pseudo-bulk, tramp, special, general, and containerised cargo.

One shipping sector which seems to be impervious to the recent declines in trade is specialised shipping — i.e. automobile carriers, special purpose and chemical tankers, heavy lift and project cargo carriers, ferries, cruise vessels, and integrated oceangoing tug barge combinations. These specialised vessels usually cater to new seaborne trades which continue to develop. These trades have suffered little from the reorganisation of trading partners or from the large oversupply, since new demands arise to supplement those only recently developed. Many of these specialised seaborne trades are the result of newly discovered opportunities.

SHIPPING AND ECONOMIC DEVELOPMENT

The value of world trade has grown rapidly in recent years and world exports which were a bare 12 per cent of World Domestic Product in 1960 have risen to 22 per cent by 1980 (19 per cent by 1982 and 21 per cent by 1984). The nations of the world rely more heavily on trade and trade linkages increasingly foster global inter-dependence. Developing country trades have grown more rapidly than those of the rest of the world. As a result, developing countries have become even more dependent on trade.

Shipping services are essential for international trade, with over 84 per cent of all international trade transported by ships. Developing countries are particularly dependent on trade with industrialised countries because of their need to market raw materials, agricultural products, and low technology manufactured products, as well as to import industrial goods.

Throughout the post-war period, and particularly in the last few decades, international trade has emerged as a major factor in world economic growth. The quest for economic development in some parts of the world, and the continued growth in others, has relied heavily on trade. Policies to cope with the current world economic situation are likely to focus again on trade expansion, despite existing protectionist tendencies in many countries.

As trade policies become increasingly important and elaborate, shipping issues are highlighted and more often subjected to governmental scrutiny and involvement. Consequently, political forces have gradually come to be dominant factors in the international shipping industry. This is demonstrated in the emergence of new national merchant marines among the LDCs and in the international trade participation by the fleets of the socialist countries. The shift in tonnage ownership has been accompanied by attempts to secure cargoes for the national fleets. This is manifested in political arrangements for bilateral and multilateral cargo sharing agreements.

As noted, developing countries are more dependent on international trade than other nations. As the average unit value of their trade is lower than that of developed countries, and the average cost of transportation per unit of cargo is usually higher, the percentage costs of transport in LDC international trade are, as a result, generally higher than those assumed by developed countries. Developing countries now seek to reduce the cost of transport of their trade, often attempting this by participation in the shipping of their own trade. They hope that such shipping will reduce foreign exchange costs as well as providing employment and other opportunities for their citizens.

In the last twenty years, the world shipping industry and world trade have undergone major structural changes. Shipping itself has similarly been subjected to major technological changes. This has introduced many new factors which influence the requirements of developing countries with respect to their role in shipping.

According to UNCTAD[1], developing countries had a deficit in the ocean freight transport balance of nearly US $33 billion in 1982. This is assumed to have contributed considerably to the existing trade and invisibles and therefore to the debt problem of developing countries.

The deficit has apparently declined somewhat in recent years, both because of slightly increased national shipping capacity in

109

developing countries and a general reduction in freight rates. Notwithstanding, there is considerable pressure for developing countries to increase participation in ocean shipping. There is no clear evidence, however, that greater participation by these countries will materially improve the balance of payment effects or achieve the other expected benefits.

Developing countries are attempting to increase their national shipping capacity to accommodate at least 40 per cent of their trade. Recent development in the shipping finance markets have exhausted most sources of finance for ship acquisition. These countries are therefore often unable to take advantage of low ship acquisition costs. On the other hand, while some developing countries (particularly in East Asia) have become very competent ship operators, others have failed to operate acquired vessels with reasonable proficiency. Developing country shipping therefore often becomes the high cost operator in the trade of a country. As discussed earlier, if the trade is served by a closed-conference, as many liner trades with developing countries are, then the freight rates charged by the whole conference will be adjusted upwards to protect the 'marginal' operator member, with a resulting general rise in freight rates and therefore transport costs of the trade of the country.

If we consider the proportion of freight charges to 1983 c.i.f. import values for developing countries, we found that these charges average twice those of developed countries (12 per cent versus 6 per cent). While this can be explained in part by the lower average c.i.f. import values, in many cases freight charges for similar commodities, carried over the same distances in roughly equal quantities per year in developing country trades, are significantly higher.

Developing country shipping generally carries a smaller percentage of developing country trade than do fleets of developed countries in their national trades. Many developing countries blame the disproportionate share of international seaborne trade for the high freight rates charged to their trade. While there is little evidence to corroborate this claim, it has served to generate political pressure for greater protection of developing country fleets.

These pressures also precipitated demands by developing countries for both financial and technical assistance to permit expansion of their fleets. Efficient, low-cost transportation is generally assumed to be a necessary condition for the maintenance and expansion of trade. There is a symbiotic relationship between transportation and trade. While many believe transportation to be a derived demand depending on trade, an increasing number of trades, particularly in developing countries, are at least in part derived from efficient, low-cost transportation.

Development requires adjustment to change, including changes in economic conditions, technology, and in policies, opportunities and incentives. Trends are more uncertain today than ever before and subject to many more factors, as a result of greater economic interdependence among nations. Since LDCs are increasingly more dependent on trade for their development, and therefore on effective shipping services, their own economic development is more dependent on the growth of the international economy. As pointed out before, LDCs on average spent over twice as much as developed countries for transportation of international trade as a percentage of the value of their trade. In fact, if we exclude the more advanced Asian LDCs, which generally have well developed shipping capacity the estimated percentage of shipping costs rises to over 3.0 times the amount spent by developed countries as a percentage of the value of their trade.

Investment in shipping by developing countries has in recent years formed a significant part of national investments (at market prices). Nevertheless, investment planning in this subsector is usually not well developed, seldomly considering competing systems, changing technology or markets. As a result, in the past, such investments have often been unplanned, spurious, and opportunistic.

Increased protectionism and intervention by governments, including limitation on free access in bulk shipping, may increase distortions in resource allocations within LDCs. This in turn would cause problems equivalent to other restrictions imposed in foreign trade policy.

Shipping and related infrastructure (such as ports, roads, etc.) constitute large investments in most coastal LDCs. There is an increasing need to improve the productivity of these investments as well as the efficiency of resource use and allocation to ensure efficient and equitable economic growth. Since shipping satisfied a demand derived from trade, and the volume of trade in many commodities depends increasingly on transportation efficiency and cost, effective shipping is critical in development. With world trade growing at a higher rate than the world domestic product, the need is urgent.

Although shipping itself, particularly modern shipping, provides few employment opportunities, it has great impact on employment generation through spin-off factors and linkage effects with trade. Effective shipping also provides incentives for improvements in

111

national freight transportation.

The foreign trade of many newly industrialised and advanced developing countries, such as South Korea, Singapore, Malaysia, and Taiwan, has grown more rapidly than that of the developed countries. This growth is often credited as a major contributing factor to their rapid development. It is interesting to note that most newly industrialised countries put a high priority on shipping development as an essential element towards their trade and economic growth.

The role of shipping in trade and in the development process has been discussed; the question is therefore whether LDCs have to own ships to assure effective, low-cost transportation for their trade.

Present participation of LDCs in shipping is not only an existing fact but grew out of political decisions which cannot readily be reversed. The political decisions by borrowers are based on a set of supposed benefits, including the following:

(1) Perceived economic and financial benefits from shipping, especially as a result of the international agreement on liner shipping with its cargo sharing provisions.
(2) Expected impact on control of rates and services through direct participation in shipping.
(3) Defence security.
(4) Public relations and national prestige.
(5) International policy.
(6) Trade and commercial relations.

Increasing integration of transport is also perceived as establishing a need for a greater role in shipping. Many LDCs have established fleets, and even landlocked LDCs are considering joining the maritime nations.

Opportunity for LDC shipping development

While the role of shipping and its contribution to development has been established, the need for LDCs to run their own shipping is still in question. Many borrowers have already put a high priority on establishing national shipping lines and made major investments. Quite apart from the question of the timing or appropriateness of these investments, many of the LDCs who have established such merchant fleets cannot back out of the decisions.

Thus, their choice is to continue inefficient operations with obsolete vessels, which drive up their own costs as well as conference rates and therefore shipping costs of their whole liner trade, or to upgrade their fleet and operations. The latter option requires financing which is not readily available.

There are a number of different opportunities which should be considered to help LDCs out of their dilemma. Several basic issues stand out:

(1) LDCs cannot afford any investment in new or second-hand tonnage without new, more innovative approaches to ship financing.

(2) To reduce shipping costs many LDCs have to upgrade their fleets and rationalise their services which may imply deviation from or domination of the 'Code' or other protectionist formula. Flexible multilateral cargo sharing may provide one such approach.

(3) LDC fleets consist largely of obsolete tonnage, which contributes to their high costs of shipping. Replacing much of this tonnage by surplus or second-hand ships of higher technology would reduce worldwide shipping overcapacity while improving LDC efficiency in the shipping of their trade.

(4) To achieve rationalised services in LDC trades, developing countries may have to combine their fleets (and probably trades), allow the designation of load centre ports served by rationalised feeder services, upgrade their fleets, and enter into joint service or venture agreements with foreign operators.

Funding sources for any investment in LDC shipping would be very hard to get. Imaginative interim arrangements, under which LDC operators might join as juniors of non-shipowning partners in some shipping service scheme is one approach. Thus newer tonnage could replace some of the obsolete LDC tonnage. Such vessels would only gradually be turned over to LDC operators as they acquire the crewing and management skills required, and would still continue to operate under the joint service or venture arrangement.

In the case of some LDC liner trades, savings of 30 to 40 per cent could be achieved to bring their costs more in line with those of developed country operators. Such savings might allow both a reduction in rates and a return to reasonable profitability for LDCs, while reestablishing the creditworthiness of some operators.

Obviously, the difficulty is how to get the ball rolling, and overcome some of the suspicion, lack of trust, and institutional or political barriers to rationalised shipping in the developing world.

Innovative commercial financing — such as low-cost lease/purchase, sale and leaseback, and other schemes — offer other opportunities for more effective LDC shipping without unduly harming the long-term interests of the traditional maritime nations.

Another possibility is barter trade of new technologically advanced, second-hand surplus shipping against the scrap value of obsolete LDC tonnage (plus some commodity volume). In essence, what is needed is limited financing of the difference in market value between young modern tonnage (which may be priced only marginally above scrap value) and the scrap value of the obsolete LDC tonnage it would replace. Clearly provisions should have to be made to assure that the obsolete tonnage would actually be scrapped.

Such a scheme would benefit both LDCs, who would acquire modern, efficient tonnage, and the world maritime industry, through acceleration of the reduction of surplus tonnage. This sort of arrangement would require very little investment. For example, the exchange of a 7 to 10-year-old medium-sized (second generation) container vessel of 18 to 25,000 DWT (700 to 850 TEU capacity) for two 15 to 25-year-old 10 to 15,000 DWT general cargo ships (valued at their scrap price of US $0.9 million total) would require an investment of only US $1.4 to US $2.4 million. Even if another US $0.5 to 1 million were spent for the installation of deck cranes on the container ship, the total investment would be recouped by operating cost savings in 1 to 2 years, depending on route and service.

Similarly, replacing two 15 to 25-year-old tramps of 10 to 15,000 DWT for one modern 5 to 8-year-old bulk carrier of 25,000 DWT would today require an investment of less than US $2 million. Again, operating cost savings alone could repay such an investment in just over one year. Most of these savings would be from reduced fuel and foreign port expenses, consisting of foreign exchange.

Upgrading the total East African national shipping fleet in this manner would require an estimated investment of less than US $26.0 million for a replacement of about 2.58 million DWT. Such a scheme might have to be introduced on a nation-by-nation basis, even though a regional approach could provide additional advantages.

The benefits of a regional emphasis are particularly attractive now that both liner (container) and bulk shipping are increasingly consolidated. The load centre concept is expected to infiltrate the operations of both liner and bulk shipping; LDCs may have to integrate their national shipping into larger regional fleets to counteract attempts by main line long distance shipping to by-pass minor trade routes and ports. To assure their participation in the benefits of the new operating scenarios, LDC regions may have to develop their own load centre ports and feeder services.

SHIPPING PROTECTION AND CARGO SHARING — ITS IMPACT ON ECONOMIC DEVELOPMENT

The economic impact of cargo sharing may take many forms. It can result from the replacement of efficient shipping with less efficient shipping, from the change in the quality and level of shipping services, the increased cost of shipping, restrictive access to markets or sources of supplies, or from limited access to shipping or selective accommodation of cargo. Jurisdictional problems, regulatory constraints or legal impediments to the movement of cargo, and the unhindered operation of shipping may also have economic repercussions. Structural deficiencies and institutional constraints also play a role.

The cost and pricing of shipping, as well as the demand for and supply of shipping, have been analysed in earlier chapters. We have shown there how restrictive practices of various sorts affect shipping costs, freight rates, and shipping supply and demand. Now we will focus on the economic impact of cargo reservations and other restrictive practices in their various forms.

It is usually assumed that there is a causal relationship between the existence of effective shipping and economic development. For example, international trade, which is largely dependent on shipping, is one of the prerequisites for economic growth.

The principal reasons for the increasing use of restrictive shipping practices — particularly cargo reservation — are the desire for greater control of shipping terms and participation in shipping benefits, including those accrued from spin-off effects such as employment in shipping, technology transfer, profits from maritime insurance, and more. Various restrictive practices have been introduced over time, as discussed before. The most important are cargo reservation in the form of exclusive or defined bilateral shipping agreements, unilaterally imposed cargo reservation, or multilateral arrangements whereby cargo shares are reserved to all trading partners. In liner shipping most cargo reservation systems require closed-conferences to service the affected trades. This study will review the effects of typical forms of cargo reservation served by closed-conferences.

The impact of restrictive shipping practices on costs, rates, and rational use of resources is pervasive. Restrictive shipping practices influence the financial and economic viability of shipping operations, and affect trading nations economically, through:

— cost of trade and cost of shipping
— volume of trade
— shipping and port investment
— technological change
— quality and level of shipping service

It is assumed that it is in the national interest of any country to encourage low freight rates and other shipping charges, lowering the trade transport costs and thereby assuring greater export competition. By lowering the price of imports, countries can also maximise consumer surplus and satisfaction.

Analysis of economic impact of cargo sharing

A simple model of the impact of cargo sharing, on the basis of a 40-40-20 or any other share allocation, is shown in Figure 3.3. The model assumes that D_1 is the demand curve on the liner route under consideration, and $D_2 = 0.6D_1$ is the 60 per cent demand curve. If P_1 was the conference freight rate before entry of the national shipping, and if, because of higher costs of the national shipping members, the conference agree to raise the freight rates to $P_2 > P_1$, then $(P_2 - P_1)Q_1$ = additional profits of non-national shipping conference members. (These had earlier accepted P_1 which included marginal profit, and $(P_2 - P_1)Q_3$ = additional cost to the country's trade of carrying Q_3.) Finally, $(Q_2 - Q_3)$ is the reduction in trading volume resulting from the increase in freight rate.

If $P_4 > P_2 > P_1$ is the c.i.f. price obtained for the commodity, and $P_3 < P_4$ is the cost per unit of the commodity, then the gross product without cargo sharing is $\{P_4 - [P_3 + P_1]\}Q_2$, and with cargo sharing $\{P_4 - [P_3 + P_2]\}Q_3$.

If this is pure export trade, then total foreign exchange revenues,

Figure 3.3: Simple model of the impact of cargo sharing

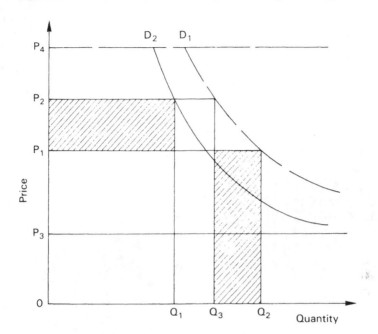

without cargo sharing (assuming all freight paid in foreign exchange), are $(P_4 - P_1)Q_2$. With cargo sharing, however, assuming freight for national shipping constitutes foreign exchange savings, these revenues are:

$$[(P_4 - P_2)Q_1 + P_4(Q_3 - Q_1)] = (P_4 - 0.6P_2)Q_3$$

Assuming:

$$(Q_3 - Q_2) = (P_2 - P_1) \text{ and } Q_1 = 0.6Q_3$$

then the difference in foreign exchange earnings is:

$$(P_4Q_2 - P_1Q_2 - P_4Q_3 - 0.6P_2Q_3)$$

which can be written:

$$P_4(P_1 - P_2) - P_1Q_2 - 0.6P_2Q_3$$

and the total cost of carrying Q_2 is then Q_2P_1 and the total cost of carrying Q_3 is then Q_3P_2.

Shipping cost and LDC foreign trade

To analyse shipping costs in the foreign trade of LDCs, consider Figure 3.4. This represents the demand and supply curves of the importing developed S_i and D_i and of the exporting less developed country S_e and D_e. For simplicity of analysis, demand and supply in both cases are assumed to be linear functions of price and quantity for the commodity under study.

At any given price, the demand for import D_i is given by the difference in quantity demanded and supplied. Obviously, at the equilibrium point F_i the demand for import is zero.

Similarly, for any given price, the demand for exports is the

Figure 3.4: Shipping cost and demand

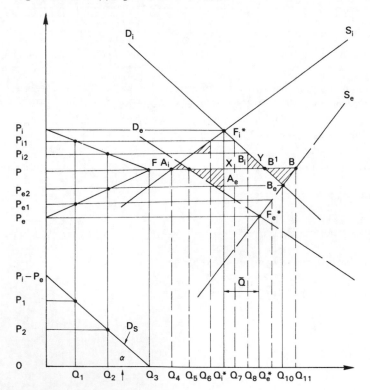

difference in quantities supplied and demanded. Here again at the equilibrium point F_e the availability of export is zero.

For any quantity of trade between the two countries defined by the distance between the supply and demand curves, such as $(A_i$ and $B_i)$ and $(A_e$ and $B_e)$, the vertical distance between these horizontal quantities gives the shipping costs (or difference of c.i.f.-f.o.b. costs in, say, US \$/ton). These shipping rates against quantities are shown by the shipping demand curve D_S. At the free trade equilibrium point F there are no shipping rates involved, and quantity $0Q_3$ would theoretically flow freely between the exporting and importing country.

Let us now presume that the import cost is US $\$P_{i1}$/ton for Q_1 tons of trade between the two countries. Country i would be paying a rate of US $\$P_{i1}$/ton (c.i.f.) to import the quantity Q_1. The f.o.b. price now is US $\$P_{e1}$/ton. Under conditions of perfect substitution the quantity imported should be equal to the quantity exported.

Now if there is an improvement in the shipping services resulting in a lower import cost, say P_{i2}/ton, then this would lead to an increase in the volume of trade (from Q_1 to Q_2, for instance). At the activity level $0Q_2$ the c.i.f. and f.o.b. prices are now P_{i2} and P_{e2} respectively. Therefore in this simple linear non-competitive model, when the price of shipping goes down, trade in the commodity between the two countries increases. Both trading countries enjoy the benefits of reduced costs.

A reduction in price from P_{i1} to P_{i2} will increase the consumer surplus if his demand is elastic, will decrease if his demand is inelastic, and will remain unchanged if demand elasticity is unitary.

If the equations of the demand and supply curves of the importing country are:

$$D_i = a - dQ$$
$$S_i = c + dQ$$

This permits P_s, or the cost of shipping c.i.f. or f.o.b. cost of commodity) in this non-competitive trade, to be expressed in terms of the commodity price differentials between importing and exporting country, when both importing and exporting country have a demand-supply equilibrium, and the gradients of the demand and supply curves of the importing and exporting country.

Changes in the elasticities of supply or demand of the importer or exporter therefore have similar effects, while a parallel shift of the demand and supply curve will move all the prices.

119

Benefits accruing to the exporting country from an f.o.b. price change, say $(P_{i2} - P_{i1})$, or to P_{i1} from P_{i2}, or supply curves of the importer, or to the area $1/2(P_{i1} - P_{i2})(Q_2 - Q_1)$. Similarly benefits to the exporter would be equal to the area $1/2(P_{e1} - P_{e2})(Q_2 - Q_1)$.

Bilateral cargo sharing

Bilateral agreements generate various economic impacts, in addition to freight rate effects, which add to the cost of trade between the countries. The modernisation of the national fleets is delayed, because competitive pressures are eliminated by the virtual exclusion of third-country carriers. (Occasionally these are chartered-in to carry national shipping shares, or admitted under special dispensation.) As noted, the shares carried by fleets of the trading partners are also uneven. This is in part a concession of the lower cost operator to the higher cost operator, permitting the less efficient operator to increase its share of net revenues through larger volume shares of cargo. On the other hand, if the higher cost operator is required to charter-in foreign flag vessels to carry its share, this siphons off valuable foreign exchange.

As a result, economic benefits are seriously compromised. The same applies for the purchase of ships to carry the national share under bilateral service agreements. The total economic impact of the bilateral liner shipping agreements can be summarised as follows:

Costs:
(a) increased costs of imports
(b) increased price of exports and resulting loss of market share
(c) foreign exchange expenditure for chartering-in of foreign vessels
(d) investment costs of fleet acquisition
(e) loss of technological improvement

Benefits:
(f) savings in foreign exchange for use of foreign shipping
(g) employment of nationals

Thus it appears that bilateral liner service agreements usually have a negative economic effect on trade, particularly on developing country barter. Although bilateral shipping agreements theoretically offer a vehicle for effective cargo sharing in liner shipping between

Figure 3.5: Perfect cargo sharing under bilateral agreement

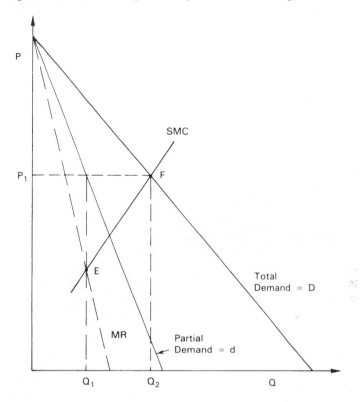

trading countries, they do not provide the incentives or mechanisms for efficient operation, resource use, and pricing, unless specifically designed into the agreement.

Bilateral agreements can only result in efficient, low-cost shipping if effective operational and investment incentives are provided. This may require reasonable participation of third-country carriers, preferably in the form of independents.

For a simple economic explanation, when both national fleets under a bilateral cargo sharing agreement have the same short run marginal costs (SMC, Figure 3.5) and agree to a share(s) of d for one and $(1 - s)D$ for the other fleet (where $d = sD$ for all D), then the price set by both would be equal to the monopoly price P_1, and the shares of the two fleets would be Q_1 and $(Q_2 - Q_1)$ respectively. If the short run marginal costs of the two fleets are different (SMC_1 and SMC_2 respectively) as shown in Figure 3.6, in which

121

Figure 3.6: Cargo sharing with differential marginal cost

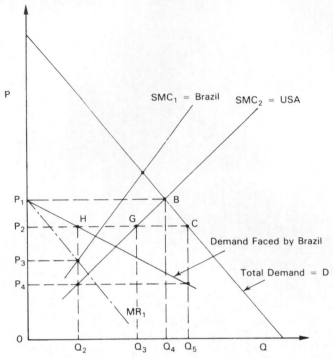

the high-cost fleet in the conference is assumed to determine the rates (price leader), then the price set would determine the market share of the fleets. For example, if the price set by the conference is P_2, then the total demand is Q_5. The high-cost fleet would supply Q_2 of this, to maximise its profits (intersection of marginal revenue and marginal cost curve for higher cost fleet). With a more realistic concave total demand and marginal cost curve, the share that the higher cost fleet would claim increases. This, in turn, would increase the profit of the lower cost fleet. In general, the price set under such conditions would be appreciably higher than the marginal cost of the lower cost fleet, with resulting excess profits for the lower cost fleet operators.

Table 3.2: Typical major LDC foreign trades and potential participation by national flag vessels

Country	Export (1,000 M.T)				Import (1,000 M.T)				% that can be carried by National Flag Vessels			
	Bulk	Petrol	G.C.	Cont.	Bulk	Petrol	G.C.	Cont.	Bulk	Tanker	G.C.¹	Cont.
1. Indonesia	34,300	70,500	–	250	21,219	–	7,050	975	7 (3,917)*	8 (4,044)	47.5 (4,270)	49.0 (4,270)
2. Korea (Rep.)	4,900	100	17,170	11,900	39,700	29,400	9,370	5,100	100 (5,115)	52 (8,930)	39.0 (5,087)	19.5 (5,087)
3. Philippines	12,000	–	6,200	2,600	6,200	9,000	8,000	3,500	61 (4,400)	28 (8,680)	23.0 (5,087)	0.5 (5,087)
4. Brazil	80,000**	68,000**	12,400**	1,600**					32 (5,405)	35 (4,740)	48.5 (4,780)	0 (4,380)
5. Nigeria	2,110	50,500	–	120	1,200	4,770	8,100	1,030	0	4 (4,200)	30.0 (5,680)	8.1

* Average one-way distance in parentheses
** Sum of export and import
¹ General cargo national flag capacity assumes 50 per cent ton-mile capacity utilisation

123

Cargo sharing

Cargo sharing and other forms of multilateral reservations of cargo are supposed to offer economic advantages to participating nations. (In this section the impact of cargo sharing in general cargo and bulk trades will be studied.)

Table 3.2[1] shows the capacity of national fleets of some major developing countries and the percentage of their foreign trade which these fleets could theoretically carry. Nigeria, as an example, could carry 4 per cent of its dry bulk trade and 30 per cent of its general cargo trade in national flag ships, but has no capacity to carry its own petroleum exports. It can handle some containers on general cargo or combination vessels.

Some developing countries can carry significant proportions of their trade. Cargo sharing therefore affects nations unpredictably, with some unable to carry anything like their share of cargo, while others are left with excess capacity.

Little information is available on the effects of cargo sharing introduced in recent years in preparation or response to the enactment of the 'Code'. Therefore, a hypothetical example is presented here, comparing trade with and without cargo sharing, and evaluating its potential impact.

EFFECTS OF SHIPPING INVESTMENT ON NATIONAL INCOME

The traditional approach taken to measure the economic effect of investment in shipping is to estimate the combined consumers' and producers' surplus generated. Applying basic principles, one could then interpret optimal shipping investment as those which maximise profits and social surplus. Figure 3.7 shows that introducing capacity Q_1 would be the ideal theoretical investment, where short-run marginal cost and marginal revenue are equal. On the other hand, long-run marginal cost for this investment is well below the marginal revenue at this point. Under free competitive conditions, or when shipping is maximised, investment would be increased to Q_2, where long-run and short-run marginal cost equals marginal revenue. If, on the other hand, social surplus is where the demand curve intersects with both the short-run and long-run marginal cost curves.

These simple principles[2] are easy to understand but difficult to apply, particularly in the framework of cargo sharing in inter-

124

Figure 3.7: Shipping investment alternatives

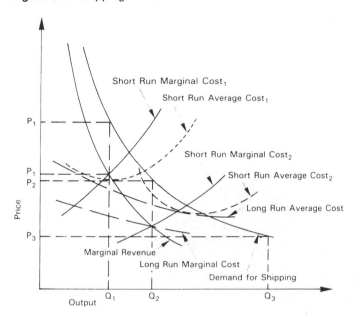

national shipping. Researchers such as Koyek[3] and Friedlander[4] have proposed the use of 'effect of transport investment' on national income instead. Still, there are some questions regarding effectiveness of such a measure as a guide to the evaluation of alternative transport or shipping investments. The difficulty arises partly from the use of macroeconomic measures in the evaluation of microeconomic decisions.

Benefits from shipping investment

There are several traditional methods for computing the benefits from shipping investments. The net present value approach is among the most popular of unbiased measured, though some organisations prefer the use of internal rate of return. Both financial and economic yardsticks of investment performance are of interest, to measure the financial viability and economic impact of such transport investment.

The Net Present Value of Shipping Investment (Financial) is:

$$NPV(F) = \sum_{t=1}^{n} \frac{[R(F)_t - L(F)_t]}{(1 + i)^t} + \frac{SV}{(1 + i)^n}$$

where:

$R(F)_t$ = expected revenue in year t
$L(F)_t$ = expected costs in year t
i   = rate of interest of capital used in investment
n   = expected life
SC   = scrap value

and the economic Net Present Value of Shipping Investment is:

$$NPV(E) = \sum_{p=1}^{k} \sum_{t=1}^{n} \frac{[B(E)_{tp} - C(E)_{tp}]}{(1 + d_t)}$$

where:

$B(E)_{tp}$ = economic and social benefit of type p in year t
$C(E)_{tp}$ = economic and social cost of type p in year t
d_t = economic discount factor in year t
k   = number of different economic and social impacts
n   = expected life of shipping investment

Determining the optimum level of investment is particularly difficult in liner shipping because participation is more affected by value than volume of cargo. The relationship of value to volume of cargo is also variable, responding to the degree of cross-subsidisation among cargoes. Usually if low value cargo is highly cross-subsidised, more will be attracted, particularly since such cargo is often highly elastic. This in turn will affect the demand for shipping (as well as marginal costs and revenues), and would therefore theoretically justify a larger investment; in reality a lesser investment, including curtailment of 'excess' capacity and pricing to reflect costs, would make better use of investments.

Structural models of cargo sharing

The economic impact of cargo sharing depends on the methods used to control cargo access, distribute revenue and share costs, employ any government aids, and organise the shipping services. In this section a number of different models of cargo sharing are presented, with discussions of their potential impact. The emphasis here is on the structural, organisational, and operational issues. Only measurable costs and benefits will be reviewed. The models presented are of two types. A general rationalised service model is considered which includes different approaches to provide the same quality of service at different costs. The second type of model introduces cargo allocations, using a number of different cargo sharing formulas to show how different allocation schemes affect rationalised use of shipping.

If we consider alternative direct and indirect service models in which service quality in terms of frequency, average time of shipping, and supply/demand balance remains essentially constant, we can develop a range of structural alternatives which are best represented by networks.

The simplest model would represent bilateral trade (liner or tramp), in which all cargo is reserved to shipping under the control of the trading partners. If the volume of liner (or bulk) exports of partners 1 and 2 is Q_1 and Q_2 respectively, and if partner 1 trades from $i = 1, 2 \ldots n$ ports and partner 2 trades from $j = 1, 2 \ldots m$ ports, where Q_{ij} is the amount of cargo exported from port i to port j and Q_{ji} is the amount of cargo exported from port j to port i, then:

$$\sum_i \sum_j Q_{ij} = Q^1 \text{ and } \sum_i \sum_j Q_{ji} = Q^2$$

Cargo imported at ports j and i is

$$\sum_i Q_{ij} = Q_j \text{ and } \sum_j Q_{ji} = Q_i$$

If cargoes exported from ports i to ports j are identified by types k, such that Q_{ij}^k = quantity of kth type of cargo shipped from ports i to ports j, and if the corresponding freight rate is R_{ij}^k, then the total average revenue obtained from the trade is

$$R_T = \sum_i \sum_j \sum_k (C_{ij}^k Q_{ij}^k + C_{ji}^k Q_{ji}^k)$$

Such a model can be used to determine the effect of alternative methods of cargo sharing and distribution, under conditions of imbalance in cargo offerings and differential rates (say $C_{ij}^k \neq C_{ij}^k$).

Cargo can be shared by total volume when each partner carries an amount as follows:

127

$$\text{Carriage by Partner} = W_i = W_j = \frac{1}{2}[\sum_i\sum_j\sum_k(Q_{ij}{}^k + Q_{ji}{}^k)]$$

Partners will then attempt to minimise the costs of carrying their allocation. If revenues are shared, then each would obtain a defined proportion of R_T as described above. If revenues and costs are to be shared, then the model must be expanded to include costs of the operators as well.

A rationalised service model assumes complete cooperation of all participants in the trade, through pooling their fleets or other cooperative arrangements. Under rationalised service, capacity between port pairs, transit times, and frequencies of service would all remain constant, but would be provided by the minimum number (and size) of ships possible. Routing, scheduling, and ship assignment would be performed centrally, and both costs and revenues shared in predetermined proportions.

Rationalised service models may include routings and schedules which differ from trip to trip, with some port calls or services provided only at intervals, or by some of the vessels. They may also involve partial or full feeder operations with one or more ports in each trading area designated as load centre ports.

Rationalisation on a trade route usually presumes cargo sharing among participating operators. Most cargo sharing arrangements are not based on a rationalisation approach, but on some formulas for cargo allocation. According to our review of several 'Codist', bilateral, and other cargo sharing arrangements, there appears to be no uniform approach to the method of cargo sharing and no general formula to apply to model the workings of such agreements. Most arrangements rely on a loose agreement for service levels and carriage, with end-of-period adjustments in carriage (or costs) in line with prevailing agreements.

FUTURE ROLE OF SHIPPING

The changes in shipping technology and operations currently underway are expected to lead to a different role for shipping in the future. Shipping will not only be more integrated with other modes of transport, becoming a true link in intermodal transport, but will also serve a more integrated role in international trade and communications. In the future, commodities are expected to be traded while underway at sea, and shipborne cargo will form part of a worldwide distribution/storage system for major commodities. At any one time traders will be able to find out what and how much of a cargo is located anywhere on land and on sea, and available for redistribution or sale. Real time decisions will then be made to trade in and reallocate cargoes in the most rational manner, minimising total cost of distribution and delivery.

Such an approach is expected to result in a dynamically efficient trading system, in which transport and storage costs (including cost of inventory holding) are minimised while transport and storage facility use is maximised. This approach also aims at reducing the risks inherent in international trade which result from currency exchange fluctuations, changes in trade barriers, regulatory obstructions, buyer credit reliability, and so on.

To accomplish this, future shipping systems must be fully integrated into intermodal transport, communications, funds transfer, booking, and other systems. Likewise, reliable tariff and commodity price information for any location and condition must be readily available. This kind of system would furthermore be tied into commodity trading — including futures trading — market systems. In fact, in the future, shipping will be studied like commodities. The different shipping terms like f.o.b., c.i.f. etc. could expand into a whole range of ship service trading terms included or excluded in the commodity trading price. For example, commodities traded while on route may be sold at a proportional difference between traditional c.i.f. and f.o.b. or similar terms.

Similarly, shipping, like other transport, will be considered simply part of the process between raw material production and delivery of the final product to the consumer. In fact, many materials or semi-finished products will probably be increasingly processed or finished on board while on route to their destination. Processing on board makes sense not only to use the time in transport which is otherwise lost, but also to take advantage of ready availability of electric power, large amounts of cooling and process water, and skilled labour. Furthermore, on-board processing may allow custom blending for particular destinations or customers, as well as escape from many restrictive regulations governing the processing of many materials, including environmental impact restrictions.

There are many examples of processing that can be carried out efficiently on board. For example, a 150,000 ton bulk vessel on a 15-day voyage could have a 10,000 ton per day processing plant installed. With 20 round trips a year, two such vessels could supply the equivalent of a 4 million tons per year/plant. While the shipboard plants would be idle more than half the time, inventory holding,

129

waste material disposal, and related costs could often be reduced. Most importantly, such an integrated intermodal system — including transport/processing/storage/packaging/distribution — would permit a large increase in the efficiencies of worldwide production, manufacture, and delivery. Preliminary studies indicate that such systems may reduce time from initial production to finished product delivery and consumption by 5 to 8 per cent, and total delivery cost by 25 to 40 per cent.

At this time, well over 30 per cent of the value of world trade is spent on holding, transport, and distribution. Shipping alone consumes a fraction of the total non-production manufacture costs. It is for that reason that changes in the role and function of shipping are not only recommended but are already gradually being introduced.

Ship technology has changed little in recent years, mainly because of the large overcapacity in most segments of the shipping industry which affected investment in new ship capacity and technology. Nonetheless, there are many technical, operational, and policy changes under consideration.

Changes in future ship technology will affect hull design, propulsion, cargo storage, cargo handling, ship handling, and ship management and communications. In the interim, the industry is shifting towards better use of these developments. Ship manning is gradually being reduced to 14 to 16 persons, and will be likely to level off at 10 to 12 crew members. Most of these will be qualified multipurpose (deck-engine-communication) personnel. As a result, shipboard staff will be able to move between ships and shipboard functions much more readily. This will make it easier to dissociate flag from crew nationality and thus reduce problems both in ship and shipping management.

Satellite communications, computerised ship management, ship weather routing, and optimum route scheduling are all technologies currently available and in use on many ships. The changing role of shipping is closely tied to these developments, allowing real time control of ship position, real time monitoring of cargoes and their condition, real time information and funds transfer, and more. Of course, all of these developments require the integration of shipping into larger transport and distribution/trading systems not only in operational, but also managerial and financial terms.

Impact of changing role on development

Consolidation of shipping, and its integration with transport and distribution systems in general, is designed to improve economies of scale, to increase link resource utilisation, reduce delivery time, and, as a result, lower cost. Unfortunately, this approach demands an amount of traffic which few developing countries generate even as a region or group. In consequence, shipping costs for these countries are expected to increase substantially in relation to those of industrialised countries. Although many developing countries are now investing heavily in containerisation and modern bulk handling technology, most lack the physical, institutional, operational, and managerial capability to integrate modern shipping and port technology with the rest of their transport and distribution systems.

In some cases, institutional obstacles are difficult to surmount, while in others there is a lack of physical infrastructure. The consequent inability of developing countries to participate in the trading of shipping/transport services is critical.

4

Financing, Revenues and Costs of Shipping

The financial management of shipping has undergone major changes in recent times. Traditional sources of ship financing are drying up, particularly for second-hand ship acquisition and more creative financing approaches are often required for shipping investments. On the shipping revenue side, the US Shipping Act of 1984, which mandated the right of independent action and service contracts to members of the 'open' conferences serving US liner trade, had the effect of transforming published conference rates from price lists into negotiable guidelines. Futures contracts, on the other hand, affect charter rates for bulk carriage in a different manner. Freight rates, as a result, are less predictable in the US liner trades now, but more predictable in bulk trades when subject to active future contract trading.

Ship costs, both acquisition and operating costs, similarly are in a large flux. Bunker costs, for example, have declined by nearly 50 per cent between early 1985 and early 1986. Similarly crew costs have been reduced in most developed country fleets by drastic reductions in crew size. As a result, total ship operating costs for similar sized vessels operating at identical speeds have sometimes declined by as much as 40 per cent over a 2 to 3 year period. If ship form and technology is furthermore improved the saving can be even more drastic. Typical container shipping costs in per container mile in 1980 were US $0.080–0.095, while the large new US Lines and Evergreen round-the-world 2700–4218 TEU vessels have costs of only about US $0.030–0.034 per TEU mile, or a reduction of about 60 per cent. Although savings in the costs of bulk and specialised shipping are less dramatic, they are still significant.

CHANGING APPROACH TO SHIP AND SHIPPING FINANCING

Shipping financing was traditionally handled by some of the largest commercial banks who accepted ship mortgages or charter parties as collateral. In recent years, the ship financing market has undergone major changes and many new approaches to ship financing have been introduced.

New ship acquisitions are usually financed by a combination of credits from sources such as:

— supplier credits including shipbuilder loans
— government export credits
— commercial mortgage loans
— commercial loans against charter agreements or other acceptable collateral
— government loans

The methods and terms of ship financing though vary widely among countries. Until a few years ago, it was common for an owner to borrow as much as 92 per cent of the price of a new vessel, usually half from commercial sources and half from government sources or with government guarantees. Government loans and supplier credits were usually for medium terms of 5 to 10 years (8 year average), while most commercial mortgage loans were for longer 15 to 20 year periods. As a result, loans against second-hand ships are usually held by commercial banks. Similarly second-hand ship financing was traditionally provided by commercial banks (including specialised merchant banks).

Ships in general are registered (and incorporated) as separate legal entities (firms or corporations) to reduce an owner's risk and exposure, in case of damage, loss, or default.

Because ship prices used to increase over time and ships were effectively insured against loss, lenders were in the past willing to write mortgages against such separate assets.

The decline of newbuilding and second-hand ship prices which started in 1981/2 has had a major impact on the method of ship financing. While some ship mortgage, government, and supplier credit financing for new ships is still available, the total amount financed by these traditional methods now seldomly exceeds 50 per cent of ship price, and commercial ship mortgage loans are usually written for periods of only ten years. If an owner requires additional financing, he will now have to post other acceptable collateral.

133

Financing second-hand ship acquisition is even more difficult, as government loans are usually not available for such transactions, and commercial mortgage financing, if at all offered, will not exceed 30 per cent of ship price, with mortgages written for periods of 5 to 10 years depending on the age of the vessel.

Ships are marketed internationally often using ship brokers. Shipbuilders though often have their own sales organisation and either offer their own designs or build to customer requirements. Newbuildings are sold as single vessels or short-run series of sister ships. Owners often contract with major equipment suppliers, such as engine manufacturers separately, to maintain their equipment choice and to obtain separate supplier credits and guarantees.

While most newbuildings are sold directly by shipbuilders, second-hand vessels are usually sold through ship brokers who maintain a worldwide data base on ship offerings and demands. Ship brokers will act for either the seller or the buyer and sometimes also represent shipbuilders who own vessels built for their own account.

Financing of new ship acquisitions has traditionally been provided by public and commercial financial institutions at reasonable rates and terms. Instruments used were export credits, ship mortgages, or loans to owners against a charter serving as collateral. In addition a number of shipbuilding countries have provided direct or indirect subsidies to their shipbuilders and/or foreign buyers of their ships through credit subsidies. Second-hand ship purchase financing, on the other hand, was mainly performed by a number of commercial and merchant banking institutions with special expertise in the field. Over-generous financing during the period 1968–78 is frequently blamed for the massive expansion of shipping in the 1970s and the subsequent crisis caused by over-tonnaging. The reasons may have been excessive optimism, the belief the fluctuations in rates were due only to short-term cyclical variations, and confidence in continued high rates of economic growth and world trade.

Another reason was probably the ambitious expansion of the banking industry in a competitive growing market with plenty of funds to lend. In recent years, largely as the result of the economic plight of the shipping industry, the attitude of lenders to shipping has changed significantly with most traditional lenders exercising great caution, suspicion, or outright reluctance or refusal to lend to all but the most reliable owners. With declining market values of new and second-hand shipping, asset values have often been insufficient to provide adequate collateral. Liquidity and quality of ownership are therefore the principal criteria considered by lenders now. The supply of finance for new and second-hand ship acquisition by less developed country or lesser owners, has as a result become quite restrictive in recent years. Developing country owners usually do not qualify for ship financing under current conditions and are, as a result, unable to take advantage of the low new and second-hand ship prices to expand, rebuild, or upgrade their fleet.

A recent survey of commercial lending for shipping[1] indicated that 89 of the world's major banks had large shipping loan portfolios. The estimated total loans of eleven banks which responded to a questionnaire was US $6.005 billion. Total commercial bank lending for shipping by the 89 major banks involved in ship lending and over 200 other commercial banks with some outstanding ship mortgage loans, is estimated to be in excess of US $50.0 billion. Lending by government export banks and similar financial institutions, as well as commercial lending with government insurance (such as under the US Title XI Ship Construction/Mortgage Program and direct lending by shipbuilders) is estimated to account for an outstanding portfolio of another US $27 billion in shipping loans, for a total balance of about US $77 billion in shipping loans.

Availability of financing

Shipping loans accounted for 20 per cent of all commercial loans extended by the 14 major commercial lenders to shipping. At the same time the proportion of the total commercial loan portfolio represented by shipping loans was about 5 per cent. Yet while only a small number of commercial banks are therefore seriously exposed to major defaults by shipping borrowers, the commercial banks have generally adopted a very cautious attitude and do not entertain financing of new or second-hand shipping for anyone but the most creditworthy ship owners.

One of the reasons why shipping loans have generally become risky is that over 80 per cent of the shipping loans were in excess of 30 per cent of the original ship price, and for periods exceeding ten years. With ship market values frequently dropping 40 per cent or more of original ship price within a couple of years of delivery, the remaining value of the asset often provided insufficient collateral after just a few years. In parallel, freight and charter rates have also dropped precariously and only infrequently now are full costs reimbursing.[2] This in turn has caused severe cash flow problems even for owners able to find employment for their vessels, while owners of unemployed vessels are frequently forced to scrap their ships, as credit extension is seldomly offered.

In addition less than 50 per cent of the ships financed by shipping loans in recent years were covered by long-term charters. While most shipping loans were made with some form of collateral, usually a ship mortgage, charter party, etc., the average value of collateral at the end of 1982 had a value less than 50 per cent of the loan. This situation has since become worse. With increasing defaults in loan payments, commercial banks have responded in different ways. While some have deferred loan repayments, others have resorted to foreclosure or outright seizure of ships. At the end of 1984, more than 110 vessels with a capacity in excess of 4.5 million DWT had been seized by lenders.

As a result, the availability of financing by commercial banks for ship acquisition has declined significantly. A recent survey of major US banks involved in ship financing by a US merchant banking and investment firm[3] indicated that few of these banks are willing to consider shipping loans at this time, unless provided to a highly reliable owner able and willing to provide acceptable non-ship equity collateral.

The major and often the only source of finance for new ship aquisitions is now a government finance agency in the country in which the new ship is built. Although new ship prices have declined significantly, terms of financing newbuildings have hardened in most cases with few newbuilding loans to foreign buyers extended over periods exceeding eight years.[4] Similarly most newbuilding loans are now limited to 40 to 60 per cent of ship price, which is significantly less than available only a few years ago when first mortgages of 70 to 80 per cent of ship price were common, often supplemented by second mortgages or other loans. Financing of second-hand ship purchases is even less available. Many of the traditional commercial lenders have incurred major losses in unpaid interest and capital repayments, and many among these have been forced to foreclose or seize ships of bankrupt borrowers. The market value of the seized assets has usually been substantially below the outstanding loan balance.

In addition banks often had difficulty disposing of seized vessels because of the glut of shipping capacity among the traditional developed country maritime nations and their unwillingness or inability to extent credit to potential buyers in developing countries. US banks, for example, who hold the largest shipping loan portfolios (and fleets of seized vessels) among the banking industries worldwide are unable to extend additional loans to most developing countries under current Federal Bank reserve rules. As a result, many of these vessels are disposed of as scrap.

The value of ship mortgages today seldomly exceed 50 to 60 per cent of the market value of a vessel and averaged only 40 per cent during 1985. Similarly security arrangements have been tightened with mortgagors requiring now among others:

(1) First secured mortgages.
(2) Irrevocable assignment of earnings.
(3) Irrevocable assignment of insurance claims.
(4) Pledge of shares of owning company.
(5) Parent or holding company guarantee.

In the past the ship owner and operator were distinct, and financial institutions obtained, as a result, first preferred mortgages and insurance assignments from the owner and assignment of earnings from the operator. This gave them two distinct sources of security. In most cases now, and particularly in developing countries, owner and operator are the same which reduces the security and increases the risk to the lender.

These tightened conditions for commercial lending and the large reduction of lending sources has made it increasingly difficult for LDC owners to obtain new ship financing and practically impossible to finance second-hand ship purchases. This condition is amplified by the request of many LDC borrowers for ship financing to permit conditions such as: acceptance of mortgages registered in the developing country; financing through sole financier versus syndication; long-term fixed interest rates; and, standardisation of loans with multi-currency options. Such conditions are usually not acceptable to commercial lenders now. For example, according to the Japanese Ministry of Transport, Japanese lending for shipping in 1983 was:

(1) Development Bank 112.5 b yen.
(2) Ex.-IM Bank 190 b yen.
(3) Trading houses 700 b yen.
(4) Leasing companies 600 b yen.
(5) Commercial banks, insurance companies, etc. 300 b yen.
(6) Others 33 b yen for a total 1983 lending of 1,936 b yen or about US $8 billion.

Recent developments in ship financing

Other ship financing arrangements now commonly used include interest swaps to reduce interest costs by exchanging floating for fixed rates and currency swaps to hedge currency risks and to acquire funds with fixed interest rates. The proposed US tax reforms have induced development of new incentive, tax-oriented ship lease financing. Until details of the US tax reforms are known, thorough estimates on the effect on availability of this type of ship financing are not possible.

Lenders for shipping are often blamed for providing too much ready financing during the period 1970–80. They have now, as mentioned before, become extremely cautious. In fact, over 80 per cent of the commercial lenders have completely withdrawn from ship financing with only a few, very large, commercial banks and trading houses still in the market in addition to government finance institutions, who usually only finance newbuildings in their domestic yards.

Although cash flow and profit projections remain important considerations in ship financing, qualitative factors such as credit-worthiness and reliability of both the owner and operator as well as external factors such as economic and trade pattern forecasts play an increasingly important role in ship financing decision-making.

Although some developed country ship owners have devised imaginative proposals such as joint ventures or joint operations with developing country operators, financing for LDC shipping from commercial sources has been difficult, if not impossible, to obtain.

Compared with the leasing of aircraft, trucks, and railcars, leasing of oceangoing ships is a very recent development, unless we consider bareboat charter arrangements as part of sale-leaseback contracts. The growth of lease financing is due to the greater flexibility and financial advantage offered to many owners, as compared with conventional ship financing. Also many owners, particularly in the industrial countries, are willing to forego their traditional preference for legal ownership because lease arrangements reduce both their operating risks and exposure to sudden ship seizures or other interventions which interfere with orderly operations. There are two basic types of ship leasing in use now:

(1) Financial leasing, where the lessee is responsible for all repairs and maintenance. The lessor signs the shipbuilding or ship purchase contract, and the lease agreement is effected by

means of a bareboat charter party over the agreed period of lease. The lease agreement may also include a right to purchase the asset at the expiration of the lease at agreed terms. This type of lease agreement often includes sophisticated leveraged lease-purchase-leaseback arrangements which are usually designed to maximise tax-advantaged treatment of the contract to the level owner of the asset. The most common is the US leverage financial lease which involves the vendor, owner, owner-trustee acting as lessor who obtains funds from a lender, and the lessee who pays lease charges to the owner-trustee or lessor. Proposed changes in US tax law may make this type of ship financing more difficult in the future.

(2) Instalment sale leasing is another lease financing arrangement. It is used when the lessor is unwilling to assume ownership of the asset because of a tax or legal position. Here the lessor purchases the vessel and simultaneously transfers ownership to the ship owner who then makes payments on instalments. To secure sale proceeds, lessors will usually take a mortgage on or place liens against the vessel.

One of the increasingly difficult issues in ship lease financing is the assumption of foreign exchange risks. With nearly 28 per cent of all ship supplier credit, ship mortgage, and ship leasing contracts written in Japanese yen,[5] affected ship owners now suffer an increase in finance cost of as much as 33 per cent as a result of the increase in the exchange rate against the US dollar. As shipping revenues in terms of rates are usually quoted and paid in US dollars, substantial exchange rate penalties are being incurred by these owners.

THE STRUCTURE OF FREIGHT RATES

Ratemaking in shipping is a complex subject. Although rates in bulk shipping, for independently-owned and other vessels in the bulk trade offered for service in the open charter market are largely subject to free market forces of supply and demand, bulk carriers in proprietary or similar service and liners serving under conference agreements usually have a complex rate structure based more on the value of service. In fact few components of the international shipping industry offer cost-based freight rates, or use marginal or average cost pricing as a basis for their ratemaking. From an economic point of view, this should result in inefficient use of resources. While this may sometimes happen, the prevailing approaches to pricing of shipping are usually dictated by the complexity of the market place, the high degree of fluctuation of demand, and rate of technical and structural change in shipping.

Freight rates are also affected by the increasing participation of government or proprietary user owned and/or controlled shipping. Governments sometimes use their shipping to attain political or strategic objectives which may be furthered by the use of less than compensatory or even predatory ratemaking. Similarly resource or trading companies which own or control large fleets on occasion use ratemaking as a means for gaining competitive advantages or achieving other commercial objectives.

The case for and against value of service conference ratemaking

Value of service conference ratemaking is often referred to as a microeconomic model of third-degree price discrimination.[6] Transportation demand elasticity usually affects value of service ratemaking, as high value goods have ordinarily rather inelastic demands for transportation, with low valued goods exhibiting quite a large demand elasticity. Similarly it is often found that the higher the ratio of freight rate to the f.o.b. or c.i.f. value of cargo, the more elastic is its demand for transportation. Value of service conference pricing is usually justified by the duality of a fixed capacity and large fixed costs. In turn, this introduces the argument that only reduced, below cost rates for low value cargo can attract the volume required to fill the offered capacity, and as a result reduce the average cost per unit of cargo carried.

Differential pricing, it is argued, enables fuller use of capacity by allowing most fixed costs to be allocated on the basis of demand. Similarly average unit costs may be difficult to determine, as they are a function of the utilisation of capacity. Therefore if a rate were cost based, high value cargo demand would barely increase as this demand is quite inelastic, while lower value cargo with elastic demand would not move. As a result, utilisation would decline with a corresponding increase in average cost for the smaller amount of cargo actually carried.

Therefore while value of service pricing can be criticised as internally subsidising, it can readily be argued that conferences use their capacity more effectively and reduce the average cost of carriage of cargo, including that of high value commodities, by the use of differential pricing. The main reason and justification for this approach is obviously the high level of fixed costs in liner shipping.

The most important argument against value of service pricing is that it fosters resource misallocation, by introducing among other factors excess capacity and by diversion of resources to high cost operations.

As shown, long-run marginal costs should provide the floor under which rates should not fall. High fixed costs though often make marginal cost pricing unrealistic, particularly if such an approach causes gross under-utilisation of capacity. Shipping capacity can usually not be subdivided into small enough units or ships so as to maintain both desired service frequency and capacity which would be fully used where pure cost of service and particularly marginal cost pricing adopted.

Conference ratemaking

Conference ratemaking is usually based more on value of cargo and not cost of service. In fact, in the absence of competition, profit maximisation of conferences depends to a large extent on the sensitivity of the volume of commodities shipped in the trade of the conference to the conference rate. In other words, conferences appear to discriminate quite extensively against cargo on the basis of sensitivity of volume shipped to rate charged. To maintain a semblance of competition and to reduce the monopoly stigma, conferences usually permit or even encourage service competition. On the other hand, price competition is not only discouraged but fought when discovered. To increase intra-conference competition, open conferences are sometimes advocated as in the US liner trade. Similarly, revenue pooling is often suggested in preference to cargo pooling as a means of improving intra-conference competition. In general, though, it is found that the greater the control and thereby monopoly the conference exerts on terms of service, such as cargo allocation, scheduling, routing, etc., the most it is able to rationalise its service and maximise its profits by increasing its revenues and minimising its costs.

In reality, conferences are imperfect monopolies and, as a result, are not as efficient as they could be if permitted to act as perfect monopolies. One question often raised is why liner shipping does not operate as competitively as tramp shipping, with shippers taking the risk of rates fluctuating with demand and supply. To provide some certainty of shipping costs, future options, forward spot rates, or other forms of forward contracts could be negotiated with 'cargo brokers' or ship owners' organisations making a market. There is a question though – how much of a premium or futures fee shippers would be willing to pay to eliminate their risk. In the past shippers of liner cargoes have generally preferred the greater certainty of conference rates and have often advocated or supported longer notice requirements and review of tariff changes, limitation of tariff changes in any particular period of time, and justification of such changes by a review of costs. The last has always been the hardest to accept because conference pricing is discriminatory and largely based on the value of the good shipped and not on the cost of transporting the good. As noted by Laing[7] such discriminatory pricing is aimed at maximising conference benefits, and it deviates from the traditional economic approach of maximising the difference between revenues and marginal costs. As value of cargo pricing invariably includes cross-subsidisation of lower valued cargo, a large number of shippers, particularly those in developing countries benefit by being able to expand their trade of lower valued exports. They would obviously object to a more cost based tariff. In reality conference prices are based only in part on value (f.o.b. price) and on some function of cargo density, as well as cargo demand elasticity. Sometimes conference pricing also considers the price elasticity of the commodity.

Although ratemaking by most conferences is not based solely on the value of service, it is usually closer to value of service than to cost of service pricing. The mix of cargoes carried by conferences depends largely on the route. While on liner routes between industrialised countries, high value manufactured goods dominate and a fair balance of trade in both directions is usually achieved (the exceptions are now US-Pacific and US-Atlantic liner routes), conference trades between developed and developing countries are usually highly imbalanced both in terms of value and volume of cargo carried (Figure 4.1). The average value of cargo carried northbound in the West Africa to Europe trade, for example, was only 28 per cent of that of southbound cargo, and the volume was a bare 48 per cent of the southbound average. With voyage costs largely sunk, liner conferences are obviously attracted to carry northbound cargo at any price in excess of marginal cost of such additional carriage.

Figure 4.1: Cumulative distribution of value of cargo on typical conference routes

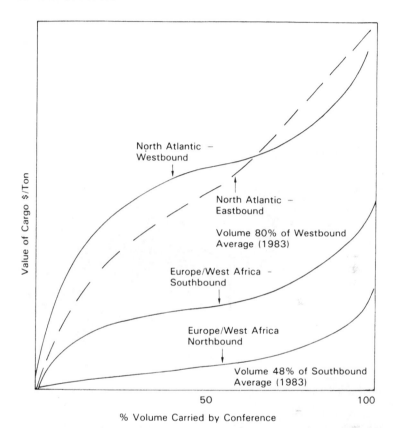

North Atlantic –
Westbound

North Atlantic –
Eastbound

Volume 80% of Westbound
Average (1983)

Europe/West Africa –
Southbound

Europe/West Africa
Northbound

Volume 48% of Southbound
Average (1983)

Value of Cargo $/Ton

50   100

% Volume Carried by Conference

Pricing of conference services has been the subject of many studies, yet many researchers differ in their evaluation of the underlying objectives of conference ratemaking. While, as a true monopoly, a conference should attempt to maximise the profits of its members, most conferences set complex rates which appear to attempt satisfaction of several – often conflicting – objectives simultaneously. As large profits would attract other liner operators, unprotected conferences will usually set their rates to be marginally profitable to the highest cost conference member; while a true monopoly supplier can set price and level of service he is prepared to offer, and his only effective constraint is the power of demand. To this end, a true monopoly will set rates above marginal and

143

Figure 4.2: Conference ratemaking

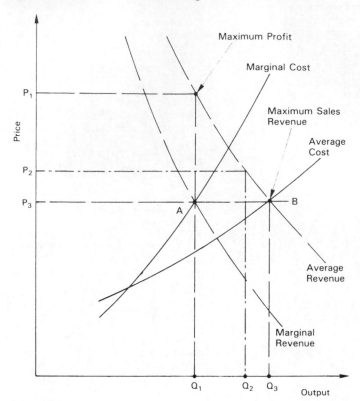

average costs to maximise profit unless demand is highly elastic. Liner conferences are seldomly in this position. Demand is often elastic, monopoly powers imperfect, and though some conferences are protected from certain types of competition, their rates and levels of service are often subject to review or approval.

The threat of outside competition obviously puts a ceiling on conference rates, while casual competition is usually dissuaded by loyalty agreements. If an outside competitor is strong and a conference recognises that in a rate war both conference and outsider would lose, then it will usually encourage the outsider to join the conference. For small assignments loyalty agreements and high ceilings effectively bar outside competition, but for large consignments, shippers obviously have charter alternatives as charters may cost less than the marginal costs of conference members.

Various theories have been advanced to explain conference ratemaking. Sturmey[8] argued that conferences try to maximise the present value of the future flow of revenues or profits. If a conference were to maximise short-run profit (Figure 4.2), it would try to carry Q_1 at P_1. In the long run though, with an objective of maximising $P_3 \times Q_3$ of total revenue, the price would be P_3. But if the conference wanted to maximise the NPV of revenue or profit, then the price would have to be between P_1 and P_3 such as at P_2, as P_1 would encourage short term competition and P_3 may not be profitable.

The effect of ratemaking of open conferences was studied by Davis[9] who considered that rates well above average costs and resulting excess profits encourage new entries which reduce market shares of all conference members. Excess capacity will then drive the conference to lower rates in an attempt to maintain profits.

If conferences are assumed to act as profit maximising monopolies, then the rate charged for each cargo on a route is related to the demand curve of that good for liner shipping service. Conferences usually discriminate by cargo and charge on the basis of demand and value of cargo and not on the basis of cost. Both the supply curve of the exporting country and the demand curve of the importing country affect the demand for shipping of a commodity. To derive the latter from these supply and demand curves, we must consider commodity supply and demand functions of the exporting and importing countries as well as world demand and supply.

Model of conference ratemaking

Demand for conference shipping capacity is determined by the supply of liner commodities in the exporting countries and the demand for such goods in the importing countries served by the conference. A model of conference ratemaking could be developed as follows. Let:

f_{ij}^k = freight rate on cargo type k between ports ij

x_{ij}^k = quantity of type k to be shipped between ports ij

$C(x_{ij}^k)$ = total ship owners' costs associated with shipping quantity x_{ij}^k of type k between port ij

$c.i.f._j^k$ = c.i.f. price of good type k in j

$f.o.b._i^k$ = f.o.b. price of good type k in i

Q_j^k = demand for good type k in j during period t

Q_i^k = supply of good type k in i during period t

$$MC(x_{ij}^{\ k}) = \text{marginal cost}$$
$$= \partial C(x_{ij}^{\ k})/\partial x_{ij}^{\ k}$$

A conference would theoretically set freight rates $f_{ij}^{\ k}$ in such a way as to maximise its total profit, on route ij

$$P_{ij} = \text{Max } [\sum_k (f_{ij}^{\ k} x_{ij}^{\ k}) - \sum_k C(x_{ij}^{\ k})]$$

subject to the constraints of the market, such as the demands of the importing country and the supply of the exporting country at the respective delivered and export price. In other words, both $Q_j^{\ k}$ and $Q_i^{\ k}$ are price dependent and, as the transport costs affect both the price the importer pays and the exporter gets, the demand and supply curves for the traded commodities and particularly their intersections are dependent on the costs of transportation. Before discussing how a conference may use information on the elasticity of demand by shippers in setting its rates, we may want to evaluate what criteria it should use if it simply wanted to maximise its profit.

Using an approach developed in a somewhat different form by Devanney et al.,[10] the objective of the conference is to maximise

$$P_{ij} = \sum_k [f_{ij}^{\ k} x_{ij}^{\ k} - C(x_{ij}^{\ k})]$$

subject to

$$x_{ij}^{\ k} \leq Q_j^{\ k} \qquad k = 1,2 \ldots m$$

$$x_{ij}^{\ k} \leq Q_i^{\ k}$$

$$f_{ij}^{\ k} \leq (\text{c.i.f.}_j^{\ k} - \text{f.o.b.}_i^{\ k})$$

Considering an individual commodity k and assuming the service is volume limited and, as a result, the cost to the ship owner of carrying any cargo only depends on its volume and is independent of the type of cargo or

$$C(x_{ij}^{\ k}) = C(x_{ij}) = \text{function of } x_{ij}$$

and $f_{ij}^{\ k} = f_{ij}$ for any cargo k, and if x_{ij} (f.o.b.) is the supply of f.o.b.$_i$ and x_{ij} (c.i.f.$_j$) is the demand at c.i.f.$_j$, then the following Lagrangian model can be constructed:[11]

$$\text{Max}[f_{ij} \, x_{ij} - C(x_{ij}) - \lambda_1(x_{ij}(\text{f.o.b.}_i) - x_{ij})$$

$$- \lambda_2(x_{ij}(\text{c.i.f.}_j) - x_{ij}) - \lambda_3(\text{c.i.f.}_j - \text{f.o.b.}_i - f_{ij})]$$

taking the derivatives with respect to the freight rate, the quantity of cargo shipped (assumed constant), the average c.i.f. and f.o.b. value of the cargo on trade route i, j, and the three Lagrange multipliers, we obtain after eliminating the Lagrange multipliers:

$$f_{ij} = \text{c.i.f.}_j - \text{f.o.b.}_i$$

and:

$$x_{ij}(\text{c.i.f.}_j) = Q_j = Q_i = x_{ij}(\text{f.o.b.}_i)$$

and:

$$f_{ij} - MC(x_{ij}) = \frac{x_{ij}(\text{c.i.f.}_j)}{\partial x_{ij}(\text{c.i.f.}_j)/\partial(\text{c.i.f.}_j)} - \frac{x_{ij}(\text{f.o.b.}_i)}{\partial x_{ij}(\text{f.o.b.}_i)/\partial(\text{c.i.f.}_j)}$$

from which we obtain the equation:

$$f_{ij} - MC(x_{ij}) = [\text{f.o.b.}_j/E_{si} - \text{c.i.f.}_j/E_{dj}]$$

or the optimum freight rate for the conference is the sum of the marginal cost of carrying an average good between i and j and the difference in the ratio of f.o.b.$_i$ to the elasticity of supply in the exporting country and the ratio of c.i.f.$_j$ to the elasticity of demand in the importing country. As the elasticities of supply and demand in the exporting and importing countries usually have opposite signs, the optimum freight rate for the conference becomes a function of the average value of the goods carried. If the elasticities of supply and demand in the exporting and importing country for example are equal to $+5$ and -5 respectively, then:

$$f_{ij} = MC(x_{ij}) + [(\text{c.i.f.}_j + \text{f.o.b.}_j)/5]$$

> = Marginal Cost of Transport of an average unit of good plus the sum of c.i.f. and f.o.b. value of the good divided by five

The more inelastic the supply and demand for the good, the larger the multiple of the values of the cargo added to marginal costs to maximise the profit of the conference. The same results were obtained by Bennathan and Walters.[12] Therefore for a conference to maximise its profit, it will introduce a value-based tariff which will be higher than its average marginal costs for the average cargo carried, and these average marginal costs should be the lower bound for its tariffs. Therefore low value cargo with high demand and supply elasticity will be charged at or near the marginal cost of carriage.

To determine an optimum tariff for the whole range of cargoes it expects to be offered on its route, a conference would ideally consider the supply and demand curves of the importers and exporters of each type of cargo and set rates which maximise profit.

$$\text{Max } P_{ij} = \sum_k [f_{ij}^k - x_{ij}^k - C(x_{ij}^k)]$$

where $C(x_{ij}^k)$ is assumed constant and f_{ij}^k and x_{ij}^k are determined from the supply and demand curves so as to maximise the product

$$\sum_k f_{ij}^k \, x_{ij}^k$$

In Figure 4.3 demand and supply curves for two commodities in a liner trade are shown as supplies of exports Q_i^1 and Q_i^2. These constitute demands for transport and for simplicity are assumed to be linear. 0E is the capacity of the fleet per unit time. To maximise profits the conference will maximise the sum of the areas 0AGD and 0BFC subject to 0C plus 0D smaller or equal to 0E. In other words we will maximise

$$\text{Max } P_{ij} = \text{Max } \sum_k [f_{ij}^k \, x_{ij}^k - C(x_{ij}^k)]$$

where:

$$\sum x_{ij} \leq 0E = \text{Total fleet capacity}$$

and:

$$f_{ij}^k \, x_{ij}^k = x_{ij}^k [f_{ij}^k(0) = Z^k x_{ij}^k]$$

where:

$$Z^k = \partial f_{ij}^k / \partial x_{ij}^k = \text{constant}$$

148

Figure 4.3: Demand and supply curves for a two-commodity liner route

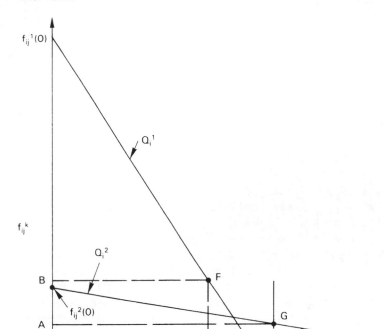

and problem becomes:

$$\text{Max } P_{ij} = \text{Max } \sum_{k}[x_{ij}^{k} f_{ij}^{k}(0) - Z^{k}x_{ij}^{k^2} - C(x_{ij}^{k})]$$

where:

$f_{ij}^{k}(0)$ = intercept of linear demand (export supply) curve

subject to:

$$\sum_{k}x_{ij}^{k} \leq x_{ij} \leq OE$$

Using this model the most profitable mix of freight rates and cargo quantities to be carried by a conference can be determined. A similar model can be established for situations where the export demand curve is not linear, and the import demand is determining, or where export/import supply demand balance is considered. Exporters trading in elastic commodities will usually have a supply curve with a greater elasticity as the demand curve of the importer unless they control a monopoly.

Considering the share importers or exporters pay for, or gain from, the deviation of the freight rate, it can be shown that the ratio of their shares is equal to the ratio of their respective supply and demand elasticities.

This is an important finding when considering liner trade between developing and developed countries. As established by Marx,[13] developing countries usually have a higher elasticity of supply in their trade than the elasticity of demand of their trading partners. Similarly in their imports their demand is usually more elastic than the supply of the exporters shipping (higher value goods) to the developing countries. As a result, developing countries would generally bear a larger share of excess transportation charges for higher value goods (import) and gain less from the cross-subsidy of transport charges of lower valued goods (export). In other words, the higher elasticity of their import demand and export supply results in developing countries bearing the bulk of the transportation charges both ways.

Tramp ratemaking

Tramp shipping is generally assumed to be a freely competitive market in which prices are determined by supply and demand. This is only partially true today because a large percentage of available tramp shipping capacity is not openly traded. Well over 35 per cent of all tramp shipping today is owned and operated by proprietary operators, like steel, oil, grain, and other bulk commodity producing, processing, or trading companies who use tonnage under their control for their own purposes. Another 15 to 20 per cent of tramp tonnage is owned by governments or government entities engaged in proprietary transport of bulk commodities.

In general, though, the private and non-proprietary sector of tramp shipping is still highly competitive. Here transport is usually engaged by chartering of whole ships for single voyages for time periods of a few months to 20 years, and rates of charters still depend largely on supply and demand. Shippers will consider spot, voyage, and short-term versus long-term charters and can protect themselves against the impact of large rate fluctuations by an adroit choice of timing and charter terms. The longer the charter the less dependent is the charter rate on present supply and demand of shipping capacity and the closer it will be to expected costs.

Relation of freight rates to shipping costs and supply of shipping

Only a few — and usually high valued — cargoes exhibit significant inelastic demand in shipping. Furthermore, there are few commodities today which cannot be replaced by others or where substitute supplies exist. As a result, demand for shipping is quite dependent on freight rates for a significant proportion of trade. On the supply side, we similarly find high elasticity in the long run. Even in the short run shipping supply is usually subjected to fairly high elasticity because of the opportunity for transfer of shipping capacity between services (oil tankers in grain trades) and the possibility of transferring cargoes among different sectors of the industry such as the transfer of liner cargoes to tramps or vice versa.

Shipping costs and freight rates

Assuming a linear relation between cost of transport and distance, Thornburn[14] argued that the optimum transport distance a commodity is moved by the ship owner can be obtained for each type of cargo from cost-freight curves as shown in Figure 4.4 by identifying the distance where the freight rate is tangential to the total cost curve. Thornburn assumed that freight rates rise continuously with declining derivatives at increasing distance. D_1 and D_2 then are the optimum distance over which commodities are carried by the ship owner when his costs are linear functions of voyage distance.

Other (non-linear) cost curves can also be introduced and their relations with freight rates used to determine the optimum distance over which cargo of a particular type could be carried. In the case of liners or parcel carriers accepting quantities of different cargoes, the optimum (most profitable) mix of cargoes to be carried can be determined by using recursive optimisation such as dynamic programming.

Figure 4.4: Shipping costs and freight rate curves

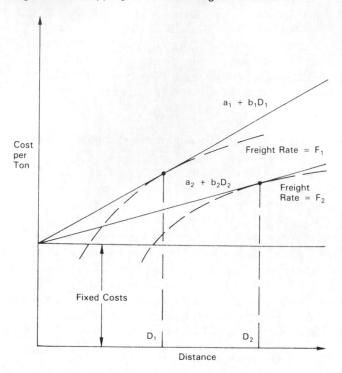

The effect of demand and supply on liner and tramp/bulk freight rates

In recent years investigators have devoted major efforts to the analysis of shipping demand and traffic forecasting, but comparatively little to the study of the underlying factors influencing shipping demand. Although many shipping demand forecasts are based on empirical data, few have identified explanatory variables and factors which would serve to produce more accurate projections. The supply and demand for goods is dependent on many aspects of national economic, political, and financial activity, which in turn influences the level of foreign trade and resulting transport and international shipping demand of nations. Shipping supply, on the other hand, is affected by factors in international trade, demand expectations, and resulting pressure on freight and charter rates which affect newbuilding and second-hand ship prices.

Many studies have been performed to forecast demand for liner shipping. It is found that the volume of demand for shipping of high value goods is usually inelastic with respect to rates, but does depend on such factors as GNP, disposable income, etc. Demand for shipping of lower value goods, on the other hand, appears to be elastic with respect to rates, but it also depends on the degree of utilisation of production or manufacturing capacity of the importing and exporting countries. In other words, large under-utilisation of low value export good production capacity will affect the demand for shipping of the good as well as large under-utilisation of the importing country's manufacturing capacity in which the good is used.

The relationship between shipping demand and actual as well as potential GNP (where the difference is a measure of unused capacity) has been studied by many researchers who found that bulk shipping demand is sensitive to changes of both capacity utilisation as well as productive capacity. Similar effects are noted in demand for shipping of low value liner cargoes, although such forecasts based on GNP and potential GNP should be supplemented by detailed studies of individual commodity markets, including utilisation of capacity in both the exporting country (production) and the importing country (manufacture). Only in this manner, and by relating such forecast results to various factors in the shipping market — particularly factors which affect the cost or price of shipping, can more reliable forecasts of shipping demand for bulk and low value liner commodities be made.

Transport demand is sensitive to freight rates or shipping costs as these constitute a fairly large percentage of delivered prices, particularly in the case of bulk commodities where shipping costs may assume a value of 30 per cent of c.i.f. commodity prices. If feeder transport, stockpile, and handling costs are added, the total transport costs often assume 40 per cent or more of c.i.f. prices to the extent that bulk and low value commodity import demand is sensitive to price, world trade and, therefore, shipping demand for transport of such commodities should be quite sensitive to freight rates.

Another related issue is the pairing of supplier and importer areas in the case of commodities with competing or substitute producers. As freight costs change, the pairing will often change as importers and exporters attempt to correct for these changes by changes in the pairing.

Obviously any change in the pairing immediately affects the utilisation of shipping capacity available. Although rational use of shipping would tend towards origin-destination pairing which

154

Figure 4.5: Relation between freight rates and per cent inefficiency in transport use

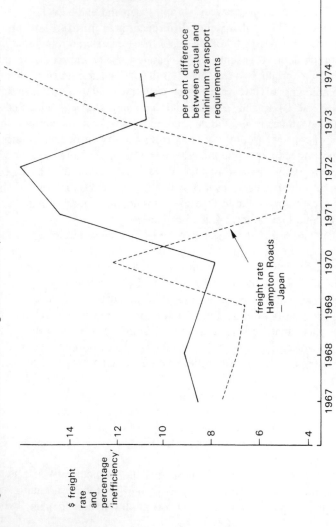

Source: Eriksen *et al.*, *Freight Markets and Trade Patterns*. Bergen, 1977

minimises transport requirements over time (ton-miles/unit time), actual pairing usually deviates appreciably from such a minimum transport requirement allocation of shipping. Eriksen[15] compared actual versus minimum transport requirements over time for major dry bulk commodities in international trade and found 'a clear negative relationship between the measured "inefficiency" and freight rates' (as shown in Figure 4.5) which indicates that when freight rates are high the inefficiency in transport use declines and vice versa.

There is some time lag in this market behaviour but in the medium run, a percentage increase in freight rates will usually reduce transport (ton-mile) demand by about 20 to 25 per cent of such a percentage increase in freight rates. About half of the decrease in transport demand is due to reduction in total import demand of the commodity, while the other half is due to rationalisation of transport use (usually shorter delivery distances).

A related issue is how the supply or offer of shipping is related to freight rates in the short run (a period too short for significant changes in overall shipping capacity through newbuilding, etc.). Devanney[16] developed supply curves in ton-miles (Figure 4.6) for

Figure 4.6: Supply curves for ton-miles

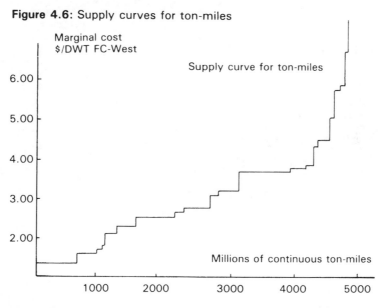

Source: Devanney, J.W. 'A Model of the Tanker Charter Market and a Related Dynamic Program' in Lorange and Norman (ed.), *Shipping Management*, Bergen, 1973

tankers as a function of marginal costs in $/DWT. These indicate that freight rates are quite important for short-run supply of capacity in the tanker trade. Similar results are projected by other investigators such as Eriksen for dry bulk trades.

Other issues which affect and are affected by freight rates and in turn influence ton-mile shipping supply are service speed, off-hire, and port turnaround. These decisions are usually quite sensitive to freight rates in the short run. To estimate the effects of these and other factors on the short term supply of shipping and in particular bulk shipping, econometric analysis may have to be performed. Such an econometric model (Ecotank) which relates freight rates to underlying demand and supply factors, user ship values of newbuilding prices and current charter rates, etc. was developed by Eriksen *et al.* and has a structure shown diagrammatically in Figure 4.7.

Figure 4.7: Model structure of 'Ecotank'

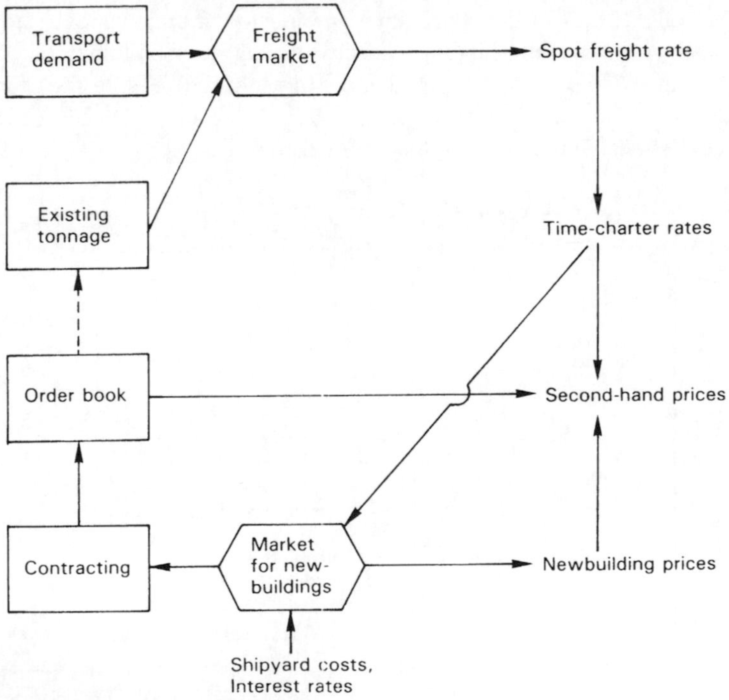

Source: Eriksen, E. *et al.* 'Ecotank' report. Institute for Shipping Research, Bergen, 1978

Liner freight revenues and cargo values

The relation between freight rates and the value of particular commodities on certain liner routes was presented in Table 2.4. Considering now freight revenues as a percentage of cargo value carried by typical conferences (Figure 4.8), it is interesting to note that these ratios are close to 20 per cent in some trades. True, the data presented here only represents major US liner routes, but it is still noteworthy that there are significant differences between inbound and outbound rates. Of particular interest is the apparent

Figure 4.8: Freight revenue as a share of cargo value
1969–1976

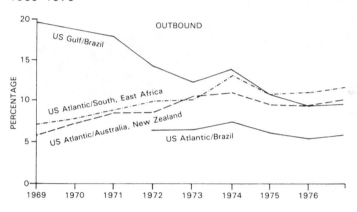

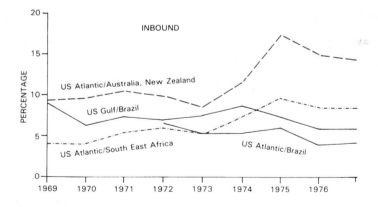

Source: Manalytics Inc., 'Impact of Bilateral Shipping Agreements in the US Liner Trades'. Office of Commercial Development, Maritime Administration, US Department of Transport, December 1979

Table 4.1: Selected maximum and minimum[a] tramp freight rates, 1972–1975

Commodity route	Currency unit (Sterling and United States dollars and cents)	1972		1973		1974		1975	
		High	Low	High	Low	High	Low	High	Low
Heavy grain:									
United States Gulf-India	Dollars	–	–	71.00	16.00	60.00	45.75	28.25	24.00
North Pacific-East Coast India	Dollars	16.50	15.50	30.50	17.50	50.00	45.50	32.00	22.25
River Plate-Antwerp/ Hamburg range	Dollars	11.65	5.30	29.60	12.75	32.00	26.50	16.00	13.00
River Plate-Japan	Dollars	9.50[c]	6.90[c]	30.25[c]	17.75[c]	45.00[d]	32.50[d]	19.50[d]	17.20[d]
North Pacific-Republic of Korea	Dollars	11.75	6.05	30.50	14.00	30.00	20.00	20.50	11.65
Coal:									
Hampton Roads-Rio de Janeiro	Dollars	2.90	2.40	–	–	–	–	–	5.65
Hampton Roads-Japan	Dollars	7.50	3.40	25.15	7.50	25.50	10.50	9.00	7.50
Sugar:									
Mauritius-United Kingdom	Sterling	7.25	4.00	11.15	7.50	13.90	11.15	10.65[e]	7.50
Philippines-USA	Dollars	12.00	7.75	17.00	14.50	30.00	29.00	16.50[e]	16.00[e]
Ore:									
Mormugão-Japan	Dollars	4.45	3.60	12.00	5.90	10.50	4.10	4.00	3.00
Brazil-Continent	Dollars	–	–	–	–	6.25	4.45	3.10	2.30
Monrovia-Continent	Dollars	3.00	1.30	7.00	3.60	–	–	–	–

	Unit								
Copra:									
Philippines-Continent	Cents	43	26½	52	4	–	–	–	–
Phosphate:									
Casablanca-China	Sterling	3.72	3.00	8.8	5.75	–	–	–	–
Aqaba-West Coast India	(Sterling)/ Dollars[b]	(2.92)	(1.90)	13.35	8.25	20.75	16.00	16.00	7.50
Rice:									
China-Sri Lanka	Sterling	6.85	6.75	8.09	6.8	–	–	–	–
Fertilisers:									
Continent-China (South Coast)	Sterling	–	–	8.55	7.55	–	–	–	–
US Gulf-India[f]	Dollars	–	–	–	–	65.25	48.00	42.50	25.00

Source: Based on information in *Lloyd's List* (London), 4 February 1974, 6 January 1975 and 5 January 1976

[a] Approximate levels
[b] In pounds sterling or United States dollars, as given by the source
[c] About 14,000 tons
[d] 20–25,000 tons
[e] From *Fairplay International Shipping Weekly*, 8 January 1976, p. 115
[f] Di-ammonium phosphate

high percentage of freight/value of cargo of US exports to Brazil and South/East Africa which consists of reasonably high value cargo (US $1,280/ton and US $1,062/ton in 1975 respectively). During the same 1968–77 period, average conference freight rates in US to Brazil and South/East Africa liner trades increased by a factor of 1.82 to 2.05.

Liner rates are subject to periodic adjustments, but more importantly are also often subjected to surcharges such as:

— Currency Adjustment Factors (CAF)
— Bunker Surcharge
— Congestion Surcharge
— Preshipment Surcharge
— Emergency and War Risk Surcharge
— Others such as landing, storage, and handling surcharges

Pre-existing surcharges are often incorporated into tariffs through corresponding increases in tariffs. In other cases and where surcharges are deemed by the conference to be truly temporary, surcharges are often lifted or cancelled without being incorporated into tariffs. Surcharges are generally universal and apply to all shipping on a conference route though congestion, emergency, war risk, and similar surcharges may be applied to a limited region or a limited number of ports.

In recent times (1975–83) 45 to 62 per cent of all conferences introduced surcharges during an average year. More than 38 per cent of these surcharges were later incorporated into the conference tariff (FMC Review 1984).

Tramp freight rates and cargo values

Tramp rates are much more volatile than conference rates as shown in Table 4.1. Rates fluctuate often by as much as a factor of two in any one year. Some trades – such as the grain trades – are subject to larger moves because of power predictability of demand than in other commodity trades such as iron ore, coal, and sugar. The ratio of tramp freight rates to cargo values is generally twice that experienced in conference ratios, as the value of tramp cargoes usually ranges from only US $160 to 600 per ton.

Considering recent tramp freight rate developments, we note that general cargo trip charter rates have fallen by over 50 per cent from their level in 1980–1. As shown in Figure 4.9, 1982 rates have stayed fairly even. Considering bulk carrier voyage rates on

Figure 4.9: General cargo trip charter rates

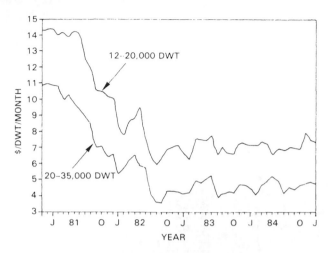

Source: H.P. Drewry, Shipping Consultants Ltd, 1984

Figure 4.10: Bulk cargo. Voyage charter rates

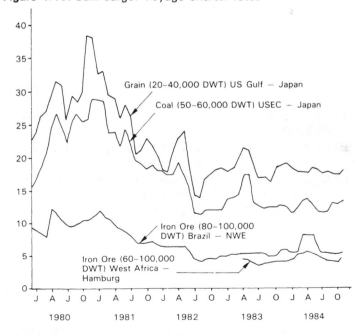

Source: H.P. Drewry, Shipping Consultants Ltd, 1984

161

Table 4.2: Dry bulk cargo voyage (single) rates in US $/ton (1980–1984)

Year	USG–JAP 20–40 KDWT Grain	HR–JAP 50–60 KDWT Coal	BRAZ–EU 80–100 KDWT Iron Ore	WAF–HAMB 60–90 KDWT Iron Ore
80.1	$24.0	$16.8	$8.4	
80.4	$29.2	$25.0	$12.3	
80.7	$26.4	$22.6	$9.1	
80.10	$31.3	$25.8	$10.8	
81.1	$33.1	$28.7	$11.9	
81.4	$28.1	$24.6	$9.5	
81.7	$26.4	$21.8	$7.9	
81.10	$23.2	$18.9	$6.8	
82.1	$18.2	$17.7	$6.5	
82.4	$23.8	$19.2	$6.5	
82.7	$14.1	$12.1	$4.6	
82.10	$17.8	$12.3	$4.8	
83.1	$18.1	$13.8	$5.0	
83.4	$21.9	$17.2	$5.5	$4.8
83.7	$16.9	$13.1	$5.5	$3.6
83.10	$18.1	$12.5	$5.2	$4.3
84.1	$18.6	$11.8	$5.8	$4.8
84.4	$18.2	$13.8	$8.0	$6.0
84.7	$17.8	$12.1	$5.8	$4.8
84.10	$17.5	$13.5	$5.6	$4.2
84 Cost	$11.37	$12.24	$3.09	$2.44

Source: H.P. Drewry, Shipping Consultants Ltd, 1985

particular routes, we find a similar development (Figure 4.10 and Table 4.2).

Similar developments are noticeable in tanker spot rates (Figure 4.11), though these rates are subject to much higher fluctuations in the short run. Voyage and spot rates have been more depressed than term charter rates and, in most cases, barely cover average costs.

In fact, while tanker voyage rates on a typical route such as West Africa to Caribbean/US east coast are just above average costs for tanker sizes of 40 to 130,000 DWT, but fall below average costs for tankers smaller than 40,000 DWT or larger than 130,000 DWT (Figure 4.12), they are below average costs for tankers on routes such as North-West Europe to Caribbean/US east coast. Voyage rates for dry bulk carriers seem to have recently been well below average costs and only slightly above marginal costs for all dry bulk carrier sizes (Figure 4.13).

Figure 4.11: Tanker spot rates

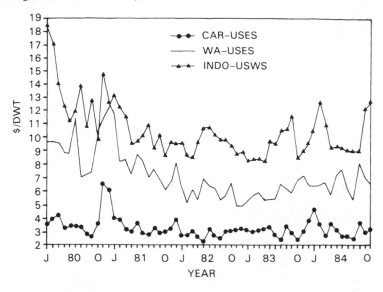

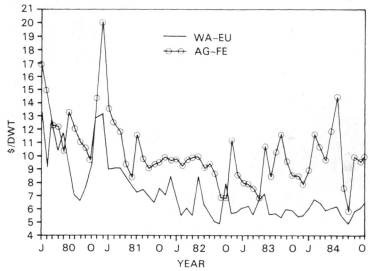

Source: H.P. Drewry, Shipping Consultants Ltd, 1984

Figure 4.12: Voyage rates compared to average and marginal costs (December 1984)

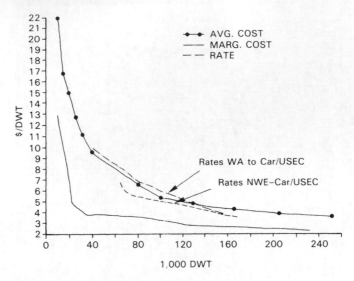

Source: Computed by author

Figure 4.13: Rate average and marginal costs

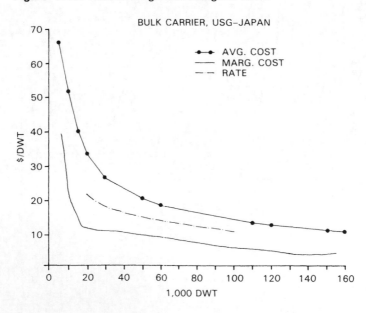

Liner conference rates

Recent liner conference rates for the Europe-Far East, Europe-US east coast, Europe-Arabian Gulf, and Europe-Australia routes in US $/TEU are shown in Figure 4.14. It is curious to note that conference rates behaved quite irrationally. Not only did they vary by a factor of more than two over the period 1981–4, but at times when some conference rates increased steeply, other conference rates declined. Conference rates also did not follow the general trend of tramp rates which, in 1982, levelled off at about half their 1980–1 rates and stayed at this low level to the middle or end of 1984. It is also interesting to note that Europe to Arabian Gulf rates did not vary at all within this four-year period. While Europe-Far East rates (UK-HK) were, in 1982–4, at only 50 per cent of their 1980–1 level of about US $2,300/TEU, rates for other, shorter routes were significantly higher. All of the rates are well above average costs even after port charges are added, assuming 100 per cent utilisation.

Recent average capacity utilisation on these routes (average of both ways) was 82 per cent for Europe-Far East, 49 per cent for Europe-Arabian Gulf, and 79 per cent Europe-US east coast. Under these conditions, the Europe-Far East rates are just barely profitable (on an average cost basis) while the other routes appear to be highly profitable now. Adjustments should be made for differentials in crew

Figure 4.14: Liners. Major conference rates

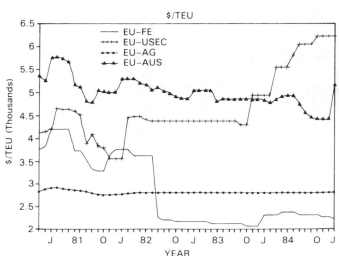

Source: Lloyd's *Shipping Economist*, various years

and other flag costs which are, for simplicity, not included in this summary.

Major reasons for the large differences in rates over time and at any one time are:

(1) Composition of cargo (value).
(2) Competitive aspects and capacity utilisation.
(3) Cargo allocation or reservation.

The approach to liner ratemaking usually assumes value of service pricing with cross-subsidisation of low-value cargoes by high-value cargoes. As pointed out, this results in a very complex rate structure, and as Sturmey suggested is based on deterrent pricing of low-value commodities which may be attracted to tramp or other occasional competitors. While this pricing approach may deter occasional tramps, it obviously offers high-class liner competitors an opportunity to offer low rates for high-value cargo and thereby siphon off the cream of the trade.

There are alternatives to the traditional value of service ratemaking in liner shipping which should become more viable as wasteful competition for high-value cargo is reduced. The approach by some container operators in recent years to charge per container independent of contents or weight was one attempt in this direction (Seatrain, etc.). Other possibilities exist which would increase incentives for more rationalised use of capacity and resources.

Risk sharing in shipping rates

A new development in shipping is the introduction of risk sharing by the use of futures contracts,[18] in the form of options such as puts, calls, or other futures instruments. Futures instruments are designed to aid transactions in two vital ways. They facilitate the price discovery process and provide a means for efficient and economic transfer of risk. Although futures have served these purposes in stock and commodity transactions for many years, these instruments have only recently been introduced into the shipping market. In the past few years, innovations in the futures markets have resulted in new types of instruments such as straddle contracts and index futures. Futures contracts are now traded also in the financial and real estate markets. While the role of index futures in the price discovery process is not clear, index futures would further enhance the transfer of shipping price risk.

Benefits of futures instruments in non-shipping markets include smoothing of prices and smoother functioning of the market. Use of futures instruments in shipping markets are expected to reduce risks to both the shipper and ship owner by introducing third or intermediary parties into the risk sharing. Another expected benefit is the possibility of increased productivity of capital used in financing shipping.

While the futures market in shipping is as yet quite limited with only a few futures instruments available and only a few market makers involved (as reviewed in the next section), the potential implications — particularly on charter rates — are great. While the use of such instruments in liner shipping is less persuasive, there are also some opportunities for use of such instruments to increase risk sharing or transfer in this component of the shipping industry as well.

Other developments in risk sharing are the introduction of third parties in ship financing, where lenders sell their variable interest in a ship mortgage, for example, for cash or for a fixed interest contract.

Use of futures contracts in freight sharing

The major uses of futures contracts in shipping are to lock in a shipping rate, usually in terms of a charter or contract of affreightment. The major advantages sought from the purchase or sale of a futures contract are:

(1) To lock in a shipping rate at low transaction cost.
(2) To protect against market risks.
(3) To improve market or charter timing.
(4) To unbundle and manage shipping contract selection and timing.
(5) To permit hedging against an expected requirement of shipping services or against availability of idle shipping capacity.
(6) To reduce market risk associated with undesired excess capacity or lack of capacity acquired in the course of business.

Futures contracts are a new development in the world shipping market which is expected to have a major impact on stabilising the market by introducing third parties as risk takers. Both liner and tramp markets are expected to be affected in the future as will international trade, because futures contracts will reduce the uncertainty of shipping freight rates and thereby assure ship owners and shippers of future terms of shipping.

There are also suggestions to expand futures contracts to include covered and uncovered options contracts which can be designed as call and put option contracts under which a shipper can call on shipping capacity at a given contracted rate during or at a fixed time, but is not obligated to take the offered shipping. Similarly, under a put option contract, an owner could place shipping capacity at a contract price during or at a specific time, but is not obliged to actually make the shipping available.

Measures of effectiveness of shipping

The effectiveness of a shipping service from the point of view of shippers or receivers is usually measured in terms of:

(1) Freight rates and related costs of shipping.
(2) Frequency of sailings, though in reality shippers are usually more concerned with transit time and frequency or average time between random delivery of cargo at the export port and its delivery at the import port.
(3) Technological developments. Here shippers are concerned with the timeliness and rate of technological change in line with shipper/consignee and integrated transport requirements.
(4) Quality of service including reliability, responsiveness, cargo care and safety, customer relations, etc.

Shippers and receivers implicitly consider all the above factors and will often prefer a service with a higher basic freight rate if, in their opinion, overall user costs are lower. This measure of effectiveness can be expressed as:

$$E = F + T + D + Q$$

where:

F = freight rate per ton of good, including surcharges, discounts, and other price adjustments
T = transit time costs which include average waiting time and storage costs for cargo arriving randomly, as well as cost from loading to delivery
D = technological cost associated with offered methods of cargo handling
Q = quality of service costs in terms of cost of cargo safety, service reliability, etc.

From a shipper/receiver point of view, E is difficult to determine. As a result, a ratio

$E = C^1/C$ = ratio of before and after costs

is often used as a measure of effectiveness. This measure of effectiveness depends on the value of the cargo, its shelf life, and the terms under which it is usually traded. For example, both high-value manufactured and low-value perishable goods are quite sensitive to transit time, though for different reasons. Similarly technological costs can be direct when the preferred physical form can or cannot be accommodated by the shipping service offered or when the ship introduces particular requirements on the cargo. Finally, quality of service costs are usually hard to determine and are often estimated using statistics of cargo loss or cargo insurance costs, where cargo loss includes partial loss or damage. In evaluating alternatives among current and rationalised services, a shipper or receiver (using c.i.f. or f.o.b. terms) will usually make his choice not on the basis of freight rate alone.

To use the measure of effectiveness, the factors influencing effectiveness – F, T, D, and Q – as defined above are usually expressed as a ratio:

$E = C^1/C$ = measure of relative effectiveness

$$= \frac{F^1 + T^1 + D^1 + Q^1}{F + T + D + Q}$$

where F^1, T^1, D^1, and Q^1 are all average existing costs. As an example, let us assume introduction of a new RoRo service in competition with a short voyage general cargo service. If:

F^1 = \$30/ton   F = \$35/ton
T^1 = \$8/ton (10-day average)   T = \$3/ton (3-day average)
D^1 = \$11/ton (packaging,   D = \$3/ton (less packaging,
     port transfers, etc.)   no port transfer)
Q^1 = \$4/ton   Q = \$2/ton

and

$E = C^1/C = 53/43 = 1.23$

A shipper/receiver would then implicitly assume that the new RoRo service was 23 per cent more effective than the existing general cargo service. Discussions with shippers and freight

Table 4.3: Shipping costs payment balances* (Freight cost and revenue – entries in SDRs (Standard Basket of World Currencies).) (Millions of SDRs)

| | Credits | | | Debits | | |
	1980	1981	1982	1980	1981	1982
Developed market economy countries:						
Original	35,452	37,886	36,342	33,852	36,151	35,058
Adjusted	50,276	56,287	53,388	33,852	36,151	35,058
Developing countries	6,346	7,683	10,745	32,670	40,088	40,439

* Adjustment for beneficial ownership of flag of convenience tonnage. UNCTAD Secretariat, 'Shipping in the Contexts of Services and the Development Process', Geneva, November 1984 (GE 84–54143)

Source: 'Review of Maritime Transport 1985', UNCTAD, New York, 1986

forwarders indicate that they intuitively or explicitly use such a measure of effectiveness in making modal and service choices.

Shipping cost payment balance

A major argument for the development of national fleets is that it may assist in reducing shipping cost payment imbalances of developing countries. There are many counter arguments — the most important of which is probably that freight rates and in particular liner conference freight rates, will usually converge on the costs of the marginal operator serving a trade. As a result, and because developing country fleets often constitute the marginal operators in such a conference trade, freight charges would usually increase.

Foreign operators will then reap additional revenues or profits which are often in excess of any revenues earned by the national operator. As a result, the balance of payment effects of national fleet participation may actually be negative by driving the imbalance even further. This effect is often amplified by the fact that expenses by national shipping operators are mostly in foreign exchange, which usually implies that little of their revenues are actually net foreign exchange earnings.

A summary of shipping costs payment balances are presented in Table 4.3. Deficits in shipping cost payments and revenues of developing countries as a block are shown to have amounted to US $34.2 billion, US $38.2 billion, and US $32.7 billion in 1980, 1981, and 1982 respectively. The situation has not improved since, and preliminary estimates for 1984 and 1985 indicate a shipping cost payment deficit by developing countries of nearly US $40.0 billion and US $39.4 billion respectively.

THE STRUCTURE OF SHIPPING COSTS

Ship costs are usually expressed in terms of voyage costs, and are broken down into the major categories shown in Table 4.4 which also indicates the breakdown of ship costs into foreign and domestic costs for ships operating in a typical developing country. Ship costs vary quite widely by year of build, age of ship, registration, ownership, crew nationality, route served, and more. Furthermore, ship costs vary over time. Capital costs or purchase prices for ships are greatly affected by the world shipping demand/supply balance as

Table 4.4: Typical distribution of ship costs for developing countries

	Usually paid in currency		Total cost %
	Foreign %	Domestic %	
Capital cost	100	–	24–38
Port cost	60–70	30–40	6– 8
Bunker	100	–	22–40
Insurance	100	–	3– 6
Ship supplies	33	67	2– 4
Food supplies	80	20	2– 3
Machinery supplies	42	58	2– 3
Repairs	70	30	4– 6
Agents	100	–	3– 4
General expenses	80	20	6– 9
Crew wages	20	80	10–18
Other crew expenses	80	20	4– 6

Therefore only 12 to 18 per cent of ship operating costs are usually in domestic currency

well as shipbuilding demand/capacity balance. Both affect the newbuilding as well as second-hand market price for ships. Another variable is the cost of financing of ships which again varies widely. As ships are traditionally heavily mortgaged, terms of financing will have a major effect on ship costs and resulting voyage costs.

Ship costs are divided into capital and operating costs where operating costs include:

C_2 = crew wages and benefits
C_3 = crew hiring and repatriation costs (transport)
C_4 = subsistence
C_5 = stores, supplies, and equipment
C_6 = insurance and reserves
C_7 = maintenance and repair
C_8 = lubricating oil
C_9 = fuel oil
C_{10} = overhead and administration
C_{11} = marketing
C_{12} = port charges

Considering operating costs first:

Crew wages and benefits are usually a linear function of flag, crew nationality, manning, and power and tonnage. In general, it can be approximated by an exponential or second-order polynomial function as shown in Figure 4.15. Crew sizes on ships with OECD crews averaged 26, while vessels with other crews averaged 35 as

Figure 4.15: Total wages and benefits cost of crew for fast-turn liner ships – mid–1983. (In millions of US dollars)

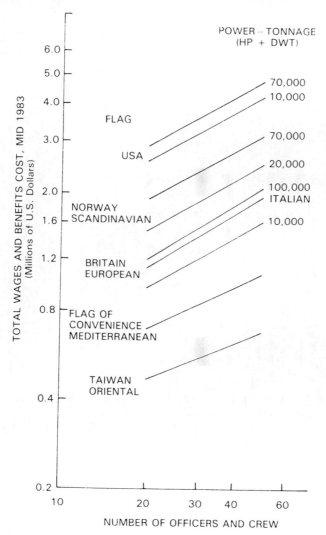

Source: Manalytics, Inc., 'Report to US Maritime Administration on Ship Operating Costs', 1984

Table 4.5: Ship manning for costing purposes (December 1983). (Average number officers and men)

Deadweight tonnage	Roll on-roll off	Liner ship types Part container	Multi-purpose	Barge carrier
5,000	26	19	23	–
7,000	29	22	25	13
10,000	32	25	28	18
12,000	34	27	29	21
15,000	37	29	31	24
20,000	40	33	33	28
25,000	43	36	35	30
30,000	45	39	36	33

Table 4.6: Manning of full containerships (December 1983)

Capacity (TEU)	Maritime* nations	Intermediate+	Oriental & flag of convenience
300	14	19	27
500	19	24	31
750	24	29	35
1,000	29	34	39
1,250	33	38	42
1,500	37	41	44
1,750	39	43	45
2,000	41	44	46

* Scandinavian and North European registered ships
+ American and Mediterranean registered ships
Source: Manalytics, Inc., 'Report to US Maritime Administration on Ship Operating Costs', 1984

shown in Tables 4.5 and 4.6 for 1983. Average crew sizes have since declined by 10 per cent.

Subsistence is again a function of crew size and origin and varies from US $5.0 to US $8.0 per man-day. *Stores and supplies* are dependent on crew origin, crew size, engine type, and engine horsepower, and varies as a linear function of crew size. It had an average cost of US $1,800 for LDC flag vessels, US $2,800 for developed countries' flag vessels, and US $3,900 for US flag vessels per man per year.

Annual *insurance* costs vary quite widely, but can be approximated by US $100,000 + 2 × DWT + 0.0043 × current ship market value.

Annual *maintenance and repair* costs depend on flag, owner, nationality of crew, engine type and size, but is usually equal to $0.03 \times$ (capital cost) $\times$ (age)$^{1.05}$. A more detailed breakdown of these costs is given in Table 4.7 in terms of ship characteristics.

Overhead and administration costs are usually 4.29 per cent of

Table 4.7: Annual maintenance and repair costs, 1984. In US dollars. (HP = horsepower)

Flag	Area	Type	
Foreign	Machinery	Diesel	$37 (HP)^{0.89} (Age)^{1.05}$
		Steam	$68 (HP)^{0.80} (Age)^{1.05}$
	Hull	Full container	$72,000 + $160 (grt)^{0.60} (Age)^{1.05}$
		Barge carrier, part container, and roll on-roll off	$78,000 + $170 (grt)^{0.60} (Age)^{1.05}$
		Break bulk, reefer	$89,000 + $180 (grt)^{0.60} (Age)^{1.05}$
United States	Machinery	All	$44 (HP)^{0.89} (Age)^{1.05}$
	Hull	Full container	$80,000 + $160 (grt)^{0.667} (Age)^{1.05}$
		Barge carrier, part container, and roll on-roll off	$89,000 + $170 (grt)^{0.667} (Age)^{1.05}$
		Break bulk, reefer	$98,000 + $180 (grt)^{0.667} (Age)^{1.05}$

Source: Private information from operators

Table 4.8: Typical crew costs (December 1983)[1] (In US dollars)

Nationality	Annual cost	Source
USA	$3,400,000	APL, US Lines, SeaLand
Denmark	1,307,000	Maersk
West Germany	1,474,000	Hapag-Lloyd
Norway	1,290,000	Knutsen, Barber Blue Sea
Japan	940,000	Japanese Consortia
Hong Kong	425,000	OOCL
Taiwan	425,000	Yang Ming, etc.
Philippines	390,000	
Korea	280,000	KSC

Source: Lloyd's *Shipping Economist*. Figures are for 1978 adjusted to 1983 via wage index from same source. The wage inflator unavailable for Taiwan, Hong Kong, Philippines, and Korea. These costs were assumed increased by 30 per cent
[1] Includes benefits and repatriation, etc. costs

operating costs of bulk carriers and 10 per cent of operating costs of liner vessels.

Fuel and lubricating oil costs depend on power used in port and at sea as well as type of engine and utilisation of installed power.

Port charges vary obviously with route, port tariffs, port efficiency, and more.

Port charges levied against liner cargo ships in European and US ports include dockage, pilotage, tug hire, line handling, watchmen, customs, launch hire, and similar items. The size of the vessel determines many of these charges, each of which is quite small. Analysis indicates that grt, a measure of the total internal volume of a ship's hull, is a suitable parameter for estimating port charges. For these charges we assume (a) one-two day port time per call for fast turnaround ships, such as full container, part container, and roll on-roll off ships, (b) five days for bulk carriers and general cargo ships, and (c) tankers are assumed to stay one-two days in port. The formulae used are:

Container etc. ship port charge ($) per day in port
= $550 + 12.5c × grt

General cargo ship port charge ($) per day in port
= $280 + 8c × grt

Bulk carrier port charge ($) per day in port = $250 + 6c × grt

Tanker port charge ($) per day in port = $180 + 4c × grt

Port charges obviously vary and are usually higher in LDC ports.

Typical *wage and benefit costs* for crews of containerships or
tankers are shown in Figure 4.15 and Table 4.8. Crew costs vary
by a factor of nearly seven (including benefits) but OECD wages
have converged recently. Crew hiring and repatriation costs usually
add another 20 per cent to crew costs.

Ship cost model

A model developed by the World Bank[19] was used for the analysis
of ship costs. Capital or financial and non-capital costs are determined separately as shown in Figures 4.16 and 4.17. Although the
diagrams show the derivation of annual costs, the model permits
computation of daily at-sea and in-port costs and, as a consequence,
voyage costs. Costs can be computed for all types and sizes of ships
under different operating (flag, etc.) and manning (nationality of
crew) conditions. The total vessel costs are computed using the
following equation:

$$C = C_1 + C_2 + N(C_3 T_i + C_4(T_{1,i} + T_{2,i}))$$

where

C_1 = annual capital costs for vessel
C_2 = annual fixed costs (excluding capital) for vessel
C_3 = variable costs including fuel per day at sea
C_4 = variable costs including fuel per day in port
T_i = average time in transit on leg i
$T_{1,i}$ = average time in loading port leg i
$T_{2,i}$ = average time in unloading port leg i
N = number of voyages per year

The above model is suitable for liners as well as contract bulk
carriers serving a regular route. If schedules and routings vary from
voyage to voyage, a second subscript j is added to indicate characteristics of particular voyages. Similarly if loading and unloading
overlaps and is performed in the same port, then $T_{1,i}$ and $T_{2,i}$ are
simply interpreted as ports in trading areas 1 and 2 respectively.

Port costs include ship waiting and turnaround costs, tonnage,
wharfage, stevedoring, and other applicable costs. (Readers interested in the details of the model are advised to consult the 'Ship
Cost' model report. Empirical data used in the model is updated

177

Figure 4.16: Ship cost cost model (annual capital costs)

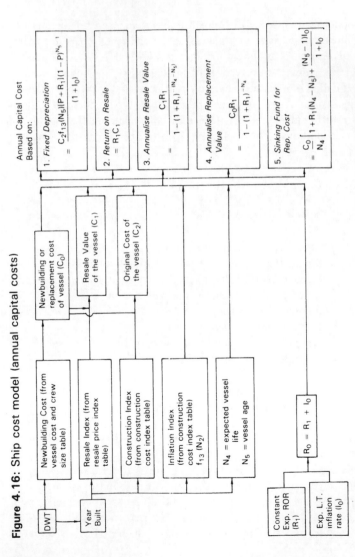

Source: World Bank, 'Ship Cost – A Vessel and Voyage Costing Model', Washington, DC, 1985

178

Figure 4.17: Ship cost model (annual non-capital costs)

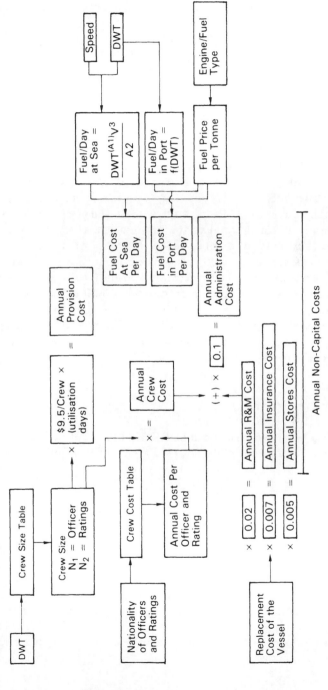

Source: World Bank, 'Ship Cost – A Vessel and Voyage Costing Model', Washington, DC, 1985

bi-annually and the information used in this report is mid-1985 cost data.)

The model of ship costs described can be used to derive fixed, variable, total, average, and marginal costs for bulk carriers, tankers, general cargo ships, and container vessels. Fixed costs are determined on the basis of annualised resale value and annualised replacement value.

Fixed costs include capital, crew, insurance, and administrative costs, while variable costs include fuel, provisions, stores, and repair and maintenance. Average and marginal ship costs are computed against DWT or ship capacity. In general, port charges as well as stevedoring and container lease costs are included in computing total, average, and marginal costs where applicable.

In the analysis of shipping costs with or without rationalisation, a measure of cost, the product of measurement tons of capacity times the nautical miles of distance sailed (MT × NM) summed for all ships in the service is used. This simple measure evaluates costs for each ship, differentiated principally by ship type, capacity, size, flag, speed, power and type of propulsion plant. It includes also port costs.

The ship cost model (1985 version – December 1984 costs) was used to determine typical vessel operating costs for various routes and ship types as shown in Appendix A.

Breakeven cost analysis

To achieve breakeven conditions, the discounted stream of net revenues over the life of the vessel, n, must equal its initial cost and:

$$C_o = \text{Initial cost of vessel} = \sum_{i=1}^{n} \frac{R_i - E_i}{(1 + x)^i} + \frac{S_o}{(1 + x)^n}$$

where:

R_i = revenues in year i
E_i = operating costs in year i
x = expected rate of return in constant value
S_o = salvage or scrap value of vessel at the end of year n

In case inflation during operating life of vessel is to be included, this equation becomes

180

$$C_0 = \sum_{i=1}^{n} \left[\frac{R_i - E_i}{(1 + x)^i (1 + r)^i} \right] + \frac{S_0}{(1 + x)^n}$$

where r = average rate of inflation

$(1 + r)^i$ could also be substituted by $\prod_i (1 + x)^n$

where r_i is the rate of inflation in year i. If I_i is defined as the net income in year i or $I_i = R_i - E_i$ then:

$$C_0 = \sum_{i}^{n} \left[\frac{I_i}{(1 + x)^i (1 + r)^i} \right] + \frac{S_0}{(1 + x)^n}$$

and if I_0 = net income in the first year then

$$I_i = I_0 (1 + r)^i \text{ or } I_0 \prod_{i}^{n} (1 + r_i)$$

whereupon

$$C_0 = \sum_{i}^{n} \left[\frac{I_0(1 + r)^i}{(1 + x)^i (1 + r)^i} \right] + S_0/(1 + x)^n$$

and

$$I_0 = \sum_{i}^{n} \left[(1 + x)^i \left(C_0 - \frac{S_0}{(1 + x)^n} \right) \right]$$

and

$$I_i = \left[\frac{(1 + r)^i}{\sum_{i}^{n} (1 + x)^{-i}} \right] \left[C_0 - \frac{S_0}{(1 + x)^n} \right]$$

which can also be interpreted as the annual net revenue required in year i in current terms to break even in the use of the vessel. To calculate the required freight rate which would provide a net return on the initial investment C_0 of say P_0 per cent, the above equation is changed to:

$$[I_i + C_oP_o] = \left[\frac{(1 + r)^i}{\sum\limits_{i}^{n} (1 + x)^{-i}} \right] \left(C_o - \frac{S_o}{(1 + x)^n} \right) + C_oP_o$$

Analysis of ship costs

Tramp or bulk carrier costs per ton are usually lower than those of a liner on a voyage cost basis because:

(1) Bulk carriers are larger on average than liners with resulting lower fixed and variable costs.
(2) Cargo handling costs per ton are lower because of cargo specialisation.

Tramps will usually charge rates based, to a large extent, on costs with variations usually affected by the supply/demand balance for tonnage. When tramps are unemployed for a percentage of time, their costs obviously go up for the limited employment secured, but rates under such circumstances would usually converge on marginal costs or less. In other words, the larger the employment of bulk carriers the lower is likely to be the cost per unit of cargo carried relative to liners. While the same applies to liner costs per unit of cargo, bulk carrier costs decline relatively faster than liner costs.

One of the reasons for this difference is that liners are burdened by proportionally higher fixed costs for capital, administration, terminal facilities, marketing and commercial representation and basic service commitment costs. The marginal costs of similar sized and otherwise identical liners are therefore usually lower than that of a tramp with the same characteristics. Assuming tramp and liner costs for identical ships are represented as shown in Figure 4.18 where C_1 and C_2 are fixed costs of the liner and tramp respectively, and total costs are assumed to be linear, Q_2 is then the quantity at which their costs per ton are equal. If traffic is less, then the liner has an average cost advantage, while above Q_2 the tramp has an average cost advantage. It should be noted though that the marginal cost of the liner is lower throughout the range. Therefore the liner committed to the voyage can quote lower marginal costs throughout the range of demand. Bennathan and Walters[20] discuss the effect of high and low demand (D_L and D_M respectively). Obviously the elasticity of demand will have a major effect on the choice of mode with highly elastic demand usually favouring the tramp operator

Figure 4.18: Relation of liner and tramp costs

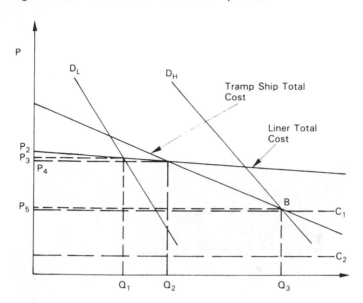

with his larger marginal costs. In reality the tramp and liner operators' marginal costs will obviously vary over the range of Q, but market evidence shows that tramp rates are generally below liner rates, subject obviously to conference discrimination or space (weight) dumping, where conference rates for marginal cargoes are set at or below marginal conference costs, for cargo filling space which would not otherwise be used.

One important factor is that conferences usually set their prices to cover long-run profits based on long-run costs, while tramps are more often engaged in short-run rate setting based on short-run costs. As a result, the theoretical long-run cost analysis, discussed above, does not represent conditions found in practice but nevertheless gives an indication of the issues. The relations between short-run and long-run average and marginal costs depend, among other things, on the existence of returns to scale.

Another interesting issue is the effect of variables such as ships' speed, number of port calls, port time, ship deadweight capacity, and ship capacity utilisation and voyage and transport cost per unit of cargo. If $D_{i,i+1}$ is the deadweight carried on leg $i,i+1$ where i is the ith port on the itinerary and $\overline{D}_{i,i+1}$ is the cargo handled in port i, then the port time in port i can be expressed as:

183

$$T_i = \left(W_i + \frac{\overline{D}_{i,i+1}}{h_i} \right) = \left(\frac{W_i h_i + \overline{D}_{i,i+1}}{h_i} \right) = \text{days in port } i$$

where:

W_i = waiting and other non-working time in port i in day
h_i = cargo handling rate in tons/day

Total port costs are then $T_i C_p$ where C_p are the daily costs of the ship in port. Time at sea for the voyage is:

$$T_S = \sum_{i=1}^{n} (X_{i,i+1}/24V)$$

where:

$X_{i,i+1}$ = distance between ports i and i+1

while:

V = Average speed of ship in knots (assumed constant independent of displacement)

If C_S are the daily at sea costs of the vessel, then voyage costs can be expressed as:

$$C_V = \sum_{i=1}^{n} \left[\left(\frac{W_i h_i + \overline{D}_{i,i+1}}{h_i} \right) C_p + (X_{i,i+1}/24V)C_S \right]$$

where:

C_p = port costs/day = $F + a_1 C_{Vp}$

and:

C_S = at sea costs (at sea or in port)
C_{Vp} = variable costs of ship in port (a function of port tariffs, cargo handled, etc.)
C_{VS} = variable costs of ship at sea (a function of ship's displacement, speed, etc.)

$$C_V = \sum_{i=1}^{n} \left[\left(\frac{W_i h_i + \overline{D}_{i,i+1}}{h_i} \right) (F + a_1 C_{Vp}) \right.$$

$$\left. + (X_{i,i+1}/24V) \, F + a_2 C_{VS} \right]$$

and:

$$\overline{D}_{i,i+1} \leq D_{i,i+1}$$

$$D_{i,i+1} \leq DWT = \text{deadweight capacity of ship}$$

The total amount of ton-miles of cargo carried on this voyage are ship productivity:

$$P_V = \sum_{i=1}^{n} D_{i,i+1} \, X_{i,i+1}$$

To obtain maximum profits or efficiency of resource use, the cost per ton-mile of transport productivity is usually desired which requires a computation of C_V/P_V and the determination under which conditions C_V/P_V is minimised.

Dividing the expression for C_V by:

$$\sum_{i=1}^{n} (D_{i,i+1} \, X_{i,i+1})$$

or P_V and differentiating partially with respect to the different variables of interest, we can obtain expressions which tell us the role that various technology and operational variables play in determining ship cost per unit output on a voyage.

The above expression can be used to compute cost/unit output with respect to changes in ship utilisation (overall or on particular legs of the voyage), with respect to port waiting time as well as port handling rate or both, fixed and variable ship costs, and more. Similarly we can use the expression to determine how a particular itinerary affects voyage costs and cost/unit on various legs of the voyage and how by-passing of some ports or other changes in the itinerary affect voyage costs and costs of cargo carried between any two ports in the voyage. These expressions can now be used to determine the relationships among variables required for minimum cost per ton-mile or per ton in the two port trade. Similar expressions can readily be obtained for the general model presented before and the sensitivity of cost/ton or cost ton/mile could be obtained as a function of particular port or voyage leg characteristics.

Considering a simple two port trade route where cargo loaded in both ports equals the ship's DWT, then:

$$\left(\frac{C_V}{P_V}\right) = \frac{1}{2XD}\left(\frac{2(Wh + d)}{h} C_P + \frac{x}{12V} C_S\right)$$

$$= \frac{(Wh + d)}{2XD} C_p + \frac{C_S}{24VD}$$

Considering non-linear expressions:

$$C_p = F + aD^h$$

$$C_s = F + bD^h$$

$$\left(\frac{C_V}{P_V}\right) = \frac{(Wh + d)}{XDh}(F + aD^h) + \frac{(F + bD^n)}{24VD}$$

and differentiating with respect to D, W, x, h, and v, we obtain:

1. $\dfrac{\partial\left(\dfrac{C_V}{P_V}\right)}{\partial D} = 0 = (n - 1)h[24VWa + Xb]D^n$
$$+ 24nVaD^{n+1} - Fh(x + 24WV)$$

2. $\dfrac{\partial\left(\dfrac{C_V}{P_V}\right)}{\partial W} = 0 = F + aD^n$

3. $\dfrac{\partial\left(\dfrac{C_V}{P_V}\right)}{\partial X} = 0 = aD^{n+1} + WahD^n + FD + hWF$

4. $\dfrac{\partial(C_V/P_V)}{\partial h} = 0 = F + aD^n$

5. $\dfrac{\partial(C_V/P_V)}{\partial V} = 0 = F + bD^n$

if n = 1 and daily costs are linear functions of D, then optimum value of D

$$D = (Fh(X + 24WV)/24a)^{1/2}$$

or deadweight is a function of the square root of fixed costs, cargo handling rate, distance, speed, ship waiting time, and the inverse square root of the coefficient of the variable port cost.

In addition shippers incur costs which usually consist of

$$\text{Cargo Loading/Unloading Costs} = \sum_i H_i \overline{D}_{i,i+1} = C_h$$

where H_i is the cost of handling one ton of cargo in port i, and if cargo is assumed to arrive at a uniform rate $D_{i,i+1}/t$ where t is the time between departures of a ship in days, then storage and interest costs are

$$\sum_i \overline{D}_{i,i+1} t/2(S + I) = C_I$$

where S are storage costs/ton per day and I are the interest or holding costs per day. Shippers are interested in minimising the sum of their 'cargo' costs $C_h + C_I$ in port i plus the cost of freight to the cargo destination.

The optimal time between departures is a function of ship size and trade volume. In fact, it is inversely proportional to the ship size employed and directly proportional to the square root of the total volume traded. In a trade between two commensurate ports, this is readily determined, but when the trade consists of multiple ports with diverse amounts of cargo handled, then a simulation model must usually be developed to determine a good frequency.

5

Shipping Operations and Management

SOCIAL AND OPERATIONAL ISSUES

Lower manning scales, higher skill requirements, and large scale internationalisation of manning of shipping, under which few crews consist exclusively of nationals of the flag of registry, has brought with it many social issues. One is the increasing demand for uniform professional standards in terms of skills and experience, which has resulted in the development of the recently announced IMO shipboard crew qualifications standards. Another is the provision of fairly uniform shipboard standards of accommodation. Obviously as crew size declines and ship technology changes, the function of the individual crew member becomes broader, but at the same time he experiences greater social isolation.

While crews are usually organised in national unions which are often divided into licensed and unlicensed seafarers, there is growing pressure towards changes in the traditional designation and classification of seafarers. Although maritime nationalism continues to encourage national union and often exclusive use of national citizens on national flag ships, more than 80 per cent of total world shipping and 43 per cent of world shipping, exclusive of shipping registered under flags of convenience by DWT, is now manned by mixed nationality crews. Crewing agents and ship management companies now provide a significant proportion of the manning requirements of world shipping. A recent entry into this field of activity is the People's Republic of China.

Operationally ships not only call less frequently at domestic ports or ports of crew domicile, but their stay is usually quite short. As a result, shipboard crews essentially spend most of their time on board. Shipboard facilities now often include in addition to single cabins and private baths, sports and recreation facilities, swimming pools, video and closed-circuit television, 24-hour (self) food services, and more. An increasing number of ships also have accommodation for spouses.

These developments have impacted on the social structure and relationship on board ships. While most vessels maintain separate eating facilities for officers and crew, the food served and most other conditions are often similar or the same. Multipurpose shipboard manning, when officers and crew perform both deck and engineering functions (bridge controlled machinery operated by qualified watch officer), has resulted in changing the traditional social and professional gap among deck and engineering officers and crews. With more highly educated and skilled crew who are performing mostly monitoring and few manual labour functions, the social separation between officers and crews is also diminishing. In the future, ships will probably have single eating and other facilities. Ship crews will not only be much smaller (10 to 15 total), but will also have fewer opportunities for shore leave. Rotation of ship crews will therefore become very common in line with the methods used in rotating aircraft crews. To make this more efficient, while assuring the reliability of vessel operations, a much higher degree of standardisation in shipboard equipment, monitors, operating and ship management procedures will be required. This has been accomplished to a large extent by the airline industry with airplane control standardisation.

Therefore with uniform professional standards introduced by IMO, the next step should be development of uniform shipboard procedures and monitoring and operating equipment. These developments need a completely different approach to shipboard manpower planning and training.

Modern communications, computer, and systems management skills have to be trained and retrained by periodic reeducation. A recent study of senior merchant marine deck officers, for example, indicated that the majority of serving officers are unable to accurately compute and project ship voyage stability and effectively use shipboard computers, communications systems, electronic instruments, and monitors.

Principles and methods used in the training of seafarers now are usually obsolete and, while they may assist the development of personality and character, most merchant officer and crew programmes lack providing effective training in modern ship operating skill and management skills.

Another issue is the archaic organisation of ship labour and hiring practices. These will have to be changed in response to the completely new technological, operational, and management environment in which shipping functions. Shipboard staff can no longer be treated as casual labour working under a strict hierarchical shipboard organisation, with only senior officers considered pseudo-permanent staff. Again, the experience of airlines will probably lead shipboard personnel employment practices in the future, with all shipboard staff permanently employed.

TECHNOLOGICAL CHANGES AND EFFECTS ON SHIPPING

Technological change in shipping has, in recent years, been largely initiated by cargo handling and cargo form technology. The use of ship volume or capacity and its effect on hold configuration, access, and internal fittings, has undergone major changes. Cellular container ships, barge carriers, Ro-Ro vessels, single or multi-purpose bulk vessels, car carriers, LNG and other gas carriers, OBOs, and other mixed use bulk carriers, are just some of the examples of this technological change.

In parallel, there have been major technological changes in cargo handling and transfer, both on shipboard and in-port facilities serving ships. Also ship management technology has changed radically. Computerised cargo, voyage, and ship condition planning now provide a capability for near real time control of ship loading/ unloading and other operational functions. Ship management is assisted by satellite communications systems, weather routing, and other modern computer-aided systems now.

Research in ship hull forms, appendices, and ship propulsion has resulted in significant improvements in energy efficiency, and in some cases seakeeping and ship manoeuvrability. On the other hand, very few fundamental changes have been introduced in hull or ship form or methods of energy conversion and propulsion.

Technological change in shipping has accelerated in recent years, a trend which is expected to continue. Technological change is a stochastic process because uncertainties are involved in its choice, performance, cost, acceptability, applicability, and use. Shipping management today faces the challenge of keeping abreast with technological developments, and managing technological change effectively. The management of technological change in shipping involves:

(1) Choice of new technology.
(2) Timing of change in technology.
(3) Scale of introduction of new technology or investment in new technology.
(4) Rate of introduction of new technology.
(5) Utilisation of new technology.
(6) Choice of application of new technology.

To manage technological change, both qualitative and quantitative analysis must be performed as shown in Figure 5.1. The management of technological change depends on the shipping company's objective, which often includes profitability (or return on investment), market share, product or service choice, and so forth. It also depends on exogenous factors such as government policy, national and international regulation, market trends, trade developments, etc., and endogenous factors such as staff and labour skills, existing capacity, port interfaces, existing service contracts, and more. The goal of management of technological change is to review existing or expected technological developments, evaluate them, and then consider the alternative technological change decisions in light of the shipping company's objectives as well as identified endogenous and exogenous factors to make the best possible management decision. The alternative technological change decisions in terms of choice, timing, etc. are usually subjected to quantitative analysis so as to determine the expected result of the management decision.

Shipping has always been a risky business, and shipping management is generally familiar with the uncertainties confronting their operations. But management of shipping was always based on short-term risks. Few ship owners considered long-term factors. Shipping demand and freight rate cycles in the past were usually of a few years' duration and short-term timing of decisions was therefore of primary importance. In fact an astute owner playing the cyclical trends of shipping demand and freight rates successfully could often expect to repay his investment in a few years, if effectively timed, and could then ride out the rest of the economic life of his ships. This was possible as ship investment costs often fell in line with decline in freight rates.

This situation has now changed and shipping demand/price cycles are stretched out over much longer and less predictable periods. Equally discerning are the implications of technological change which usually have long-term impacts. Shipping management must

Figure 5.1: Diagrammatic of relationships of factors of management of technological change

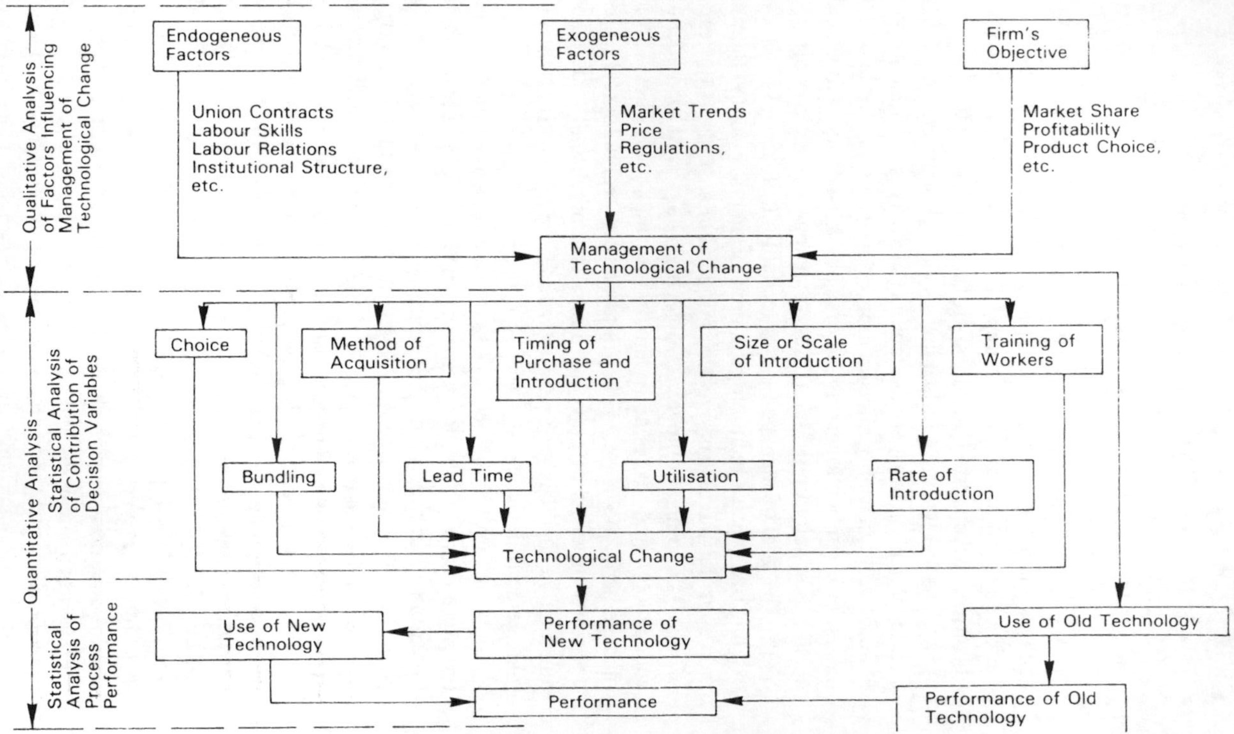

192

now become accustomed to making formal evaluations of the impact of technological change to be successful. Traditionally, new shipping technology was introduced by newcomers to the shipping industry or the rare innovators among its members. The shipping industry, as a whole, has spent little on research and development of technology with the exception of improved shipping management technology.

By and large, the industry followed the leaders in technological change by observing and imitating the few risk takers among its members or newcomers who introduced new technology. The new technological pressure requires shipping companies to employ much more highly educated and skilled staff and managers now. This pressure influences the structure of the shipping industry in which small traditional owners may find it increasingly difficult to compete with larger and often integrated companies who can afford a high level of technical competence and continuous training of their staff. Technological change therefore has become a major force in influencing change in the ownership and operational structure of the shipping industry. It has resulted in much greater concentration and vertical integration of shipping. The number of 'active' shipping companies in international liner trade has fallen by 42 per cent between 1976 and 1985, largely by mergers or joint ventures. As bulk carriers are often incorporated as individual ship owning corporations managed by some larger operating company, it is more difficult to determine the change in concentration in the bulk shipping industry.

Technological change in shipping

Technological change has become the most important management issue in shipping in recent years. Not only has ship and ship interface technology changed drastically, but technological changes are also being introduced into communication, control, guidance, and ship condition technology. Technological change, as a result, no longer affects ship performance in terms of ship speed and power, ship seakeeping, ship carrying capacity to displacement ratios and so forth, but now impacts also on cargo handling operations and stowage and thereby port turnaround. Ship manning, intermodal transfer effectiveness, ship condition and operations management, ship maintenance, and more, are all affected by technological change.

The management of technological change is a difficult problem because technological change in shipping usually involves large amounts of capital and large financial and operational risks. Technological change in shipping can be divided into change in:

(1) Ship Design Technology
   — Hull Form
   — Hull Structure
   — Hull Subdivision
(2) Ship Services
   — Steering and Direction Keeping
   — Accommodation
   — Cargo Containment
   — Ship Engineering
(3) Ship Propulsion Technology
   — Ship Machinery
   — Ship Propulsors
   — Energy Conversion
   — Fuel Processing
   — Machinery Monitoring and Control
(4) Ship Condition Technology
   — Ship Steering and Routing
   — Trim and Stability and Control
   — Fire and Safety
   — Cargo Maintenance
   — Ship and Machinery Maintenance
   — Air, Temperature, and Humidity Condition
(5) Ship Management
   — Ship Communication
   — Ship Information Management
   — Ship Control
   — Ship Inventory and Supplies

Technological change and its effect on shipping operations

Technological change has resulted in larger and faster ships, and new cargo handling techniques. In addition to the effects that technological change had on manpower, ship management, use of port, and cargo handling and carrying effectiveness, particular developments can be identified. Flexible combination carriers, such as the oil-bulk-ore ships, have made the carriage of dry and liquid bulk cargoes interchangeable. These two major segments of bulk trade are now increasingly tied together so that surplus tonnage in the oil market can more readily move into dry bulk trades and vice versa. This is what happened in the bulk markets, for example, when in the economic slump after 1974, the oil trade declined substantially. Similarly containerisation has made major inroads into general as well as pseudo-bulk trades. In the early stages, the use of containers differentiated very clearly between the carriage of general cargo and bulk. At a later stage, however, it brought the two sectors closer together as general cargo put into containers became homogeneous and some pseudo-bulk commodities were also moved in containers.

More recently some bulk vessels were equipped to carry deck loads of containers. As a result, liner conferences are today meeting increased competition from bulk as well as independent liner operators. The final result is oversupply in container ship tonnage capacity which has caused a weakening of conference participation in terms of the share of liner cargo carried (60 per cent in 1984 versus 85 per cent in 1980). While tramps have traditionally been considered the potential competitors of conference liner operators, the sophisticated technological change embodied in container shipping was assumed to promote more specialised carriage of liner cargo and thus reduce tramp and bulk ship competition. As it happens, traditional competitive relationships between the various shipping markets remain basically intact or have actually been sharpened by recent technological developments. The whole industry is increasingly closely tied together so that all major types of cargo form and all methods of operations increasingly affect each other competitively. Competition though occurs at higher levels of technological sophistication and efficiency than was previously the case.

New shipping technology requires effective land-based support facilities, both physical and human, as technologically advanced ships require similarly technologically advanced ports and inland transport services. But ports cannot be divorced from their hinterlands and the necessary domestic transport infrastructure. To maximise the benefits of advances in cargo handling and transport technology, the whole system – ships, ports, internal distribution – must be technologically consistent. Such technological consistencies are unfortunately seldomly available in LDCs. Yet such requirements must be considered when assessing investments in advanced shipping technology to serve developing countries.

The efficiency and operational capacity of ships has increased dramatically in recent years, thus allowing for more cargo to be carried by fewer ships. This is, in large part, the cause for the large

195

surplus tonnage today. In a period of stable or declining trade, operators see the capturing of cargo share as a zero sum game and there is a distinct movement toward mergers and increasing scale of operations – a trend particularly noticeable in, but not limited to, liner operations in developed countries. To maintain advanced technology in shipping on an international scale in a highly competitive environment requires large capital resources as well as high level expertise. Many shipping companies have, as a result, resorted to cooperative operations in the form of consortia, joint services, joint ventures, space charters, mergers, and leasing arrangements.

Demands for advanced managerial skills and ability are increasing and we are rapidly moving into a situation in which high technology shipping will be concentrated on a few, very large, and financially-strong operators capable of combining managerial skills and technological capability with advanced methods of ship financing.

By necessity, large liner operations will be focused on a few high volume trade routes connecting with feeder services, such as the round-the-world services offered by US Lines, Evergreen, and K-Line who use the 'load centre' systems concept to reduce the number of port calls. They are likely to spawn new services to and from intermediate volume ports in competition with the feeder services. That is, cargo from a feeder port in one range destined to another feeder port in another range would move directly from the former to the latter by-passing their respective load centres. This may well be an area for LDC involvement as it seems to be a case in which domestic shipping may indeed promote trade, i.e., it would establish services not otherwise available on that route.

TECHNOLOGICAL DEVELOPMENTS IN SHIPPING

Recent overtonnaging and the resulting decline in rates has caused delays in the introduction of many technological developments in shipping which are readily available or could be adapted from other fields without much effort. Operators in general are deferring major investments now until a clearer picture of the trend of the shipping market emerges. This though has not affected the development of new ideas, technologies, or operating concepts.

As soon as the current shipping recession comes to an end, major technological developments are expected to be introduced. We will attempt to hypothesise the form, technology, and operational approach used by shipping companies of the future. For the purposes of this study, the future horizon is contemplated as any time after 1995. Our discussion will be divided into the following major technological areas:

(1) The structure and method of management of the shipping company of the future.
(2) The operational approach used by the shipping company of the future.
(3) Ship, ship management, and cargo handling technology of the shipping company of the future.

Future structure and method of management of shipping

As noted, the structure of the shipping industry and the role of shipping companies is expected to change dramatically. Shipping companies are expected to increasingly merge with other transportation companies to form highly integrated transportation systems, capable of controlling the movement of goods from origin to destination. The management of shipping in other words will be largely subordinated to and integrated with the management of total through transportation systems which may involve physical form change of cargo at various intermodal transport interfaces.

Cargo booking, as a result, will not be done by the shipping company (or for that matter individual modal operators serving the system) but by the system operator, who is responsible for the allocation of cargo to the various modal link operators or subsystems.

Shipping management will function as a modal division of total systems management. Cargo will be booked electronically and capacity as well as storage and other requirements for each leg of the origin to destination transport will be determined and committed. Any sequence delays at modal interfaces will be noted and alternative routing (or modal choice) investigated. Changes in itinerary, arrival/departure times, capacities, etc. of individual modal operations will be transmitted to the central booking system which will immediately reorganise bookings and routings of individual consignments. This process continues and the system, as a result, maintains a real time record of all flows, operations, and resource or capacity uses, including the need for intermodal storage. The function of shipping management will be to control the operations of the fleet and assure timely departure and arrival. Marketing and similar functions will be performed by the central organisation as will be cargo planning, with the exception of cargo loading plan review for shipping condition control.

The above will apply not only to integrated bulk transport but increasingly also to break bulk cargo transport involving liner type shipping operations. The most important change will be that shipping management will no longer attempt to optimise shipping operations (for example by trying to reduce cost of shipping) but manage the shipping mode of the total system so as to optimise the performance of the total integrated transport system. In other words, optimise total system performance (and cost) instead of allowing each modal link to attempt to suboptimise its performance (and costs).

Obviously the combined performance or cost of a series of individually optimised operations is seldomly as good as the performance and cost of a total optimised transport system. Integrated systems can achieve much higher utilisation of resources employed and because of their size and diversity of services offered can usually obtain larger market penetration.

There is some fear that the increasing number of large integrated transport enterprises, and the decline in the number of modal operators, including shipping companies will reduce competition, lead to monopolistic or at least oligopolistic behaviour including price fixing. Deregulation of transport (including antitrust immunity extension) in countries like the USA have been a major impetus towards transport integration. At the same time, deregulation has allowed extended competition among operators and services, facilitated entry and merger, and permitted more effective pricing of services.

Future operational approach to shipping

The most important change in ship operations will be automation of most ship functions including ship condition management. To assist in this and allow ship manning to be reduced to a skeleton crew of 9 to 11 men for the average new vessel put in service at the end of this century, full use of computer controls, artificial intelligence and expert systems will be made. The use of expert systems will allow more effective direct and real time diagnostic analysis and corrective action than professional operators could possibly achieve.

Expert systems for each of the many operational systems on a ship will incorporate the experience, analytical, and decision-making approach of a large number of the top professionals and incorporate them in a computer decision model which analyses the readings of various monitoring devices and ship management objectives and goals and determines the best course of action under the circumstances. Expert systems are already used in many complex systems. Their use frees operators to spend their time on supervision. Even if conditions occur for which corrective actions are not programmed into the system, the expert system will provide the operator with a full diagnostic and a review of alternative actions and their prospective outcome. As a result the operator should be able to make more intelligent and fully-informed decisions.

In the future, ship manning will be composed of a small group of highly trained, multipurpose deck-engine-communications experts who will manage the ship. Practically all ship functions from line and anchor handling, engine operations, hatch cover handling, cargo handling equipment operations, and more will be remotely and often automatically operated. Central monitors with backup, central computers with expert systems programs all tied into integrated communication systems will be used for most ship conditions and operational management functions. In the future ship routing will largely be under the control of ship traffic controllers who assign ships a route (and often speed) within narrow bounds. Vessel traffic control systems are expected to encompass most major shipping lanes by the end of this century. This is expected to reduce the size of ship manning and increase vessel safety.

Future ship and cargo handling technology

Several new hull types are expected to be in use before the end of this century. For example, vessels carrying volume intensive cargoes such as containerships, Ro-Ro vessels, car ferries, and so forth, will often use catamaran or semi-submerged catamaran hulls. The wing or bridge connecting the two hulls will serve as a large area and volume cargo carrying platform. For example use of such hull forms may also allow more effective ship-port interface by allowing such vessels to straddle finger piers or similar structures for direct block transfer of cargo.

Other hull developments are full bodied, shallow draft, two screw and skeg type bulk carriers which should reduce steel weight (and

199

therefore costs) of tankers and dry bulk carriers by 10 to 20 per cent and the drafts of such vessels by up to 33 per cent, with a resulting impact on total bulk shipping costs, particularly on draft limited trade routes.

New bulk carrier hull technology is largely based on developments in ocean barging which are continuing. Large 85,000 DWT integrated, open water decoupable, tug barge systems are in operation now. Drop and swap capability of such systems also provides a high degree of flexibility and allows reduction of shore-based storage facilities.

Other hull developments may include bottom loading/unloading tankers, and bottom (gravity) unloading bulk carriers discharging their cargo through bottom sluice gates onto a bottom trench-mounted conveyor encased in a concrete channel which seals itself temporarily to the flat part of the ship's bottom by a membrane seal.

Self-unloading of bulk carriers will become more popular as ship-board carried bulk unloading equipment becomes cheaper, more efficient, and lighter. In the future containerships will be cell-less, and allow the block handling of containers of different sizes. Similarly, traditional Ro-Ro vessels will probably be replaced by warehouse-type vessels which permit blocks of cargo (including stacked vehicles) to be rolled on and off the decks of such vessels.

In propulsion, ships will use much lighter, smaller, less volume consuming, fuel efficient, energy conserving devices or engines. The internal combustion (or diesel) engine will remain the main shipboard energy converter or propulsion motor, but slow- to medium-speed diesel engines with turbocharging and various types of economisers (water and exhaust heat extracting devices) will be used. Although sail assistance will be incorporated on some vessels, greater use of solar-powered devices (particularly in remote parts of the ship where savings in wiring, etc. are significant) is expected.

SHIP LOGISTICS

Reduced ship manning, faster ship turnaround, and larger capital investment in ships will all put pressure on higher ship system reliability, availability, and maintainability as well as more effective ship supply systems. In the future, on-board maintenance will be restricted to adjustments and minor repairs. As in the aviation industry where engines, pumps, and other mechanical, electrical, and electronic components are replaced periodically for in-shop overhaul with on-aircraft repair and maintenance restricted to very minor adjustments, ship repair will in the future similarly be largely removed as an on-board function.

Most repairs in the future will be periodic and preventative under ideal ship conditions. This will require a higher degree of standard-isation of components, and better ship design of easy (modular) removal and replacement of components from main engines to pumps and motors. On-board spaces will be drastically reduced with resulting savings in both on-board spare inventory weight and cost which can be quite appreciable.

In the future bunker intakes will be placed at the shipsides to eliminate hose handling by ship crew, with remote tank sounding and inflow controls monitored by either ship crew or bunker supplier. Ship consumable supplies will be delivered in prestacked containers, lifted on or off shipboard by remotely controlled hoists, and moved into their position against a deckhouse seal. Inventory control will be performed by shore staff who will control both delivered and returned consumable supplies.

IMPACT OF TRANSPORT INTEGRATION AND INTERMODALISM

The post-war period has seen a vast development and expansion of roads and railroads throughout the world. Together with the technological developments in shipping, transport became inter-modal. The phenomenon is seen in many parts of the world in the concept of the land-bridge. The effects are much more far-reaching. Inter-coastal seatrade in North America, for example, is virtually gone. The same holds for Europe where the British short-sea trades are severely affected; similarly UK trade with the Continent is largely by land-based transport, with trucks using ferry services across the Channel. Also the Scandinavian trade with the Continent is mainly by land transport as is the trade with the Mediterranean and the Near East. Similarly some European trade with the Far East is now transported overland via the USSR.

What were once major traditional short distance liner routes have largely disappeared as the cargoes increasingly move by intermodal transport. The areas where shipping encounters competition from land-based transport are growing as technology makes the transport system increasingly intermodal. The tendency towards more value added in traded goods may also argue for more intermodal transport, which in turn may influence ocean shipping demand. In the short term, therefore, while world economic recovery will result in a resurge in international trade, it may not have as strong an impact on the growth of seaborne trade as expected.

There are some very broad policy implications for this view. First. as mentioned, growing international trade need not, as in the past, result in a commensurate growth in seaborne trade. Much depends on where the growth occurs. Second, intermodalism brings international shipping onto the domestic scene; domestic economic and development policies must consider the interface with international shipping. Since governments are usually involved in domestic transport regulation and because of the imperatives of national trade policy, governments must now balance international economic and domestic political factors. Shipping, including coastal shipping, will expand where land transport is not, or cannot be, sufficiently developed to provide competition. This applies to many LDC countries or regions. The same holds where the trade is not suited for land transport – this would seem to apply to major bulk cargoes.

The introduction of new technology at the interface of modal transportation links is perhaps the most relevant development in transport integration. Intermodal transport change, largely introduced at modal transport interface terminals, is bringing intermodal freight-forwarding within the grasp of both developed and developing countries and with this the possibility of controlling transport costs and revenues of the import-export trades. New intermodal developments include:

(1) Systems such as 'trailer-on-flat-car' (TOFC), 'swap-body, Lo-Lo, piggyback rail operations', Ro-Ro/Lo-Lo ship/shore transfers, etc.
(2) Generations of intermodal ships (Ro-Ro/Lo-Lo/Con-Ro, etc.).
(3) Intermodal freight terminal (truck terminal, TOFC terminal, inland container depot, container freight station, etc.).

In general, most technological changes have been introduced at intermodal transport terminals which provide a pool of services to the various interfacing modes of transport. Economies of scale created by these terminals have influenced introduction of improved information and documentation systems, as well as better procedures.

Deregulation of transport has also often contributed to the

introduction of technological change in intermodal transport. One area is simplification of contraction for freight-forwarding and shipping. Shippers or consignees can now control freight movements in many countries from origin to destination at no additional investment or cost.

The change in priorities in intermodal transport investment from purely physical infrastructure hardware, towards improved systems and procedures is now pervasive, as the potential savings in transit time, security and revenue control through use of improved intermodal transport management systems far outweigh any savings which could accrue through hardware investments.

Requirements for efficient intermodal transport[1]

Intermodal transport is not a new concept as many goods, particularly in international trade, have always been transported by several modes of transport in series. What is new is the recognition that efficient intermodal transport requires a systems approach in which the integrated requirements of the chain of transport are considered in preference to the requirements for efficient transport by individual modal links. In other words, we are looking for efficient operation of the system and not a combination of efficient subsystems or modal links. This approach demands that the requirements of individual modes or links be subordinated to those of the total system.

The objectives of efficient intermodal transport are to move cargo from origin to destination in minimum time and at minimum costs. To achieve this the technology, operations, and management of each modal link must be integrated with the overall systems requirements. Links in intermodal transport consists of both transport and transfer links. Transfer links are usually provided by intermodal terminals and ports. They are usually designed to perform cargo transfer (loading/unloading), buffering or storage, and physical form change operations. Buffering or storage is required to accommodate the mating of different capacities of interfacing transport modes such as a large ship of 20,000 tons and trucks with a 10-ton capacity. Physical form change is similarly undertaken to match the cargo to the requirements of subsequent modal transport and transfer operations.

203

The structure of intermodal transport

Intermodal transport requires close coordination of all the modal links of transport in terms of technology, operational control, and information flow. The capacities, frequencies of service, and schedules of each link must be closely coordinated with those of other links in the system and in particular with interfacing transport links. Intermodal transport is usually designed around a few basic requirements:

(1) Compatibility of all equipment used in transport and for transfer.
(2) Standardisation of physical form and dimensions of cargo units such as pallets, trailers, containers, and tanks.
(3) Balancing of capacity of sequential transport links to allow effective utilisation of employed capacity, independent of . . .
(4) Provision of effective transfer equipment at intermodal terminals which allows maximum direct transfer between transport modes.
(5) Adequate buffer storage capacity to allow for storage of cargo at intermodal terminals accumulated as a result of differences in scale, intermittency and services among interfacing modal transport links.
(6) Provision of effective capacity to allow turnaround of modal transport carriers at intermodal terminal in minimum time.
(7) Standardisation of cargo and unit load codes, read off, and recording information; information transfer must be closely coordinated in terms of form, format, accessibility, etc.
(8) Standardisation of rate structures, interservice rate computations, etc., transfers and accounting.
(9) Coordination of transport service schedules and operations to achieve as close as possible 'just in time' arrival of shipments.

Intermodal transport has become highly complex and requires close coordination of the operations of many separate carriers and terminal operators. The structure of intermodal transport today is based on closely coordinated management and control of operations, sharing of information and data, and the use of an integrated multimodal transport strategy or plan which subjugates the objectives of individual operators of modal links to those of the total intermodal system.

Intermodal transport usually involves modal carriers such as ship operators, barge companies, trucking companies, railways, pipeline companies, conveyors, and other modal transport operators which may be public or private common carriers, contract carriers, or private proprietary transport providers. They may be involved in a limited service or operate a large network and compete with other modal transport providers on at least some links. It also involves ports, public or private port and intermodal terminals, and private common user or proprietary terminals. In addition to all these providers of services in intermodal transport, there are numerous users or user representatives such as shippers, agents, freight forwarders, and cargo brokers who are involved in the process of intermodal transportation. The most important requirement for efficient intermodal transport is the coordination of these parties and their diverse interests and requirements. An efficient intermodal transport system is required.

In some countries intermodal transport has been organised on a systems basis with centralised control or by one of the operators assuming the coordinating (or control) functions. In the US where, until recently, such coordination was illegal under antitrust laws, some operators acquired control of container terminals, trucking, and inland terminals to assure integrated control of intermodal transport. Others acquired control of container terminals and unit train operations. An interesting development is the entry of the Port of Seattle into unit train operations in a move designed to provide integrated intermodal services to its customers.

There are various degrees of intermodal transport integration. One approach is that of SeaLand and many proprietary operators of oil and dry bulk intermodal transport which involves ownership and/or control of the links of the intermodal transport chain. Another approach provides for control of some, but not all, the transport links by a major operator who then serves as the coordinator and contractor for the remaining services. Finally there is the alternative of independent and often competing providers of transport services for all the diverse links in the intermodal chain. In this case there is usually a designated and often neutral (or non-competing) agent who provides for the integration of the intermodal services.

Incentives for efficient intermodal transport

A recent study of non-integrated intermodal transport in the US traced a number of general break bulk cargo shipments from the

Table 5.1: Comparative intermodal operations

Item	Break bulk cargo		Containerised cargo	
	Time (days)	Cost as % of total for break bulk cargo	Time (days)	Cost as % of total for break bulk cargo
Shipper to inland terminal	0.10	2.1	0.10	2.0
Unloading/loading of inland terminal	0.12	3.2	0.04	2.1
Storage at inland terminal	2.01	2.6	0.84	1.4
Inland terminal to long distance (rail or truck terminal)	0.06	0.9	–	–
Unloading/loading at long distance terminal	0.48	4.7	–	–
Storage/consolidation at long distance terminal	3.42	2.8	–	–
Long distance (feeder) transport	0.84	5.2	0.79	4.9
Unloading at port	0.30	5.4	–	2.2
Storage at port	9.83	3.8	4.62	2.0
Loading at port	3.08	10.8	0.84	7.2
Shipping to foreign destination	9.00	26.0	6.94	36.2
Transport in foreign country	1.04	7.8	0.84	6.4
Non-transport in foreign country	4.82	23.7	3.42	10.6
Total	35.20	100.0	18.43	74.0

Source: E. Frankel, *Study of Intermodal Transport Costs*, MIT, 1978

Chicago area to southern Germany. It was found that on average these shipments required 35.2 days from dispatch to delivery. As shown in Table 5.1, only 30 per cent of the time was spent in actual transport and less than 42 per cent of the total origin-to-destination costs were spent for actual transport. The rest of the time and money were expended on non-transport activities or services such as cargo transfer, storage, classification, stacking, overstowing, checking, and more. The same table also shows what happened after the cargo was containerised. Total average time to delivery declined to just over 18.43 days (or by nearly 50 per cent). While total costs declined by much less because freight rates for containerised cargo were higher than break bulk cargo, a significantly smaller percentage of the total costs were spent on non-transport related activities (one-third of total containerised origin-destination costs versus 58 per cent in case of break bulk cargo origin-to-destination costs).

If the cost of time of cargo in transport is added, which in the case of high value cargo may be quite appreciable, then the cost differentials become even larger. If the cargo is shipped using intermodal through-bills, then the time factor obviously becomes an important consideration in setting discount rates. There are incentives for the reduction of time and the number and cost of non-transport services and operations in intermodal transport which call for attempts towards maximising and minimising the number of transport, as well as other, links in the intermodal transport chain. These incentives are higher when the intermodal system is more complicated. Break bulk cargo values now often exceed US$10,000/ton when the value of time becomes readily US$2 to 4 per ton per day. The saving of 10 to 20 days in origin-to-destination time may then result in a saving of cargo in transit costs of US$20 to 80/ton.

There is similarly an incentive to increase the utilisation of all links of intermodal transport chains by assuring continuity of flow compatibility of link capacities and service frequencies, and a minimum of intra-link or buffer storage or cargo. Such an approach will both reduce the time in transit and utilisation of resources employed in the transport links. To achieve this requires close intermodal coordination and in some cases integration of services.

Intermodal freight terminals

Intermodal freight terminals provide for the transfer of cargo between different modes of transport. They are usually located at

Figure 5.2: Luff system — for prestacked transfer of container-pallet or break bulk cargo

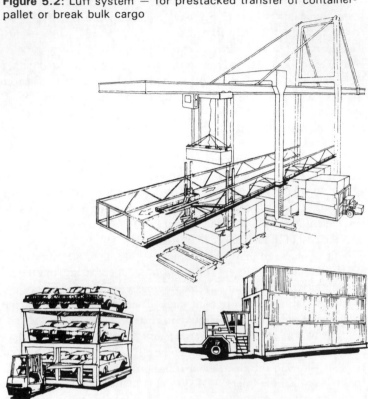

Source: Luff Systems, Salen-Wicander Terminal Systems AB, Sweden

strategic interfaces which provide convenient access by the modes served by the terminal. Such freight terminals also provide for the consolidation/deconsolidation and storage of cargo, as well as for administrative control of modal transport services. Freight terminals often also provide a location for various services to modal transport operators and other users, such as vehicle storage, repair, fuelling, and more.

Intermodal freight terminals are preferably located so as to relieve urban transport congestion and minimise transport delivery and distribution cost and time. They should provide ready access to major modal transport links and facilitate the marshalling of trucks, railcars, and barges. Terminals must be equipped for direct transfer of cargo between modes and therefore provide for effective layouts.

There are many technological developments affecting intermodal terminals. Luff frames (Figure 5.2) which allow transfer of pre-stacked containers, automobiles, pallets, and break bulk cargo are one innovation which can significantly reduce storage and handling capacity requirements in terminals by allowing unloading and stacking operations as well as unstacking and loading operations to be integrated. In other words, unloading and stacking is performed by one machine in one cycle at one location instead of in two cycles at two locations.

High rise automated break bulk, pallet, and container silos or warehouses are another important development. Such terminals offer perfect selectivity, immediate access, and identification and control of each piece of cargo. Although such terminals are more expensive, their economy in land use and operational costs, as well as their efficiency, make them effective choices under many conditions. The most important terminal developments though are probably in the area of automation, control, communication, and data handling which will be discussed in a separate chapter.

Efficient intermodal handling by rail

Intermodal handling between rail and road, water and other transport takes place at ports, inland intermodal terminals, small railway terminals, and at temporary or dedicated (often private) terminals. In recent years rail transfer has become an increasingly significant factor in intermodal transport over medium to long distances. While rail has traditionally provided the intermodal link for many dry bulk and pseudo-bulk liquid cargoes, it is now increasingly being used in trailers on flat car (TOFC) and container unit train operations as part of an integrated intermodal service.

Coal, for example, is loaded by conveyors from stockpiles on to unit trains which are run through car dumpers which discharge the coal on to the conveyor at the other end of the run. Similar arrangements are used in the transport of liquid bulk and also liquefied gas cargoes.

The most important recent developments are in rail container transport. Double stack cars, each car carrying 2 or 4 × 40 ft (12.19 m) containers or 4 to 8 TEUs, have made a major impact on container unit train operating costs in the US. Nearly 20 per cent of all unit train container transport is now on double-stacked cars and equipment is under test now which will allow the loading and unloading of two prestacked containers in one lift. Container handling equipment must obviously be compatible with equipment used for container handling generally. An important development is the mobile container transfer crane developed by 'Freightliners' which offers a low-cost, highly flexible container transfer capability.

Intermodal railyards are now largely automated with winch-controlled train movements often tied into yard container crane operations. Completely automated intermodal railyards are under consideration both in the USA and in Europe. Other developments are conveyor-supplied scissor lift container transfer equipment, designed to load/unload containers to or from railcars for transfer. Integrated port unit train facilities now use gantry crane operator, rail movement controls designed to move strings of railcars along the tracks beneath the crane between arrival of container lifts.

Data and movement controls

Sophisticated intermodal system management information systems have been developed which tie the various intermodal system links together in terms of information hookup and transfer. These are usually tied together by satellite communications systems to provide real time data transfer which in turn allows identification of the location and condition of any piece of cargo or unit of equipment at any period in time. Delays are immediately recorded and alternate routings, equipment, or space assignments are then made.

For effective use of such a system all intermodal links must be operationally integrated, their intermodal use cost predetermined, and intermodal systems management override be incorporated which allows intermodal management to superimpose its requirements over and above those of individual modes and their operators.

Computerised intermodal movement and routing controls are available now and have been installed by several integrated inter-modal operators. These computer methods perform planning, scheduling, routing, modal choice, tracking, and accounting functions, and are available for use on small and large computers. They simulate possible alternatives and select the best in line with cargo requirements, available capacity, costs, and other factors. They also perform billing functions and store booking as well as movement information for short- and medium-term operational and investment planning.

Deregulation of intermodal transport

Intermodal transport has successfully demonstrated its ability for reducing transport time and costs in recent years. Although principally used in the transport of containers or trailers, other physical forms of cargo have started to benefit from the use of the concept as well. Deregulation of modal as well as intermodal transport[2,3] virtually eliminates entry controls by the ICC and FMC in the USA, for example, and protects intermodal carriers from antitrust action. Since 1981, rail and intermodal and subsidiary truck joint services are also exempted from ICC regulation.[4] Deregulation of intermodal transport has introduced the ability for companies to change rates without notice and to enter or exit a market without restriction.

Since deregulation, intermodal transport has expanded significantly. It has also been able to introduce major cost savings by effective rationalisation which allowed it to operate profitably even during the recent recession. Although the opportunities in intermodal transport are evident by now, railroads, contrary to truckers and ship operators, have been slow in making commitments to intermodal transport.

The reason may be that railroads have traditionally earned most of their revenues (and profits) from the carriage of bulk cargoes such as coal and grain. Another is probably the lack of knowledge or ability to effectively rationalise its service, consistent with intermodal service requirements. Many railways, particularly in the US, also seem to have difficulty adjusting to the deregulated environment.

Trucking economics have also improved due to the liberation of truck size and increasing use of double trailer rigs. But even with these economies, rail intermodal transport appears to be gaining as the economic distance over which rail can provide cheaper distance continues to come down. Today rail in the US, for example, can compete over distances of about 800 miles, while in Europe it is probably less than 500 miles.

Intermodal technology

To become truly efficient, intermodal operators must maintain and offer the most advanced technology. Double stacked railcars are increasingly used in the US, and some truck operators are considering double stack, double trailer rigs now for use on routes without overhead restrictions. Similarly as longer, 48 ft (14.63 m) and wider, 102 in (259 cm), containers are being considered by shippers, rail and road operators are considering trailer and railcar technology to deal with this new demand.

Lightweight, trailer-carrying articulated cars are now being introduced with four tandem rail bogeys. Another development is the flexible length railcar which consists of 4-wheel platforms linked together by the containers locked upon them. Although most intermodal rail transport is carried by container unit trains, there is still a significant amount of trailer-on-flatbed railcar transport in both the US and Europe.

Different technologies for the loading/unloading of trailers or containers are now available, some of which can be carried or installed right on the railcar to make the operation of the intermodal train flexible and independent of terminal equipment capabilities.

Institutional developments

UNCTAD's Convention on Multimodal Transport adopted in 1980 is a long way from acceptance and ratification. Its purpose is to regulate transport using several modes. Its salient feature is that integration of several modes into one company may be held back. The conventions call for multimodal transport to be arranged by licensed and regulated multimodal transport operators who would act as agents for shippers, not carriers. On the face of it the convention goes counter to the observed structural changes in the industry which indicate that concentration and the creation of large multimodal transport companies is taking place in many parts of the world. Formal integration under an independent and disinterested 'third party' is really required if multimodal transport is to achieve its potential.

Conclusions

For efficient intermodal transport, all participating modal links must be effectively integrated, share information, subjugate their operational requirements to those of the intermodal chain, and adjust their rates to those of a part of integrated intermodal rates. Today we have the means to effect such integration and real time controls. Obviously such an approach will not benefit all modal transport or terminal interface service providers equally. In fact intermodal terminal operators would ultimately see a reduction in the need for much of the interface storage capacity offered by them.

The payoff though is great. In most cases, reductions in costs and time required for point-to-point intermodal transport could be reduced to a fraction (30 to 50 per cent) of what is required today. Similarly such integration by making more effective use of equipment and facilities should allow major reductions in the investment requirements for intermodal transport and terminals.

6

Shipping Policy Initiatives

Various countries, groupings of countries, and international agencies concerned with shipping as well as different private and commercial organisations have proposed, introduced, or undertaken policy initiatives or changes which are expected to have profound effects on world shipping. While the UNCTAD Liner Code of Conduct may have been the single most important international agreement affecting shipping ever, many developments such as bilateral and multilateral agreements between the US and Argentina and Brazil and among others as well as unilateral policy pronouncements or legislation have recently been advanced which are not only to have a larger effect than the Code, but may actually negate many of the recommendations and provisions of the Code.

As bilateral shipping agreements affected the Code by eliminating rightful participation by cross-traders and other provisions of the Code in the trade covered by the bilateral agreements, so did unilateral legislation such as the US Shipping Act of 1984 affect the traditional function and role of liner conferences, particularly in the trade of the US.

This act not only undermines the major powers of liner conferences by reducing their ability to enforce conference rates and terms of affreightment, but it also provides rights to the shippers and individual conference members which may make it difficult for a conference to maintain its membership as there is less advantage or inducement for ship operators to join.

In this section, some of the principal shipping policy initiatives of recent years are briefly presented and discussed.

Policy makers face difficult problems in deciding how to weigh different interests affecting shipping policy. National economic interests, for example, may demand different policy initiatives from

214

national defence, industrial development, and employment interests. Although ultimately all these conflicting interests should be comparable in terms of the overall national interests, this is seldomly possible and even more rarely done. Over and above policy makers are usually influenced or accountable to a national and sometimes even international political process.

Policies are usually designed to achieve some objectives. These though can usually only be achieved at the expense of some other objectives. Although policies are supposed to be the result of policy analysis in which the alternative allocations of resources in the achievement of different objectives are compared, most shipping policies are the results of political negotiations.

Shipping policies are usually based on diverse political and national objectives such as the promotion of foreign trade, employment generation, national defence capability, promotion of industrial development, control of transport costs, and economic growth and protection.

Many interests are usually involved in the promotion, planning, design, and implementation of shipping policies. These interests are not only concerned with maritime or shipping policy, but also by what means such policy will be achieved. The major interests concerned with shipping policy include:

(1) Public at large.
(2) Producers and consumers of goods traded internationally.
(3) Domestic producers catering to the domestic market.
(4) Shippers.
(5) Transport and ship operators.
(6) Shipbuilders and repairers.
(7) Organised labour.
(8) Defence community.
(9) Political parties.
(10) Financial community.

The definition of objectives and identification of interests in shipping policy does not really bound the problem as each interest involved and/or affected by such policy considers it from a different viewpoint.

Although most shipping policy is developed from a national perspective, it must recognise international aspects and implications. As most nations depend on trade for their economic development, and as most trade requires shipping, shipping policy cannot be introduced in isolation.

Shipping policy often tries to tie shipping regulation to trade and shipping promotion. The purposes of regulation though are often opposed to the objectives of promotion. It is for that reason that direct shipping regulation such as protectionism and preferential cargo access are usually detrimental to trade and economic development. There are many shipping policy issues which are of concern now such as:

(1) The US Shipping Act of 1984.
(2) Registration of ships and growth of national shipping.
(3) Cabotage and coastal/inter-island, domestic and national shipping including effects on feeder shipping.
(4) Definition of national shipping and the relation between ownership and control of shipping.
(5) Protectionism in non-liner shipping, including contract carriage.
(6) The future of the Code of Conduct of Liner Conferences.

US SHIPPING ACT OF 1984

This Act has several policy objectives, the most important of which are probably the mandated requirement that conference members be free to agree to independent arrangements (or actions) with shippers, and to enter into service contracts between a shipper and the conference member. Furthermore, the Act allows conferences to set intermodal or through rates or to offer shippers conference intermodal tariffs. Similarly, members in conferences serving US trades may now enter into rationalisation agreements such as joint services, operating consortia, space charters, and more.

Other provisions of the Act protect US flag operators' access to cross-trades. Although formal shippers' councils are not called for or encouraged by the Act, it does suggest shipper associations as less formal bodies in negotiations with liner conferences. Shipper, freight forwarders, non-vessel operating commercial carriers, brokers, trading companies, and related organisations all may now join shipper associations.

The Act has a major impact on liner conference operations in the US trades. By early 1986 or just over 18 months after enactment, well over 50 per cent of all liner cargoes in US conference trades were carried under terms of service contracts. This has affected both the role and power of the conferences and provided shippers with new leverage. As mandated, independent action by conference members requires only ten days' notice which is often too little for effective response by the conference.

The increased antitrust immunity should have a positive effect on shipping by allowing improvements in rationalisation of shipping as well as stability of both shipping and intermodal services. One issue which is suggested in evaluating regulatory decision making under the Act is contestability and competitiveness. It is assumed that a shipping market is competitive if it is contestable. This is obviously a highly theoretical argument.

With carriers now able to enter into rationalisation agreements such as joint ventures, space sharing or chartering, shipping consortia, partnerships, and more, efficiency and rationalisation of shipping operations in the US liner trade should improve. Operators can now share equipment, arrange for joint schedules, and otherwise integrate their operations. Other sectors affected by the Act are port, terminal, and intermodal operators who are now covered by increased antitrust immunity, and an ability to negotiate intermodal agreements.

There are serious questions regarding the impact of the Act. At this time of large overtonnaging, operators obviously suffer under low service contract rates, particularly as many shippers insist on clauses that require service contract terms to be adjusted to the lowest terms offered by the operator at a time. On the other hand, shippers may argue that when there is a shortage of tonnage, the situation may well be reversed and rates quoted actually exceed standard conference rates.

The new US Shipping Act of 1984 was enacted on 20 March 1984, after a conference resolution of the differences between the House's and the Senate's versions. The Act has a number of objectives:

(1) It is designed to clarify the antitrust position of the government in relation to liner conference operations.
(2) It authorises various aspects of intermodal transportation.
(3) It makes various innovative forms of rationalisation of shipping easier to accomplish; such as joint venturing, joint service operations, and pooling.
(4) It streamlines the oversight, review, and approval procedures of the FMC.

The primary goals of this Act are to improve the effectiveness of shipping in US foreign trade, to reduce costs of shipping, to enhance the defence responsiveness capability of US flag shipping, and to assure more effective use of intermodal transport in US foreign trade.

This Shipping Act replaces significant portions of various maritime laws passed since 1916. As noted, the principal provisions of the Act are designed to ease government regulations of carriers and strengthen shippers' negotiating powers. These provisions can be summarised as follows:

(1) Exemption from antitrust laws are broadened to include:
   (a) antitrust immunity for the collective setting of rates for through transportation
   (b) substantive and procedural changes in government review of multicarrier agreements
   — expedition of process, so carriers promptly know whether their agreements will be allowed to go into effect
   — review of agreements to give much less weight to policies of antitrust laws which is expected to result in the reduction in US government resistance to implementation of carrier agreements.

(2) 'Shippers' Provisions' are intended to increase carrier responsiveness to shippers for better service and lower rates by increasing shippers' ability to bargain for better rates and services, by placing pressure on carriers to consult shippers. As a result, shippers' demands are expected to effectively replace government regulation. It is expected that shippers' needs will be better met than by previously existing constraints on carriers – i.e. carriers are freed to meet shippers' needs. These provisions are imbedded in changes in Section 10 entitled Prohibited Acts.

   Provisions strengthening shipper negotiation power consist of:
   — *Independent Action* – Here member carriers of conference agreements have the right to act independently. This provision allows greater conference flexibility and increases competition. Independent action though is not prohibited on service contracts.
   — *Service Contracts* – Authorisation for conferences and ocean common carriers to offer service contracts.

Therefore, alternative means for ratemaking expectation that carriers will be more willing to grant favourable rate and service terms in return for a shipper's commitment. Therefore, shippers stand to benefit.

— *Essential Terms of Service Contracts* – To be filed with FMC and carrier or conference. To include: origin and destination points/ports, commodity/commodities, minimum volume of cargo revenue, contract rate of rate schedule, duration of the contract, service commitments, liquidated damages (does not apply for forest products, recycled metal scrap, waste paper, or paper waste).

— *Service Contracts and Time-Volume Contracts* – Time-volume contracts sanctioned in 1916 Act. Similar regulatory treatment as service contracts by the FMC. Rates may vary with the volume of cargo over a specified period of time.

— *Shippers' Associations* – To improve the small shippers' negotiating position, and protected from antitrust exposure for such negotiations/collective activities.

— *Factors of Importance in Examining the Lawfulness of Associations* – (i) Question of market power. (ii) Composition of the association.

(3) *Changes in Prohibited Acts*

New prohibition: Section 10(b)(9). A carrier may not use a loyalty contract, except in conformity with the antitrust laws (potentially the most significant new prohibition).

Other prohibitions: Section 10(c)(5) – two or more common carriers may not concertedly deny compensation to an ocean freight forwarder (in US export trades). Section 10(b)(13) – a common carrier or a group of common carriers may not refuse to negotiate with a shippers' association. While there are new provisions overall, the 1984 Act's prohibitions do not differ from the prohibitions of the 1916 Act.

As stated, the principal objectives of the Act are the minimisation of government regulation and intervention, and as a consequence the reduction of the costs of shipping regulation. Regulation by government is to be replaced with a more effective regulation by the market place. In other words, reliance in the Act is largely to be placed on regulation by shipper/consignee demand. To this end, shippers/consignees are allowed or in fact encouraged to consult and formulate joint approaches. Similarly, shippers are assisted by statutory requirements such as the clause which requires conferences to provide their members with freedom to take independent action, for example, in response to shipper demands.

The Act explicitly recognises conferences, and introduces substantive and procedural changes in rate filing and other requirements, such as changes in review of multicarrier agreements, including reductions in antitrust considerations in such multicarrier agreements.

Carriers may also receive antitrust immunity for collective setting of rates for through, multimodal, or intermodal transportation. Similarly, antitrust immunity is expanded to cover carriers involved in collective actions.

One purpose in strengthening shippers'/consignees' negotiating powers is to provide some balance to the easing of regulations affecting ship operators.

Intermodal ratemaking

Since the introduction of containerisation in international shipping the advantages of through documentation and through billing of intermodal transport of containers have been recognised and demanded. As shippers showed increased interest in the purchase of through intermodal transportation (often under one management or control), ship operators attempted to incorporate feeder and terminal costs in their quotes. On several occasions the FMC approved conference intermodal even before the 1984 Act provided explicit immunity from antitrust action to intermodal ratemaking. The Justice Department challenged FMC's decisions, and the intermodal agreements were declared moot as the 1916 Act did not resolve the right of carriers to set collectively intermodal through rates.

One of the principal features of the Act of 1984 is the broadened antitrust immunity carriers may receive for the collective setting of intermodal rates, by which rates are quoted for origin to destination, origin to destination port, and loading port to final destination transport. This freedom to set through rates has become a necessary feature of integrated multimodal transportation.

Similarly, collective agreements between carriers on how they will cooperate with each other in rate setting, service, or resource (capacity) allocation are now largely exempt from government regulation under antitrust laws.

Government review of such agreements will, under the Act, be greatly simplified and expedited. As a result, carriers should know relatively quickly if proposed agreements will be allowed by the FMC, to go into effect.

The effect of the ability to enter into intermodal ratemaking agreements is to permit:

(a) better rationalisation of use of transport resources in door-to-door container and trailer transportation
(b) more effective routing of cargo
(c) improved consolidation of services
(d) effective competition with alternative services (such as through shipping services)
(e) greater stability of total door-to-door transport costs, as fluctuations in costs of one modal link are more readily absorbed in total intermodal rate

As a result, intermodal ratemaking is expected to provide both lower total costs to users and higher profits to transport providers.

The effect of the Shipping Act on marine terminal owners and operators

The Shipping Act of 1984 gives specific recognition and definition for Marine Terminal Operators (MTOs). It includes provisions for antitrust immunity for MTOs, but does not provide for any change in FMC's jurisdiction over MTOs and their services. The Act is designed to permit cooperative agreements among MTOs, to fix or establish rates for services, free time, credit terms, as well as all kinds of other arrangements. Antitrust immunity to such agreements is now provided though they must be filed with the FMC as before, and becomes effective 45 days after filing unless additional information is requested or objections are filed and allowed.

The Act provides MTOs with more flexibility in their operations. At the same time certain duties and restrictions are written into the Act, such as the prohibition of boycott or other unreasonable discrimination in the provision of services to any terminal user or shipper. Similarly, penalties for violation of the Act are larger now.

The Act therefore maintains FMC's jurisdiction with some changes in oversights and omissions regarding MTO services.

The Act is expected to effect credit terms offered to and payments made by users as a result of the ability of MTOs to take collective measures or to offer joint services by several MTOs. This may result in greater financial responsibility by terminal users and, as a result, improve the financial conditions of MTOs by improving their cash flow and reducing their risk. At the same time competition among MTOs will only be slightly reduced because of the large number of user operated and proprietary terminals, as well as the inherent competition among MTOs.

In general, the Act should result in greater terminal user responsibility and loyalty, with a resulting impact on greater rationalisation in terminal investment and a higher utilisation of facilities and equipment. This, in turn, should improve the profitabililty of MTOs and allow them to maintain or introduce more advanced technology and operations.

This is particularly appropriate now, when terminal users are increasingly bound together in joint operations and services and the concept of load centring becomes more popular, not only in container shipping but also in general cargo and bulk shipping. In a way the Act provides the MTOs with freedom of operation similar to that provided carriers and now shippers as well.

The economic implications are the potential for greater concentration of terminals, with commercial opportunities because of scale and more equal participation in the market place.

Shippers' agreements

Shippers' negotiating powers are enhanced under the Act by the mandatory right of independent action for conference carriers, the recognition of 'shippers' associations' and the statutory recognition of service contracts in liner operations.

Under the Act, conference members have the right to act independently, which should increase inter-conference competition and greater service flexibility of the conference members. It is also expected to induce independent carriers to join a conference, as under these new rules conference member carriers can better respond to the market place in terms of shipper demands.

The Act stipulates that conference agreements must allow members to take independent action in terms of rates or service, and carriers may under a conference agreement filed with the FMC exercise such a right of independent action within ten days of notice to the conference. The right to independent action applies only to rate of service items which must be filed in a tariff under Section

8(a) of the Act.

Under the Act shippers can talk directly to individual operators to conclude more favourable terms in exchange for volume and/or frequency undertakings. The Act provides for independent action by operators (Section 5(b)(8)) with respect to rate of service items required to be filed in a tariff (Section 8(a)), but the right for independent action does not extend to entering into the service contract. On this point the Act is open in that it does not prohibit independent action with regards to service contracts, but leaves it up to the conference to determine if and on what terms independent action by conference members with respect to service contracts is to be allowed.

Service contracts provide a ratemaking alternative. Under the Act conferences and operators are given statutory authority to enter into service contracts in place of traditional liner ratemaking. Under the Act (Section 8(c)) service contracts are filed confidentially with the FMC, and only their 'essential terms' are to be published in tariff format. The FMC, in fact, introduced interim rulings that such public filing of 'essential terms of service contracts' be part of the operators' or conferences' tariffs. This may be difficult to implement because the definition of 'essential terms' of a service contract is subject to many interpretations. The FMC's interim rules require filed terms to include origin and destination points or ports, commodities covered by contract, minimum volume of cargo at the contract freight rate, contract rate and rate schedule, duration of contract, service commitments, and conditions for liquidated damages or penalties.

The filing requirements do not apply to commodities such as forest products, recycled metal scrap, waste paper or paper waste, etc.

Under the 1916 Act, time/volume contracts between shippers and conferences were specifically sanctioned. Such contracts – similar to service contracts – involve a contractual obligation among the parties. Although such contracts are not mentioned in the 1984 Act, the FMC has decided to treat such contracts as not distinct from service contracts. As a result, conferences are not required to provide its members with the right of independent action with respect to the offering of time/volume contracts.

There is a question though if the FMC will be able to continue to support the conferences' right to regulate independent action of operators with respect to service contracts or time/volume contracts. The US Justice Department appears to be of the opinion that the Act

223

guarantees individual operators the right of independent action at least as far as time/volume contracts are concerned. We will probably witness discussions on this issue which may take some time to resolve.

Service contracts and volume incentives, for example, have already been introduced on the Trans-Pacific trade in response to this change in legislation. While some conferences may restrain their members from negotiating with shippers directly, there appears to be a cautious move in this direction. Service contracts may involve the securing of a certain amount of space at a certain rate for a specified period of time or number of voyages. Most existing service contracts are for periods not exceeding six months, as shippers are usually unwilling to commit themselves for longer periods. This new freedom of direct negotiation between shippers and operators adversely affects smaller shippers who do not have the leverage to negotiate favourable terms. Some way may have to be found to encourage (and permit) smaller shippers to combine their shipments or negotiate as a group.

Another issue is the potential for large differences in outbound and inbound freight rates. For example, shippers in some countries (such as Japan) are often the sellers and ship mostly c.i.f. In other words, they negotiate the freight and as these exporters control larger volumes than say importers in Japan (or in the US for that matter), they are usually able to negotiate much more favourable terms.

Although meetings between conferences or individual operators and shippers are held, they usually only cover service conditions and freight rates. There is an increasing need to also cover issues such as currency exchange rates, credit terms, bunker surcharges (or discounts), congestion charges, and terms and conditions of loyalty contracts. Many conferences (and individual operators) have adopted dual or multiple rate systems, or exclusive-patronage contracts. Freight rate differences of up to 10 per cent between contract and non-contract shippers are often experienced. Shippers are also affected by advance notice of rate changes. While the long-term notice recommendation of the 'UNCTAD Code' is probably unrealistic, one to three month notice is often too little for effective planning by shippers who are sometimes required to bid for one year or longer delivery of goods.

Shippers' associations

The Act recognised that small shippers may require special negotiating powers, *vis-à-vis* conferences or operators, which only an association or grouping of shippers can provide. A provision of the Act provides therefore for statutory recognition of 'shippers' associations' and protection of such associations from antitrust action resulting from collective activities and negotiations performed by such associations.

The Act also prohibits operators (alone or as a conference) from refusing to negotiate with such shippers' associations.

One unresolved issue in this regard is the amount of traffic that shippers' associations should be allowed to control. Market shares have not been defined as yet, and the issue still waits to be resolved.

The composition of shippers' associations is another issue. The US Department of Justice is interested in discouraging competitors in a trade from negotiating jointly with carriers. They do not object to individual shippers' direct negotiations. As a result, while shippers' associations are now legal, and are in fact encouraged, some restrictions on their formation and activities continue.

Changes in prohibited acts

All the US shipping acts include prohibitions and the 1984 Act is no exception. The most important of these is probably the prohibition for operators to use loyalty contracts, unless such contracts are in 'conformity with antitrust laws' (Section 14bg – 1916).

Other prohibited acts concern the 'concerted denial of compensation to an ocean freight forwarder' by two or more operators, or limiting such compensation by concerted action.

Operators and conferences similarly may not refuse to negotiate with shippers or shippers' associations.

Impact of the Act

The basic objectives of the Act were to reduce government regulations of operators by permitting them greater freedom of action within the liner conference system, and increasing the negotiating posture of shippers with operators or conferences so as to allow market forces to play a larger role in ratemaking and service regulation.

The policy is aimed principally at improving the conditions of US liner trades by encouraging more competition and better resource utilisation. It is difficult to predict the impact of the Act on liner shipping in US trades, particularly now, when many liner rates are not compensatory.

The increasing capital intensity of the largely containerised liner shipping in US trades has encouraged both use of very large container vessels to capture economies of scale and use of joint venture or joint service operations. These measures are all aimed at reducing unit costs and have allowed some operators to remain profitable even under the current depressed freight rates. Although open conferences will continue to serve US liner trade, the Act, together with the requirement for open conferences, reduces the functions and powers of conferences. In the future, small numbers of joint ventures or services will serve individual trades, and the identity of individual operators may be submerged under such entities. The right of independent action and negotiation between shippers or shippers' associations and individual operators may become less meaningful as individual operators may be represented by a joint venture of service company in such meetings.

A major impact of the Act is expected to be in the area of inter-modal services, where the Act can beneficially affect both rates and service quality. This, in turn, and in combination with increasing use of service or time/volume contracts, could result in lower total cost of transportation in US liner trades, as larger utilisation of capacity and greater integration as well as coordination of services permits a reduction of rates at profitable levels.

REGISTRATION OF SHIPS AND GROWTH OF NATIONAL SHIPPING

Ships are registered in the registry of particular countries. Such registration usually confers on the ship the right to fly the flag of the country of registry and to protection by the country or registry. Registration is associated with a port of domicile of the ship or home port. Rules for registration of ships differ widely among countries. Some countries, for example the USA, require qualifying ships to be majority owned by US citizens and exclusively manned by US citizens. At the other extreme, there are countries like Panama, Liberia, Honduras, and so forth who require no genuine link between a ship and the country of registry. In other words, ships can be wholly owned, manned, and controlled by foreign nationals, and yet in fact have no role in the trade, transport, or economics of the country of registry. Such countries are often termed nations of open registry conferring flags of convenience.

For many years, UNCTAD has struggled to resolve the issue of ship registration and many nations have demanded a genuine link, such as national ownership, control, and manning as a prerequisite for registry under a flag.

There are many arguments for and against the provision of open registry. While many developing countries blame open registry for loss of employment by their nationals, loss of trading markets of their ships, and reduced safety at sea, others including some major maritime developing countries feel that freedom of registry must be preserved to encourage free competitive trade.

United Nations convention on conditions of registration of ships

The stated purpose of this convention was the introduction of new standards of responsibility and accountability for the world shipping industry, by defining the elements of the 'genuine link' that various international conventions suggested (starting with the 1958 Convention on the High Seas and the 1982 Law of the Sea Convention). While embodied as a concept in various conventions, it had never been defined before, and the question is how will this new convention drafted on 7 February 1986 succeed in defining the concept in a meaningful and implementable manner? The key economic links between ships and a flag state are defined by the convention as the participation of flag state nationals in the manning, ownership, and management of the ships. The convention maintains options between several of the so-called mandatory links, and in particular among ownership and manning.

In addition to the establishment of the links, the convention attempts to introduce improvements in shipping by charging states of registry with:

(1) Financial responsibility of nationals responsible for the management and operations of ships.
(2) Establishment of a 'competent and adequate' national maritime administration.
(3) Safety of ships registered under its flag and the competency

of officers and crews manning ships under its flag.
(4) Identifiability of owners and operators of ships under its flag.
(5) Prevention of pollution by ships under its flag.

The objective of the convention in strengthening the genuine link between states and ships flying its flag and the exercise of effective jurisdiction and control over such ships by the country of registry, while well conceived, may be rather difficult to obtain. Countries of registry are supposed to assure identification and accountability of ship owners and operators for example, yet the provisions allow arm's length type of arrangements. The convention similarly requires manning and/or ownership to provide the genuine link, but both requirements are stated loosely and can be interpreted in different ways.

The most basic issue is the ownership link. As banks usually hold the dominant equity interests in ships, the citizenship of the ship owner should really not be considered the genuine link as his interest in the ships' equity may be as little as 5 to 10 per cent.

A similar problem arises in the area of management as the 'nationality' of management is readily subject to many interpretations. Is it the nationality of the management company or firm? The citizenship of its principal officers of the company or firm? The place of the principal offices of the company or firm? Or a combination of them all? The convention talks of a ship-owning company (or a subsidiary of a ship-owning company) established or having its principal place of business in the country of registry in accordance with its laws and regulations.

Manning is probably the most easily identifiable link, but even there problems arise as many countries convey temporary or permanent residence to persons of particular skills or qualifications and allow such persons to be considered nationals for purposes of establishment of a genuine link.

The effectiveness of the convention in resolving the issue of a genuine link between flag state and ships registered under their flag is doubtful, particularly as ships remain easily transferred assets.

The effect of registry under a flag on the national economy, balance of payment, and employment of nationals remains elusive. The convention provides a first attempt at establishing some measures of a genuine link between a country of registry and the ship, yet few believe that it will accomplish basic objectives such as growth of developing country fleets, better ownership accountability, and so forth.

228

There are many developed and developing country-owned ships that cannot operate economically under their own flag or where registration under the national flag would cause difficulty in ship financing, manning, or management.

Even if the traditional flags of convenience or open registry were to be abolished, other nations would probably offer similar terms of registry under a different disguise.

Nations deemed to offer open registry are, as a result, difficult to define. Various international agencies for example have differed over the years on which countries should be so defined. At some time or other, countries like the UK, Singapore, Cyprus, Lebanon, Liberia, Panama, Honduras, Costa Rica, Bermuda, Moldives, Bahamas, Oman, Vanuatu, and so forth have all been considered countries with open registries, but this list changes over time as well as a result of the perspective of the reviewer.

CABOTAGE AND DOMESTIC SHIPPING

Coastal and inter-island domestic trade has traditionally been protected under cabotage or other laws which restrict access to this trade to national shipping. In some cases the restriction is even more rigid when the trade is reserved to only certain segments of national shipping. In many countries, for example, national shipping engaged in international trade may not engage interchangeably in domestic trade such as coastal traffic. Although domestic shipping offers many economic advantages, requires comparatively small investments, uses largely low level technology and provides flexible transport and distribution capacity, few developing countries have developed this transport sector effectively.

In fact in most developing countries, domestic – including coastal, inter-island, and inland – water shipping has fallen in disuse. The average age of vessels employed is extremely high, port and other facilities are in disarray, dredging and river training is largely discontinued, with a resulting decline of the whole domestic shipping industry in terms of capacity and service.

Considering the eleven developing countries with the largest domestic fleets, it is noted (Table 6.1) that over 54.8 per cent of their fleet is 15 years or older and 36.7 per cent is 20 years or older. If we consider the domestic fleets of all developing countries, the average age is even higher (17.6 years). Equally important is the lack of effective maintenance of many domestically used vessels,

Table 6.1: Number of vessels (steam and motor) under 3,999 grt, from selected countries over 15 and 20 years old in 1984. (Vessels under 100 grt excluded)

Country	Total	20+ years	%	15+ years	%
Algeria	97	7	7.2	8	8.2
Argentina	375	190	50.7	258	68.8
Brazil	427	179	41.9	214	50.1
India	377	91	24.1	157	41.6
Indonesia	1,388	514	37.0	685	49.3
Korea (South)	1,518	412	27.1	901	59.4
Malaysia	360	124	34.4	185	51.4
Mexico	557	89	16.0	133	23.9
Philippines	775	344	44.4	546	70.5
Turkey	637	207	32.5	285	44.7
Venezuela	196	72	36.7	102	52.0

Source: Lloyd's *Register of Shipping*, 1984

which often are subject to little if any safety and other inspection.

Although coastal vessels (100 to 3,990 grt) comprise only 52 per cent of the total number and 11 per cent of the capacity of the world seagoing fleet (100 grt plus), they accounted for over 89 per cent of the ship casualties in recent years. In most countries, access to coastal shipping is not only restricted to nationally owned and manned vessels, but also often to vessels built domestically and licensed to serve particular domestic routes. In some countries, some domestic trade is reserved exclusively for government owned vessels. Most developing countries restrict entry into coastal shipping and have mandatory licensing and registration requirements. Licensing furthermore may restrict use of vessels not only to certain routes and services, but also carriage of a restricted number of goods at prescribed frequencies of service. Similarly, rates are often set by government.

Many countries have, in recent years, recognised the great contribution domestic shipping can make to economic development. The industrialised nations of the OECD, for example, have encouraged large expansion of domestic shipping, including coastal barging. To encourage such expansion though requires changes in restrictive policies affecting rates, entry, merger, registration and licensing.

NATIONAL SHIPPING – OWNERSHIP AND CONTROL

Recent international agreements, as well as national legislation, in different countries refers to national shipping and confers various rights, benefits, and duties to it. In only a few examples is national shipping explicitly defined. In fact, it appears that politicians and legislators purposely define national shipping in rather loose terms subject to various interpretations. This has resulted in many problems as well as often unexpected opportunities for ship operators. National shipping can be defined in a number of ways. The most restrictive definition would be shipping owned and manned by citizens of the country, operating in the trade of the country, under the control of an entity owned and registered in the country.

PROTECTIONISM IN NON-LINER SHIPPING

Protectionism in bulk shipping is often based on a desire for self-reliance, control of shipping rates, and of terms of trade. The difficulty is that most developing countries are exporters of bulk goods in oversupplied buyers' markets. Buyers, as a result, often not only select or determine the terms of trade but also choose and control shipping used in the trade. This situation has, in recent years, stymied attempts by developing countries to introduce cargo reservation or other protective measures into the bulk shipping market. At the same time, it is recognised that developing countries as a group (excluding countries with open registry) control a disproportionately small share of bulk shipping (15.9 per cent in 1984, most of which was controlled by Asian LDCs). Other factors weakening the prospects of demands for greater protectionism in the bulk shipping trades are (as discussed in Chapters 1 and 2) a growing trend toward partial or total processing of bulk materials by producers. Many LDCs face the dilemma of conflict between a policy of benefiting from greater added value of exports versus larger revenues from shipping. Trends in the shipping markets also indicate that developing countries will not acquire a larger share of bulk tonnage in the near term. The distribution of both newbuilding bulk deliveries as well as second-hand bulk tonnage acquired by LDCs has been under 10 per cent of world total since 1982, when 12.1 per cent of all newbuilding deliveries and 11.8 per cent of all bulk carrier newbuilding deliveries were made to developing countries (all in grt).

The question is, therefore, what purpose would international agreements or national legislation protecting developing country bulk shipping serve?

THE FUTURE OF THE CODE OF CONDUCT OF LINER CONFERENCES

Although the Code entered into force in October 1983, when an adequate number of countries signed the agreement, serious questions regarding its future have been raised. A number of agreeing countries have done so only conditionally, while many others have reinterpreted many aspects of the Code. As a result, there is little conformity even among agreeing parties on the terms and conditions of the Code. In fact a number of agreeing countries have enacted legislation which extends, modifies, or reinterprets terms of the Code, and several agreeing countries have introduced unilateral or bilateral cargo reservation and other protectionist measures not in strict conformity with the terms of the Code. In addition, as noted before, the US (a non-agreeing party) by enactment of the Shipping Act of 1984 has introduced measures which severely affect the functioning of conferences operating in the US liner trades by curtailing their powers of rate setting.

By mid-1986 over 57 per cent of all liner cargo in US liner trades moved at negotiated and not conference rates (usually under shipper-operator negotiated service contracts). Similar approaches are now under consideration in trades between other countries. This development may affect the future of liner conferences as we know them today, and result in new types of operator associations.

Returning to the Code, the introduction of unilateral legislative actions by agreeing parties which deviate widely from the terms of the Code are seriously undermining this agreement. The Code is firmly based on the concept of closed conferences which is – by many – considered obsolete. Closed conferences are oligopolistic and depend on strict adherence to its rules by conference members.

Even before the US enacted the Shipping Act of 1984, which introduced the mandatory right of independent action (or directly negotiated rates) by individual conference members – which as discussed has greatly weakened the open conferences serving US liner trade, penetration by non-conference operators in major liner trades had become significant; Table 6.2 indicates that well over 36

Table 6.2: Non-conference penetration in major liner trades (per cent of traffic carried by non-conference operators)

Route	1980*	1983**
Transpacific	30	35–50
Far East – Europe	19	30–40
Transatlantic	28	50
Europe – Australia	10	20
Far East – Australia	–	30
South Europe – East Africa	3	0+

* 'The Competitive Dynamics of Container Shipping', University of Liverpool, Marine Transport Centre, Liverpool
** Extracted by author from data published in *Fairplay* and *Journal of Commerce* articles

per cent of liner trades worldwide were carried by non-conference operators. The situation appears to have stabilised somewhat, particularly in the US-transpacific and transatlantic trades, but it is difficult to verify if this is the result of the new rate-setting freedom provided to operators in these trades by the US Shipping Act of 1984 or a lessening of competition. Continuous overtonnaging appears to induce independents to compete with established conferences. Similarly, fleets of socialist countries will probably maintain their practice of offering non-conference liner services on selective conference routes and thereby destabilise the conference system. This is done notwithstanding the avowed support by socialist countries of the UNCTAD Code and its provisions under which conferences have exclusive access to liner trade.

The future of the Code is therefore in some doubt as nations and their operators search for ways to maintain more effective participation in liner trade and a more efficient rationalised approach to liner shipping operations.

7

Future Prospects of Shipping

GENERAL

Shipping is developing an increasingly global and integrated transport perspective. After serving colonial shipping expansion of Great Britain, France, Spain, Japan, etc. for many years, it became a principal tool of economic expansion of countries such as the USA and Great Britain before World War II and Japan after World War II. Shipping nationalism formed part of these developments throughout history but has become a more specific objective of newly independent countries who consider national shipping not only a prestigious and an effective shortcut to industrial and economic prowess, but also a tool of economic and political influence.

The global world recession, debt crisis, and stagnation of LDC development affects shipping not only in terms of inadequate demand but is expected to have a longer term impact. The narrow perspectives of shipping nationalism – which advocate shipping protection and support on a national scale – are running into problems.

Both the objectives and needs of most countries, particularly of most developing countries, have become much more complex to allow simplistic solutions such as cargo reservations. The economic objectives of countries can no longer be universally advanced by reserving cargo to national shipping. These objectives may, for example, be better served by processing the previously exported material for domestic use (instead of re-import of finished goods) with only a fraction of the previous export volumes traded, and now handled as semi-finished or finished goods. In turn, these would probably be shipped in different forms and to different markets. In other words, total national economic objective global perspective now replaces the narrow national shipping perspectives of many countries.

INTERNATIONAL SHIPPING POLICY

While national shipping policy is usually designed to satisfy the perceived interest of a country or power group within a country, international shipping policy should satisfy the interests of a majority of countries of a rule or policymaking organisation. As developing countries have the majority of votes in all such bodies, international shipping policymaking is usually skewed towards perceived LDC interests, notwithstanding the fact that these countries account for less than 41.1 per cent of the volume and 14.9 per cent of the value of world seaborne trade.

Attempts are often made to achieve a compromise between the national interests and international regulations, but in recent years the differences have become much more focused and have resulted in four major policy groupings – developing, advanced developing, socialist, and developed countries. International shipping policy increasingly emphasises the political interests of nations instead of their public, economic, resource use rationalisation interests, and concern with the standards of service quality.

The prospects for greater cooperation in international shipping policymaking are not good, yet with shipping increasingly more integrated, operational cooperation will become essential. It is likely that nations and their operators will increasingly enter into informal and purely commercial arrangements and ignore the increasingly irrelevant or inapplicable international shipping policies. The exception will be in the area of shipping safety and environmental regulation where near consensus has been reached.

OPERATIONAL PROSPECTS

Economies of scale in ship design or size will be largely replaced by economies of scale of integrated ship operations. As noted before, an increasing percentage of world tonnage is now owned and/or operated by government, industrial company, or integrated trading or transport company owned enterprises. The participation of specialised ship operator companies will decline in world shipping not only in the bulk but also in the liner trades.

Considering container shipping, an increasing percentage of capacity is concentrated in very large container ships. In fact, ships of 2,400 TEU plus capacity are expected to comprise over 36 per cent of total world mainline container shipping capacity by 1988.

At the other extreme, a resurgence of specialised container feeder vessels with capacities of 200 to 600 TEUs is expected. These vessels will serve transshipment of containers to and from very large container ships at load centre ports.

Load centre ports have become a controversial subject, particularly after the introduction of the round-the-world (RTW) container ship service by operators like Evergreen, US Lines, and others. Yet the use of this concept is irreversible and will eventually benefit both ports and operators by distributing part of the sea transport cost savings arising from the economies of scale of very large container ships to feeder and transshipment ports as well as feeder transport operators. Feeder ports would normally continue to maintain their traffic share but serve feeder instead of mainline vessels. Increased service frequency and quality should increase traffic through feeder ports. Transshipment load centre ports would benefit from the addition of feeder service.

This concept has been in use in other trades such as coal import trade to Japan, oil import to UK (Bantry Bay), and other bulk trades for a long time. It not only assures economic transportation, but also reduces requirements for investment in fixed port and channel dredging, etc. In the long run this concept is expected to greatly reduce the wasteful duplication in port improvements, many of which do not generate adequate traffic to pay for the investment as they are often based on the assumption that the new facilities will attract traffic which competing ports expect to attract with their new investments.

As a result it is expected that before the end of this century, load centre type of operations with feeder-mainline transshipment will become common in all large volume distance trades. Feeder transport will often be performed by integrated tug-barge combinations with drop and swap operations. Barges will then provide facilities for temporary inventory (stacking, silo, holding, and so forth) operations which should reduce port cargo handling and storage systems requirements.

Another expected development is increased use of offshore (artificial island) type ports as major load centre transshipment facilities. Multipurpose ships, particularly self-sustaining bulk carriers with deck-mounted containers and/or Ro–Ro storage facilities, will probably become increasingly popular in North-South trades between developed and developing countries.

INSTITUTIONAL PROSPECTS

Notwithstanding the increase in public shipping nationalism voiced at international meetings, there is evidence that shipping – including liner shipping – is becoming more and more international. National shipping companies increasingly enter into joint venture, joint service, or other international cooperative shipping agreements. It is expected that world shipping will become much more internationalised before the year 2000 as governments and operators recognise the benefits of integration of shipping, international cooperation in transport, pooling of resources, complementation of capabilities, and more.

This trend will be accelerated by the EDP (Electronic Data Processing) revolution in information handling, automated funds transfer, and use of expert systems and other computer-aided management approaches which can be expected to allow effective real time total systems management of integrated shipping and intermodal operations.

Through-transport management from origin to final destination will become common and will include cargo routing and form changes to accomplish the overall origin to destination transport more efficiently. The objective is obviously delivery at the best combination of total cost and time and assured reliability of service. Shippers are mainly interested in this overall objective and increasingly emphasise their lack of interest in modal link efficiency or special terms offered by modal operators.

This trend is expected to encompass practically all major trades and commodities. As noted earlier, shippers are particularly concerned with the high cost, large time loss, and lack of accountability at intermodal transfer links. It is they who therefore encourage integrated management of intermodal transport. Intermodal interface costs in trades vary between 30 to 52 per cent in origin to destination container transport, 42 to 67 per cent in origin to destination general cargo transport, and 20 to 34 per cent in origin to destination bulk transport, excluding lost time which varies from a fraction to a multiple of productive transport time, and added significant additional costs to the shipper.

Integrated intermodal transportation can reduce interface costs and time loss by 50 per cent or more while increasing transport system and interface terminal or link resource utilisation. With origin to destination transport costs in excess of 18.9 per cent of the value of world trade (7.4 per cent of the value of world trade is consumed by shipping freight charges), total transport cost of world trade could be significantly reduced by more effective intermodal integration. This process is well underway in OECD trade, but little progress has been achieved in this direction in the trades of developing countries which spent as much as 80 per cent more than developed countries for transport of their international trade (in value of trade terms). While this is partially due to the fact that the value of trade of developing countries is less than half that of developed nations in terms of value per unit weight or volume of cargo, the lack of effective moves towards intermodal integration does play an important role.

REGULATORY AND TRAINING DEVELOPMENTS

International standard setting and regulation has been most successful in the areas of safety, pollution prevention, and qualification of ship manning. This is largely due to the leading role played by IMO which has been able to obtain wide agreement to its rules and standards. It is expected that international design and operational standards will be accepted, ratified, and enforced by nearly all maritime nations before the year 2000. Similarly, universal standards of training, qualification (experience), examination, and rank will also be in force by that time. This may permit more effective transfer of seagoing staff among vessels registered under different flags, and the establishment of worldwide registry of seafaring licensees. It may also allow more effective development of regional instead of national maritime training centres. The traditional 'Merchant Marine Academies' are under pressure to upgrade their curricula and many have developed university-type degree programmes.

At the same time the majority of these schools suffer under overcapacity and a lack of capability to develop and teach increasingly more advanced and technical subjects. Regional integration of merchant ship officer training under international supervision appears to be an attractive solution, particularly if combined with the training of shipping management personnel.

Appendix A

Typical Ship Operating Costs

Table A.1: Containers – 1984 vessel operating costs
(per one way voyage)

		UK-HK 2800TEU-7200MI		UK-USEC 2800TEU-3300MI	
		Total ($1,000)	Per TEU ($/TEU)	Total ($1,000)	Per TEU ($/TEU)
Orig-dest.*	Oper. cost	248.34	88.69	151.72	54.19
	Cap. cost	246.72	88.11	150.73	53.83
	Fuel cost	249.17	88.99	115.90	41.39
	Total cost	744.23	265.80	418.35	149.41
	Adj. T.C.		441.89		248.40
Dest-orig.	Oper. cost	178.36	63.70	81.74	29.19
	Cap. cost	177.21	63.29	81.21	29.00
	Fuel cost	246.04	87.87	112.76	40.27
	Total cost	601.61	214.86	275.71	98.47
	Adj. T.C.		357.21		163.70

		UK-AG 2800TEU-6500MI		UK-AUS 2800TEU-11,200MI	
		Total ($1,000)	Per TEU ($/TEU)	Total ($1,000)	Per TEU ($/TEU)
Orig-dest.*	Oper. cost	228.44	81.59	347.42	24.08
	Cap. cost	226.95	81.05	345.15	123.27
	Fuel cost	221.73	79.19	385.85	137.80
	Total cost	677.12	241.83	1078.42	385.15
	Adj. T.C.		402.04		640.31
Dest. orig.	Oper. cost	158.46	56.59	277.45	90.09
	Cap. cost	157.43	56.23	275.63	98.44
	Fuel cost	218.59	78.07	382.72	136.99
	Total cost	534.48	190.89	935.8	334.21
	Adj. T.C.		317.35		555.63

From 'Shipcost' IBRD 1985. Excludes any port charges
* Origin/destination costs include port time costs at both origin and destination ports

Table A.2: Dry bulk carriers – 1984 vessel operating costs (per one way voyage)

		USG-JAP 30K-9000MI Grain		HR-JAP 55K-13,100MI Coal		BRAZ-UK 90K-4200MI Iron Ore		LAGOS-HAMB 75K-3000MI Iron Ore	
		Total ($1,000)	Per DWT ($/DWT)	Total ($1,000)	Per DWT ($/DWT)	Total ($1,000)	Per DWT ($/DWT)	Total ($1,000)	Per DWT ($/DWT)
Orig-dest.*	Oper. cost	128.94	4.30	189.90	3.45	89.99	1.00	70.62	0.94
	Cap. cost	65.02	2.17	118.79	2.16	72.11	0.80	53.83	0.72
	Fuel cost	201.94	6.73	445.75	8.10	185.00	2.06	182.28	2.43
	Total cost	395.9	13.20	754.44	13.72	347.1	3.86	306.73	4.09
Dest-orig.	Oper. cost	105.46	3.52	164.05	2.98	61.90	0.69	42.34	0.56
	Cap. cost	53.18	1.77	102.61	1.87	49.60	0.55	32.27	0.43
	Fuel cost	182.52	6.08	406.71	7.39	166.90	1.85	108.09	1.44
	Total cost	341.16	11.37	673.37	12.24	278.4	3.09	182.7	2.44

From 'Shipcost' IBRD 1985. Excludes any port charges
* Origin/destination costs include port time costs at both origin and destination ports

Table A.3: Tankers – 1984 vessel operating costs (per one way voyage)

		VENEZ-NY 85K-3700MI		LAGOS-UK 85K-3000MI		LAGOS-NY 85K-3400MI		INDON-LA 85K-7700MI		AG-JAP 85K-6200MI	
		Total ($1,000)	Per DWT ($/DWT)	Total ($1,000)	Per DWT ($/DWT)	Total ($1,000)	Per DWT ($/DWT)	Total ($1,000)	Per DWT ($/DWT)	Total ($1,000)	Per DWT ($/DWT)
Orig-dest.*	Oper. cost	72.34	0.85	60.67	0.71	65.22	0.77	138.76	1.63	113.88	1.34
	Cap. cost	63.33	0.75	53.25	0.63	53.48	0.63	121.80	1.43	99.96	1.18
	Fuel cost	148.63	1.75	120.63	1.42	136.54	1.61	307.90	3.62	248.23	2.92
	Total cost	284.3	3.34	234.55	2.76	255.24	3.00	568.46	6.69	462.07	5.44
Dest-orig.	Oper. cost	56.2	0.66	45.55	0.54	51.67	0.61	116.94	1.38	94.16	1.11
	Cap. cost	49.33	0.58	39.98	0.47	45.36	0.53	102.64	1.21	82.65	0.97
	Fuel cost	134.79	1.59	109.24	1.29	123.93	1.46	280.44	3.30	225.82	2.66
	Total cost	240.32	2.83	194.77	2.29	220.96	2.60	500.02	5.88	402.63	4.74

From 'Shipcost' IBRD 1985. Excludes any port charges
* Origin/destination costs include port time costs at both origin and destination ports

Table A.4: General cargo vessels – 1984 vessel operating costs

	16,000 DWT	28,000 DWT
Annual Operating Cost ($1,000)		
– with crew cost	1,359	1,580
– without crew cost	562	783
Annual Capital Cost ($1,000)	530	976
Fuel in Port ($1,000/day)	0.3	0.4
Fuel at Sea ($1,000/day)	9.8	12.6
$/DWT/Month – without fuel	9.83	7.6
$/DWT/Month – without fuel		
without crew	5.68	5.23
Typical Costs (excluding port charges)		
5 days port/25 days sea	25.24	18.93
10 days port/20 days sea	22.28	16.75

Appendix B

United Nations Convention on International Multimodal Transport of Goods

On 24 May 1980, a United Nations conference, under the auspices of UNCTAD, adopted, after seven years of negotiations, the United Nations Convention on International Intermodal Transport of Goods. The new instrument, which will be open for signature in New York from 1 September 1980 to 31 August 1981 and will remain open for accession thereafter, will enter into force internationally when 30 states have become contracting parties either by definitive signature, ratification, or accession.

The new Convention describes the various terms used in international multimodal transport and the persons involved in multimodal transport operations. The Convention, *inter alia*:

(1) Defines the Multimodal Transport Document (MTD) which, either in negotiable or non-negotiable form, contains particulars concerning:
   (a) the general nature of the goods, the leading marks for their identification, the information on the quality and quantity of the goods and their apparent conditions;
   (b) information on the place of taking in charge and delivery of the goods;
   (c) information on the journey route, the various modes of transport, places of transshipment, etc.;
(2) Indicates the basis, period, and limitation of the liabilities of the multimodal transport operator (MTO) and the responsibilities of the consignee.
(3) Describes the procedures for claims and actions, the limitations of actions, the juridical proceedings and possibilities and basis for arbitration relating to international multimodal transport.

(4) Indicates, in its annex, the customs transit procedure relating to the international multimodal transport of goods.

The Convention is a complement to unitisation in the sense that it permits full advantage to be taken of through multimodal transport. It introduces one agreed system of 'through liability' over the existing unimodal regimes, in which liability was segmented, each unimodal carrier being responsible for his own stage of journey. With the new Convention, the multimodal transport operator (MTO) is responsible for the goods for the entire transport from the time the MTO takes them in charge until delivery, irrespective of the modes of transport that may be involved.

Notes

Chapter 2: Institutional, Policy, and Regulatory Issues

1. UNCTAD, 'United Nations Conference of Plenipotentiaries on a Code of Conduct for Liner Conferences'. Vol. II, 1979, Final Act No. E.T.S.II. p. 12.

2. These include for example, countries such as Benin, Cameroon, Gabon, the Ivory Coast, Morocco, Senegal, Togo, Zaire, Bangladesh, Sri Lanka, Chile, Cuba, Mexico, Peru, Venezuela, and the People's Republic of China. Source: Shipping Division, Transport Department, 1985, OECD.

3. Wijkman, P.M. 'Effects of Cargo Reservation'. *Marine Policy*, October 1980.

4. Vanags, A.H. 'Flag Discrimination: An Economic Analysis'. *Maritime Studies and Management*, 1973.

5. Sturmey, S.G. 'The Development of the Code of Conduct for Liner Conferences'. *Marine Policy*, April 1979.

6. Heaver, T.D. 'A Theory of Shipping Conference Pricing and Policies'. *Maritime Studies and Management*, November 1973.

7. Laing, E.T. 'The Rationality of Conference Pricing and Output Policies'. *Maritime Studies and Management*, No. 1975 and No. 3, 1976.

8. Bennathan, E. and Walters, A.A. *The Economics of Ocean Freight Rates*. Praeger, New York, 1969.

9. Bohme, Hans. 'The Changing Framework of Shipping: Trends in Trade, Technology, and Policies'. *Marine Policy*, July 1984.

10. Devanney, J.W., Livanos, V.M., and Stewart, R.J. 'Conference Ratemaking and the West Coast of South America'. *Journal of Transportation Economics and Policy*, May 1975.

11. Ellsworth, R.A. 'Competition or Rationalization in the Liner Industry'. *Journal of Maritime Law and Commerce*, Vol. 10, No. 4, 1979.

12. Frankel *et al.* 'Impact of Cargo Sharing on U.S. Liner Trade'. *Marine Policy*, January 1981.

13. Frankel *et al.* 'Bilateral Agreements in Liner Trades - The Case of the U.S./Brazil-Argentina Liner Trade'. *Federal Maritime Commission Report*, 82--3.

14. Goss, R O. *Shipping and Competition Policy*. University of Wales,

Institute of Science and Technology, Cardiff, September 1982.

15. Goss, R.O. 'Economics and the International Regime for Shipping'. *Maritime Policy and Management*, Vol. II, 1984.

16. Goss, R.O. *Studies in Maritime Economist*. Cambridge University Press, London, 1978.

17. Davis, J.E. 'The Economics of Open Conferences'. *Marine Policy and Management*, Vol. 7, 1980.

18. Walgreen, J.A. 'Liner Nationality and Steamship Conference Ratemaking'. *Journal of Industrial Economics*, 1969.

19. Devanney, J.W., Livanos, V.M., and Stewart, R.J. 'Conference Ratemaking and the West Coast of South America'. *Journal of Transport Economics and Policy*, May 1975.

20. Zerby, J.A. 'On the Practicality of the UNCTAD 40-40-20 Liner Code of Conduct for Liner Conferences'. *Maritime Policy and Management*, 1979.

21. UNCTAD. 'The Liner Conference System'. Geneva, 1970.

22. This does not apply to Argentinian pools. There the national flag lines may carry more than their allotted 80 per cent.

23. 46 Code of Federal Regulations, US Government, §522.2(a)(3).

24. Joint service agreements between common carriers in the US foreign trade are subject to Section 15 of the Shipping Act of 1916 (46 USC 814, 1976). The agreements must be filed with and approved by the FMC before they become effective. There are presently 12 joint service agreements covering the US-Far East Trade on file with the FMC.

25. In the US such notice must be given to the FMC.

26. For the text of the UNCTAD Code, see UN Conference of Plenipotentiaries on a Code of Conduct for Liner Conferences, Vol. LL Final Act. No. E.T.S.II.D.12.

27. 'The Implementation of the UN Code of Conduct for Liner Conferences: A Study of U.S. Options'. TRC, Inc., Washington, 1981, p. 2.

28. *Aide memoire* of the EEC regarding 28/6/82 negotiations, p. 6.

29. Frankel, E.G. 'Tonnage Redistribution Requirements Under Cargo Sharing', Internal Working Study, World Bank, 1985.

30. Shrier, E. 'Implementation of Rationalized Ocean Liner Service'. US Federal Maritime Commission Report No. 3–195, June 1980.

31. Shrier, E. 'Implementation of Rationalized Ocean Liner Service'. US Federal Maritime Commission Report No. 3–195, June 1980.

32. Binkley, John. 'The Possible Effect of Rationalization on Maritime Fuel Consumption'. Webb Institute of Naval Architecture for US Maritime Administration. NTIS, 1975.

33. Hapag-Lloyd A.G., Corporate Planning Department. 'Comparison of Open and Coordinated Competition on the North Atlantic Container Trade'. Hamburg, 1976.

34. Gilman, S., Maggs, R.P., and Ryder, S. *Containers on the North Atlantic: An Economic Analysis of Ships and Routes*. University of Liverpool, Marine Transport Centre, Liverpool, 1977.

35. Bast, G.H. and Keist, M.C. of the Royal Netherlands Ship Association. 'Cost Consequences of Cargo Reservation in The Future of Liner Shipping'. Bremen: Institute of Shipping Economics, 1976.

Chapter 3: Trade and Economic Development

1. 'Shipping in the Contexts of Services and the Development Process', UNCTAD, 1984, TD/B/10/3.
2. Button, K.J. *Transport Economics*. Heinemann, London, 1982.
3. Bos, M.C. and Koyek, L.M. 'The Appraisal of Road Construction Projects', *Review of Economics and Statistics*, Vol. 43, 1961.
4. Friedlander, N.F. *The Interstate Highway System: A Study of Public Investments*. North Holland, Amsterdam, 1965.

Chapter 4: Financing, Revenues, and Costs of Shipping

1. Banking Survey: Shipping Loans. Drewry Shipping Consultants Limited, London, December 1982.
2. 'Nautical Upheaval: Shipping firms are hit by shake-out as rates drop'. *Wall Street Journal*, 5 November 1985.
3. Recent terms extended for newbuildings in Korea and Japan.
4. Brown & Son, Investment Portfolios in Shipping of US Banking, Internal Memorandum, 5 July 1985.
5. Japan Maritime Research Institute, Ship Finance, JAMRI Report No. 12, November 1985.
6. Davis, G.M. and Combs, L.J. 'Some Observations Regarding Value of Service Pricing in Transportation'. *Transportation Journal*, Vol. 14, 1975.
7. Laing, E.T. 'The Rationality of Conference Pricing and Output Policies — Part I and II'. *Maritime Studies and Management*, No. 3, 1975 and No. 3, 1976.
8. Sturmey, S.G. *Shipping Economics: Collected Papers*. Macmillan Press, London, 1975.
9. Davis, J.E. 'The Economics of Open Conference Systems'. *Maritime Policy and Management*, Vol. 7, 1982.
10. Devanney, J.W., Livanos, V.M., and Stewart, R.J. 'Conference Ratemaking and the West Coast of South America'. Technical Report 72–1 MIT, Commodity Transportation and Economic Development Laboratory.
11. In liner shipping the cost of shipping quantity x_{ij} is equal to a large fixed cost plus a small variable cost and therefore $C(x_{ij}) = F + Vx_{ij}$ where F = fixed cost and V = variable cost.
12. Bennathan, E. and Walters, A.A. *The Economics of Ocean Freight Rates*. Oxford University Press, Oxford, 1969.
13. Marx, D. *International Shipping Cartels*. Princeton University Press, Princeton, New Jersey, 1953.
14. Thornburn, T. 'Supply and Demand of Water Transport'. The Business Research Institute — The Stockholm School of Economics, Stockholm, 1969.
15. Eriksen, E. *et al. Freight Market and Trade Patterns*. Institute for Shipping Research, Bergen, 1977.
16. Devanney, J.W. 'A Model of the Tanker Charter Market and a Related Dynamic Program' in Lorange and Norman (ed.), *Shipping

Management, Bergen, 1973.

17. Eriksen, E. *et al*. *Ecotank: An Econometric Model*. Institute for Shipping Research, Bergen, 1978.

18. A futures contract is a firm legal agreement between a buyer (or seller) and an established exchange in which the parties agree to take (or make) delivery of shipping services (or capacity) at a specified price at the end of (or during) a designated period of time.

19. Arnold, J.H. and Chang, Y.W. 'Ship Cost — A Vessel and Voyage Costing Model for Project Appraisal'. World Bank, Washington, DC, September 1985.

20. Bennathan, E. and Walters, A.A. *The Economics of Ocean Freight Rates*. Praeger, London, 1969.

Chapter 5: Shipping Operations and Management

1. Adapted from presentation by author at 'Transmat Conference' at Kuala Lumpur, Malaysia, April 1986.

2. Staggers Act – Motor Carriers Act of 1980.

3. Shipping Act of 1984.

4. *Ex parte* 230 Proceedings.

Chapter 6: Shipping Policy Initiatives

1. Public Law No. 98–237.98 stat 67.47, US Congress app #1701 *et seq*, referred to as S.47, the Act of the '1984 Act'.

References

Abrahamsson, J. (1980) *International Ocean Shipping: Current Concepts and Principles*, Westview Press

Abrahamsson, B.J. (1977) 'The Marine Environment and Ocean Shipping: Some Implications for a New Law of the Sea', *International Organization* (Spring)

Abrahamsson, B.J. (1969) 'A Model of Liner Price Setting', *Journal of Transport Economics*

Abrahamsson, B.J. (1972) 'Liner and Tramp Rates', *Journal of the Israel Shipping Research Institute* (Winter)

Alexanderson, G., and Norstrom, G. (1963) *World Shipping*, John Wiley & Sons, New York

Athay, Robert E. (1972) *The Economics of Soviet Merchant Shipping Policy*, Oxford University Press, Oxford

Barker, J., and Brandwein, Robert (1970) *The U.S. Merchant Marine in National Perspective*, D.C. Heath & Company, Lexington, Mass.

Barros, J. and Johnston, D.M. (1974) *The International Law of Pollution*, Free Press, New York

Bennathan, E., and Walters, A.A. (1979) *Port Pricing and Investment Policy for Developing Countries*, Oxford University Press, Oxford

Bennathan, E., and Walters, A.A. (1969) *The Economics of Ocean Freight Rates*, Praeger, New York

Bes, J. (1975) *Chartering and Shipping Terms*, 7th edn, W.S. Heinemann, New York

Bilder, A.W. (1970/1) The Canadian Arctic Waters Pollution Prevention Act: New Study on the Law of the Sea, 69 Mich. L. Rev. 1

BIMCO Bulletin (1983) 'Memorandum of Agreement', Copenhagen

Blackwell, Robert J. (1974) 'Implementation of the Merchant Marine Act of 1970', *Journal of Maritime Law and Commerce* (January)

Blood, D. (1972) *Inland Waterway Policy in the U.S.* (February 1972)

Boczek, B.A. (1962) *Flags of Convenience: An International Legal Study*, Harvard University Press, Cambridge, Mass.

Bohme, Hans (1984) 'The Changing Framework of Shipping: Trends in Trade, Technology and Policies', *Marine Policy* (July)

Bosies, Jr., William J. and Green, William G. (1974) 'The Liner
Conference Convention: Launching An International Regulatory
Regime', *Law and Policy in International Business*, The International
Journal of Georgetown University Law Center, Vol. 6, No. 2 (Spring)

Branch, Alan E. (1977) *The Elements of Shipping*, 4th edn, Chapman &
Hall, London

British Shipping Laws. Stevens & Sons, various years, London. (This is a
set of volumes each by a different author on a different subject. Volume
13 gives much information on international organisations and classification agencies in shipping.)

Bross, S. (1956) *Ocean Shipping*, Cornell Maritime Press, Cambridge, Md.

Bush, William L. (1972) 'Steamship Conference Contract Rate Agreements
and the Dual Rate System', *I.C.C. Practitioner's Journal*, (November–
December)

Canadian Transport Commission (1976) *Study of the Economic Implications
of the International Convention on a Code of Conduct for Liner
Conferences*, Ottawa, ESAB 76–13 (February)

Churchill, R., and Nordquist, M. (1973) *New Directions in the Law of the
Sea*, Dobbs Ferry, New York and Oceana Publications. (This set, in
many volumes, gives the original texts of conventions and amendments.)

Cohen, D., and Schneerson, D. (1976) 'The Domestic Resource Costs of
Establishing or Expanding a National Fleet', *Maritime Studies and
Management*, No. 4

Comité Maritime International. *International Conventions on Maritime
Law*. Secretariat of the International Maritime Committee, 17
Borzestraat, B2000 Antwerp, Belgium, 1982

Comment (1941) Regulation of Water Carriers by the Interstate Commerce
Commission, 50 Yale L.J. 654

Committee of American Steamship Lines (1964/5) *Studies Re-examining
National Maritime Policies and Requirements*, 6 Vols., Washington, DC

Committee of American Steamship Lines (1964) *Government Aids to
Foreign Competitors*, Washington, DC

Cotton, A.R. (1984) 'Conference-shipper Loyalty Contracts: Time for a re-
think?', *Maritime Policy Management*

Council of European & Japanese National Shipowners' Associations (1984)
Information Bulletin, No. 26, London (February)

Couper, A.D. (1972) *The Geography of Sea Transport*, Hutchinson,
London

Coyle, D. (1971) 'The Compatibility of the Rule of Rate Making and the
National Transportation Policy', 38 ICC Prac. J. 340

Croner's Directory of Freight Conferences (1982), Croners Publishers

Cufley, C.F. (1974) *Ocean Freights and Chartering*, Crosby Lockwood
Staples, London

Darling, H.J. (1974) 'The Elements of an International Shipping Policy for
Canada', *Transport Canada Marine*, Ottawa

Davies, J.I. (1980) 'The Economics of the Open Conference System',
Maritime Policy Management

Deakin, B.M., and Seward, T. (1973) *Shipping Conferences: A Study of their Origins, Destinations, and Economic Practices*, Cambridge University Press, Cambridge

Deakin, B.M. (1974) 'Shipping Conferences, Some Economic Aspects of International Regulation', *Maritime Studies and Management* (July)

Department of Defense (1972), Sealift Procurement and National Security Study

Devanney, J. (1974) *Marine Economics*, Massachusetts Institute of Technology, Cambridge, Mass.

Devanney, J.W., Livanos, V.M., and Stewart, R.J. (1975) 'Conference Rate Making and the West Coast of South America', *Journal of Transportation Economics and Policy* (May)

Doganis, R.S., and Metaxas, B.N. (1976) *The Impact of Flags of Convenience*. Research Report No. 3, Polytechnic of Central London, Transport Studies Group, London (September). (This report was followed by a discussion paper by Ken Grundey.)

Dover, Victor (1975) *A Handbook to Marine Insurance*, 8th edn, H.F. & G. Witherby, London

Drewry, H.P. (Shipping Consultants, Ltd.) (1978) *Organization and Structure of the Dry Bulk Shipping Industry*, Study No. 63. London

Dubow, M. (1982) 'Third UN Conference on the Law of the Sea', 4:172 *Northwestern Journal of International Law and Business*

Ellison, A.P. (1984) 'Regulatory Reform in Transport: 'A Canadian Perspective', *Transportation Journal*, Vol. 23/No. 4 (Summer)

Ellsworth, Robert A. (1979) 'Competition or Rationalization in the Liner Industry?', *Journal of Maritime Law and Commerce*, Vol. 10, No. 4 (July)

Eversheim, F. (1958) *Effects of Shipping Subsidization*, Institute of Shipping Economics, Bremen

Federal Maritime Commission (1965) *Fact Finding Investigation No. 6: The Effect of Steamship Conference Organization, Rules, Regulations, and Practices Upon the Foreign Commerce of the U.S.*

Ferguson, Allen, and associates (1961) *The Economic Value of the U.S. Merchant Marine*, Northwestern University, The Transportation Center, Chicago

Frankel, E.G. (1983) *Economics of Cargo Sharing*, Massachusetts Institute of Technology, Cambridge, Mass.

Frankel, E.G. (1984) 'Shipping: Redefining Functions', *Marine Policy* (April)

Frankel, E.G. (1984/5) *Impact of Socio-Economic and Technological Changes on Future U.S. Port Developments*, Massachusetts Institute of Technology, Cambridge, Mass.

Gilman, S. (1977) 'Optimal Shipping Technologies for Routes to Developing Countries', *Journal of Transportation Economics and Policy* (January)

Gilmore, G., and Black, C. (1975) *The Law of Admiralty*, 2nd edn.

Gold, Edgar (1978) *Canadian Admiralty Law: Introductory Materials*, 2nd edn, Dalhousie University, Faculty of Law, Halifax, Nova Scotia

Gold, Edgar (ed.) (1978) *New Directions in Maritime Law 1978.* Dalhousie University, Faculty of Law, Halifax, Nova Scotia

Gorter, Wytze (1956) *United States Shipping Policy.* Harper Brothers, New York

Goss, R.O. (1970) 'Some Financial Aspects of Shipping Conferences', Ealing Technical College, Transport Economics Seminar, London

Goss, R.O. (1984) 'Economics and The International Regime for Shipping', *Maritime Policy and Management,* Vol. II, No. 2, pp. 135–45

Goss, R.O. (1982) 'Shipping and Competition Policy', University of Wales Institute of Science and Technology, Cardiff (September)

Goss, R.O. (1978) *Studies in Maritime Economics,* Cambridge University Press, London

Goss, R.O. (1968) 'The Turnaround Time of Cargo Liners and Its Effect Upon Sea Transport Costs', *Journal of Transport Economics*

Goss, R.O. (ed.) (1977) *Advances in Maritime Economics,* Cambridge University Press, Cambridge

Goss, R.O. (1964) 'The Regulation of Liner Shipping', University of Haifa – ZIM Symposium, University of Wales Institute of Science and Technology, Cardiff

Goss, R.O. (1982) 'The Measurement of Productivity in Shipping', University of Wales Institute of Science and Technology, Cardiff

Grammenos, Costas (1979) 'Bank Financing for Ship Purchase', Bangor Occasional Papers in Economics, No. 16, University of Wales Press, Cardiff

Grossman, William (1956) *Ocean Freight Rates,* Cornell Maritime Press, Cambridge, Md.

Grundey, K. (1978) *Flags of Convenience in 1978.* Discussion Paper No. 8 (November). Polytechnic of Central London, Transport Studies Group, London. (This is a follow-up of the study by Doganis and Metaxas.)

Hansen, Harald (1981) 'The Developing Countries and International Shipping', World Bank Staff Working Paper No. 502

Hanson, Philip (1970) 'Soviet Union and World Shipping', *Journal of Soviet Studies* (July)

Healy, N.J., and Sharpe, D.J. (1974) *Admiralty: Cases and Materials,* American Casebook Series. West Publishing, St Paul, Minn.

Heaver, T.D. (1972) 'Trans-Pacific Trade Liner Shipping and Conference Rates', *Transportation and Logistics Reviews* (Spring)

Heaver, T.D. (1973) 'The Structure of Liner Conference Rates', *Journal of Industrial Economics*

Heaver, T.D. (1973) 'A Theory of Shipping Conference Pricing and Policies', *Maritime Studies and Management,* No. 1

Heaver, T.D., Taplin, J.H.E., and Aandahl, C. Loren (1981) 'Terms of Shipment and Efficiency in Overseas Trade', University of British Columbia, Faculty of Commerce, Vancouver, *Maritime Policy Management.* Vol. 8, No. 4, pp. 235–52

Horn, Johan (1969) 'Nationalism and Internationalism in Shipping', *Journal of Transportation Economics and Policy* (September)

Houthaker, H.S., and Magee, S.P. (1969) 'Income and Price Elasticities in

World Trade', *Review of Economics and Statistics* (May)

Institute for International Economics (1973) 'Shipping Conferences Rate Policy and Developing Countries', Hamburg
Institute for Shipping Economics (1975) 'Future of Liner Shipping', International Symposium in Bremen (23–25 September)
Institute for Shipping Economics, *Shipping Statistics Yearbook* (annual), Bremen

Jessup, P. (1927) *The Law of Territorial Waters and Maritime Jurisdiction*
Jones, W. (1976) *Cases and Materials on Regulated Industries*, 2nd edn

Kearney Management Consultants (1983) 'The Impact of Bilateral Shipping Agreements: An Analysis of Service, Rates, and Shipper Responses' (January)
Kendall, Lane C. (1973) *The Business of Shipping*, Cornell Maritime Press, Cambridge, Md.
Kilgour, John G. (1975) *The U.S. Merchant Marine: National Maritime Policy and Industrial Relations*, Praeger, New York

Laing, E.T. 'The Rationality of Conference Pricing and Output Policies', Part I (1975) *Maritime Studies and Management*, no. 3. Part II (1976) *Maritime Studies and Management*, no. 3. (See Schneerson's commentary in the latter issue.)
Laing, E.T. (1976) 'The Rationality of Conference Pricing and Output Policies', Part II, *Maritime Studies Management*, No. 3, pp. 141–51
Larner, R. (1975) 'Public Policy in the Ocean Freight Industry', in *Promoting Competition in Regulated Markets*, edited by A. Phillips. Brookings Institute, Washington, DC
Lawrence, Samuel A. (1972) *International Shipping: The Years Ahead*, Lexington Books, Lexington, Mass.
Lawrence, Samuel (1966) *United States Merchant Shipping Policies and Politics*, Brookings Institute, Washington, DC
'Liner Shipping in the U.S. Trades' (1978) *Maritime Policy and Management* (July). (This is a special issue and is an answer to the 1977 report by the US Department of Justice, *The Regulated Ocean Shipping Industry*.)
Lowe, E. (1976/7) 'The Right of Entry into Maritime Ports in International Law', 14 *San Diego L. Rev.* 597

Manalytics, Inc. (1980) 'Rationalized and Induced Trans-Atlantic Liner Shipping Services and Costs', The Federal Maritime Commission, Bureau of Industry Economics (June)
Manalytics, Inc. (1979) 'Limited Rationalization of Liner Ship Service, United States and Gulf Ports to Northern Europe' (September)
Manalytics, Inc. (1979) 'The Impact of Bilateral Shipping Agreements in the U.S. Liner Trades', US Department of Commerce (May)
Marcus, Henry S. (1980) 'Challenges for the Maritime Industry'. *Sapanut*, Journal of the Israel Shipping Research Institute, Vol. 10, No. 1, Haifa (Spring/Summer)
Marcus, Henry S. (1981) 'In Search of National Maritime Policies',

presented at the Law of the Sea Institute Conference, Honolulu, Hawaii (October)

Marcus, Henry, and Devanney, John W. (1972) 'International Relations and the U.S. Merchant Marine', Report No. MITCTL 72–16 (August)

Marx, Daniel (1953) *International Shipping Cartels*, Princeton University Press, New Jersey

McCarney, W. (1968) 'ICC Rate Regulation and Rail Motor Carrier Pricing Behavior: A Reappraisal', 35 *ICC Prac. J.* 707

McDougal, M.E., and Burke, W. (1952) *The Public Order of the Oceans*

McGehee, (1967) 'The Inherent Advantages of Carrier Modes Under the National Transportation Policy', 34 *ICC Prac. J.* 722

McLachlen, D.L. (1963) 'The Price Policy of Liner Conferences', *Scottish Journal of Political Economy* (November)

Metaxas, B.N. (1978) 'Notes on the Internationalization Process in the Maritime Sectors', *Maritime Policy and Management* (January)

Metaxas, B.N. (1971) *The Economics of Tramp Shipping*, Athlone Press, London

Moore, K.A. (1984) 'Viewpoint UN Liner Code and Shares of Trade', *Marine Policy* (July)

Morris, Michael A. (1978) *International Politics and the Sea: The Case of Brazil*, Westview Press

Moyer, Charles (1974) 'A Critique of the Rationales for Present U.S. Maritime Programs', *Transportation Journal* (Winter)

Naess, Erling D. (1972) *The Great PanLibHon Controversy*, Gower Press, London

Northwestern University Transportation Center Forum (1978). *Proceedings: In Search of a Rational Liner Shipping Policy*. Northwestern University Transportation Center, Evanston, Ill. (March)

Note (1965) Rate Regulation in Ocean Shipping, 78 *Harv. L. Rev.* 635

OECD (1967) *Ocean Freight Rates as Part of Total Transport Costs*, Paris

OECD (1984) *Maritime Transport* (annual), Paris

OECD (1974) *Export Cartels*, Paris

O'Loughlin, Carleen (1967) *The Economics of Sea Transport*, Pergamon Press, London

Panzar, J.C., and Willig, R.D. (1982) Free Entry and the Sustainability of Natural Monopoly', *The Bell Journal of Economics*

Pearson, Charles C. (1975) *International Marine Environment Policy: The Economic Dimension*, Johns Hopkins University Press, Baltimore

Peet, G. (1984) 'The 1984 North Sea Conference: A Preview', *Marine Policy* (July)

Ram, M.S. (1969) *Shipping*, Asia Publishing House, New York

Reese, H.C. (ed.) (1963) *Merchant Marine Policy*. Proceedings of the Symposium of the Fifteenth Ocean Shipping Management Institute of the American University's School of Business Administration. Cornell Maritime Press, Cambridge, Md.

Restrictive Trade Practices Commission (Canada) (1966) *Shipping*

Conferences Arrangements and Practices, Queen's Printers, Ottawa

Rinman, T., and Linden, R. (1978) *Shipping – How It Works*, Gothenburg, Sweden

Rogers, W. (1973) 'Inland Waterways', 40 *ICC Prac. J.* 636

Role, (1971) Regulation of Intermodal Rate Competition in Transportation, 69 Mich. L.R. 1011

Ryder, Inger, and Von Schirach-Szmigiel, Christopher, (eds.) (1980) *Shipping and Ships for the 1990s*, Stockholm School of Economics, Stockholm

Schneerson, D. (1977) 'On the Measurement of Benefits from Shipping Services', *Maritime Policy Management*, 4, pp. 277–80

Schneerson, D. (1976) 'The Rationality of Conference Pricing and Output Policies: Commentary', *Maritime Studies and Management*, No. 3

Schneerson, D. (1976) 'The Structure of Liner Freight Rates', *Journal of Transportation Economics and Policy* (January)

Shah, M.J. (1982) 'The UN Liner Code Revisited', UNCTAD secretariat

Shipping and Ocean Freight Rates (1982) Regional Economic Cooperation Series No. 5

Singh, Nagendra (1973) *International Conventions of Merchant Shipping*, 2nd edn, Stevens & Sons, London (This is vol. 8 of *British Shipping Laws*.)

Skinner, G. and Noakes, R. (1979) 'Cargo Reservation and Liner Conference Shipping Serving Canada'. An Analysis Related to the UNCTAD Code of Conduct (July)

Smith, A. (1776) *The Wealth of Nations*

Smith, (1976) 'The Politics of Lawmaking: Problems in International Maritime Regulation – Innocent Passage vs. Free Transit, 37 *Pitt. L. Rev.* 487

Stigler, G.J. (1982) *The Theory of Economic Regulation*, University of Chicago Press, Chicago

Sturmey, S. (1965) 'National Shipping Policies', *Journal of Independent Economists*

Sturmey, S.G. (1984) 'Administering the Code of Conduct', *Marine Policy* (July)

Sturmey, S.G. (1982) *Pricing of Tramp Freight*, Institute for Shipping Research, Bergen

Sturmey, S.G. (1979) 'The Development of the Code of Conduct for Liner Conferences', *Marine Policy* (April)

Sturmey, S.G. (1968) 'Economics and International Liner Services', *Journal of Transport Economics*

Sturmey, S.G. (1975) *Shipping Economics: Collected Papers*. Macmillan Press, London

Sturmey, S.G. (1962) *British Shipping and World Competition*, The Athlone Press, London

Sturmey, S.G. (1965) *A Consideration of the Ends and Means of National Shipping Policy*, Institute for Shipping Research, Bergen

Svendsen, A.S. (1957) 'Liner Conferences and the Determinations of Freight Rates', Paper No. 5, The Institute of Economics, Bergen

Tache, S.W. (1982) 'Constraints to the Effective Implementation of the

U.S. Maritime Policy'
Tanker Register (1970), E. Clarkson & Co., London
Thuong, L.T. (1982) 'Competition versus Cooperation in Liner Shipping: A Marketing Orientation Viewpoint', University of Toledo (November)
Till, G. (1984) 'Strategic Forum – The USA, its Navy and the Pacific', *Marine Policy* (July)
Totland, Terje (1980) 'Protectionism in International Shipping and Some Economic Effects', *Maritime Policy Management*
Tramp Shipping Freight Rates (1968) UK Publications, London (September)
Turner, H.A. (1971) *The Principles of Marine Insurance*, Stone & Cox Publications, London

UNCTAD (1968) Commodity Survey 1968, TD/B/C.1/50
UNCTAD (1978) Consultation in Shipping, TD/B/C.4/20
UNCTAD (1979) Containers, Pallets, and Other Unitized Methods for the Intermodal Movement of Freight, New York, St/Eca/120
UNCTAD (1981) Control by Transnational Corporations Over Dry Bulk Cargo Movements, TD/B/C.4/203/Rev. 1, New York
UNCTAD (1974) Convention on a Code of Conduct for Liner Conferences, TD/CODE/11/Rev. (April)
UNCTAD (1979) Development or Expansion of Merchant Marines in Developing Countries, TD/B/C.4/42
UNCTAD (1977) Economic Consequences of the Existence or Lack of a Genuine Link Between Vessel and Flag of Registry, TD/B/C.4/168 (March)
UNCTAD (1968) Establishment or Expansion of Merchant Marines in Developing Countries, 69.II.D.1
UNCTAD (1984) General Debate Concluded at Conference on Conditions for Registration of Ships (July)
UNCTAD (1969) Handbook of International Trade and Development
UNCTAD (1974) International Trans-oceanic Transport and Economic Development, TD/C/C.4/46
UNCTAD (1980) Level and Structure of Freight Rates Conference Practices and Adequacy of Shipping Services, TD/B/C.4/47
UNCTAD (1970) Liberalization of Terms and Conditions of Assistance, TD/B/C.3/77 (January)
UNCTAD (1967) Liner Shipping in India's Overseas Trade, TD/B/C.4/31, Sarangan
UNCTAD (1970) The Liner Conference System, TD/B/C.4/62, New York
UNCTAD (1969) Maritime Transport and Economic Development (September)
UNCTAD (1979) Port Administration and Legislation Handbook, ST/E/108
UNCTAD (1979) Program for the Liberation and Expansion of Trade in the Commodities of Interest in Developing Countries, TD/B/C.1/32
UNCTAD (1969) Review of International Trade and Development 1969, TD/B/257/Rev. 1
UNCTAD (annual) *Review of Maritime Transport*
UNCTAD (1976) Rules of Origin in the General Scheme of Preferences in

Favor of the Developing Countries, TD/B/AC.5/3

UNCTAD (1978) Shipping and the World Economy – Report of a Seminar on Shipping Economics, 67.II.D.12

UNCTAD (1968) Shipping and Ocean Freight Rates, No. 5, New York

UNCTAD (1972) Shipping in the Seventies, UN Sales No. 72, II.D.15

UNCTAD (1969) Technical Assistance in Shipping and Ports, TD/B/C.4/48 (February)

UNCTAD (1974) Terms of Shipment, TD/B/C.4/36

UNCTAD (1976) Trade Expansion and Economic Integration Among Developing Countries, TD/B/85

UNCTAD (1969) Trade Projections for 1975 vs 1980, TD/B.264

UNCTAD (1969) Trade Relations Among Countries Having Different Economic and Social Systems, TD/B/251 (July)

UNCTAD (1976) West African Shipping Range. D. Tresselt, TD/B/C.4/32. Prepared for the Institute of Shipping Research, Bergen

US Congress (1977) House Committee on Merchant Marine and Fisheries. *Third Flag*. Hearings before the Subcommittee on the Merchant Marine 94th Congress, 1st and 2nd sessions, serial no. 95–35

US Congress (1977) Senate Committee on Commerce, Science, and Transportation. *Illegal Rebating in the U.S. Ocean Commerce*. Hearings before the Subcommittee on Merchant Marine and Tourism. 95th Congress, 1st session, serial no. 95–13

US Congress (1965) Joint Economic Committee. *Discriminatory Ocean Freight Rates and the Balance of Payments*. 89th Congress, 1st session (January)

US Department of Commerce (1978) *Effective U.S. Control of Merchant Ships: A Statistical Study*, Maritime Administration (MarAd), Washington, DC

US Department of Commerce (1980) *Development of a Standardized U.S. Flag Dry Bulk Carrier*, Maritime Administration (MarAd), Washington, DC (June)

US Department of Commerce (1984) *A Statistical Analysis of the World's Merchant Fleet* (annual), Maritime Administration (MarAd), Washington, DC

US Department of Commerce (1984) *Foreign Flag Ships Owned by U.S. Parent Companies* (annual), Maritime Administration (MarAd), Washington, DC

US Department of Justice (1977) Antitrust Division. *The Regulated Ocean Shipping Industry*. Report (stock #027–000–00474–1)

'US Maritime Objectives Continue to be Elsewhere' (1976), No. 49, *Shipping World* (December)

Vanags, A.H. (1982) 'Maritime Congestion: An Economic Analysis'

Vanags, A.H. (1983) 'Flag Discrimination: An Economic Analysis', *Maritime Studies and Management*, Nos. 18, 19

Walgreen, J.A. (1969) 'Liner Nationality and Steamship Conference-Rate-making', *Journal of Industrial Economics*

Wanhill, S.R.C. (1978) 'On the Cost Benefit Analysis of Port Projects', *Maritime Policy Management*, 5, pp. 315–26

Warner, D.W. (1983) 'Merchant Fleet Feasibility', *Maritime Policy Management*, Vol. 10, No. 4, pp. 251–64

Whitehurst, C.H. (1984) 'U.S. Flag Passenger Ships and National Security', *Marine Policy* (September)

Wijkman, P.M. (1980) 'Effects of Cargo Reservation – A Review of UNCTAD's Code of Conduct for Liner Conferences', *Marine Policy* (October)

Winter, W. (1952) *Marine Insurance – Its Principles and Practice*, 3rd edn, McGraw-Hill, New York

Yang, C.I. (1980) 'Shipping Practice, War Risks Clause', *Asian Shipping* (November)

Zannetos, Z. (1973) 'Persistent Misconceptions in the Transportation of Oil by Sea', *Maritime Studies and Management*, No. 1

Zeis, P.M. (1938) *American Shipping Policy*, Princeton University Press, New Jersey

Zerby, J.A. (1979) 'On the Practicality of the UNCTAD 40-40-20 Code for Liner Conferences', University of Wales, *Maritime Policy Management*

Zoll, B. (1945) 'The Development of Federal Regulatory Control Over Water Carriers', 12 *ICC Prac. J.* 552

Index